...AND SOME FELL
ON GOOD GROUND

Mother M. Catherine McAuley
Foundress, Sisters of Mercy

...AND SOME FELL ON GOOD GROUND

A History of the Sisters of Mercy
of California and Arizona

Sister Mary Athanasius Sheridan

A Hearthstone Book

Carlton Press, Inc.   New York, N.Y.

INTRODUCTION

In the light of the directives enunciated in *Perfectae Caritatis* religious institutes have been urged to make an in-depth study of their religious life at all levels. For this they were given specific guidelines: 1) to return to the source of all Christian life (Scripture) and to the original inspiration or charism of their founder; 2) to make an adjustment of their institute or Order to the changed conditions of our times. Such a renewal would then move forward according to the inspiration of the Holy Spirit and the guidance of the Church. The very much loved Pope John XXIII spoke of "the fresh air" he longed to see flow through the Church to sweep away the accretions of time and witness the breath of the Holy Spirit in renewal.

A perusal of Sacred Scriptures does not reveal any definition of religious life nor specify its essentials, but it does testify that the fundamental norm of religious life is the following of Christ as proposed in the gospel and the latter is regarded by all religious as their supreme law. It not only invites to the imitation of Christ but it points out the means to union with God through the profession of the evangelical counsels. Of course, it does not spell out the vows, as such, but there is ample evidence that Christ showed a clear preference for a life of chastity, poverty, and obedience, and He declared Himself to be the Way, the Truth and the Life. He even established a communal unit when He called to Himself the apostles, and He imbued this company with His spirit. He was the living rule. He taught by the way He acted, as well as by the words He used and in this way He inculcated the importance of prayer and the apostolic goals for the spread of the Kingdom of God, while He ministered to the needs of men.

Each religious institute in its call to adaptation and renewal has been asked to renew its unique character as delineated by the founder. Therefore an earnest study has been made of the nature of Catherine McAuley's contribution of an approved institute of religious women whose spirit is mercy toward all those afflicted by ignorance, poverty and illness or suffering in its manifold forms.

With this background the rest of this work is devoted to the history of the Sisters of Mercy, California and Arizona. This study, too, is limited in scope because it will tell only the story of those foundations of Sisters of Mercy made in the nineteenth and twentieth century in California, New Mexico and Arizona which became amalgamated as one organization by 1923.

It is also of interest to note that the Sisters of Mercy moved with the course of history and sought to meet the needs of time and place. Because the works of Mercy are so many-faceted the Sisters of Mercy have found a very fertile apostolate in California and the Southwest.

The book falls quite naturally in three parts:

I   *Roots*, the origin and nature of the Institute of the Sisters of Mercy as founded by Mother Catherine McAuley;

II *Shoots and Offshoots*, the story of the foundations in California, New Mexico and Arizona up to the amalgamation in 1923;

III *Grafting for Growth*, the amalgamations (1917 - 1923).

Doubtless the reader can gain some insight into the nature of this Institute by following the story of the pioneer Sisters of Mercy in the Far West. These women who dauntlessly faced great hardships and showed heroic self-sacrifice as they ministered to the needs of their fellowmen were living examples of the spirit of Mercy and the meaning of religious life. As true daughters of Mother Catherine McAuley they found strength for their life of service in their total dedication to Christ.

No one would be more ready than the noble women who undertook the several foundations in California, New Mexico and Arizona to acknowledge that they were but instruments in the Hands of God. He was the "Sower."

A sower went out to sow some seed. . .*and some fell on good ground.* Lk 8: 1-8

CONTENTS

M. Catherine McAuley—Frontispiece

PART I—ROOTS

PART II—SHOOTS AND OFFSHOOTS

ILLUSTRATIONS—
following page 275

M. Baptist Russell
M. Camillus McGarr
M. Paul O'Grady
M. Bonaventure Fox
M. Michael Cummings
Magdalen Asylum
Our Lady's Home
Motherhouse, Burlingame
St. Mary's Hospital, San Francisco
Mercy Hospital, San Diego
St. Joseph's Hospital, Phoenix
Refugees

PART III—GRAFTING FOR GROWTH

...AND SOME FELL
ON GOOD GROUND

PART I – ROOTS

Chapter 1

LED BY THE SPIRIT
Catherine McAuley: Her Life and Work
(1778-1841)

Few nations have suffered so long and relentlessly at the hands of an oppressor as the Irish Catholics during the three centuries of British rule.[1] It would be hard for a student of history in the world of today to understand the injustice, the tyranny and the inhumanity of the English Penal Laws.[2] This was evidenced in the legislation on land tenure, restrictions on education and the economic laws that formed the basis for the Protestant ascendency. Most of these could be said to offer a pattern for the persecution of those loyal to the Catholic faith.

A new era was introduced gradually by the Bogland Act in 1771, which enabled the Roman Catholics to take leases for sixty-one years of not more than fifty acres of rather unpromising land; a poor concession, but at least it lifted somewhat the long ostracism of the Irish from their own land. In 1778, by the Gardiner Relief Act, Catholics were able to get leases of indefinite tenure if they had taken an oath of allegiance. Finally in 1782, by the second Gardiner Relief Act, the Irish Parliament permitted Roman Catholics who had taken the oath of allegiance to purchase, hold and bequeath even freehold lands and leases on the same terms as the Protestants.[3]

A glance at these dates prompts the reader to guess that it was to the interest of Parliament to face facts and note the trends of the times. For it was a denial of basic rights and the enforcement of unjust economic laws that had caused her American colonies to assert themselves, and, between 1776 and 1783 to cut "the apron strings."

In his *History of Ireland*, Professor Edmund Curtis tells us that in 1782 Ireland entered upon a period of prosperity thanks to the wise legislation of the Irish Parliament.

> . . .By the abolition of the greater part of the Penal
> Laws the upper and middle classes of Roman Catho-
> lics were enabled to acquire property and to have the
> status of citizen. . . .[4]

The Constitution of 1782, however, did not represent all the
people of Ireland and there was still too much opportunity to
disregard the basic rights of many. Yet the new order showed
what Irishmen could do if not restricted by the government.

Then came the Act of Union in 1800. Ireland was, by this
act, merged into one kingdom to be known as the United
Kingdom of Great Britain and Ireland. In Parliament, Ireland
was represented in the House of Commons by one-hundred Irish
members as against 660 other members. The interests of the
Catholic majority were submerged. Because all members of the
United Parliament were required to take an oath which of its
nature excluded Roman Catholics, the Catholic majority was at
the mercy of the Irish Protestant minority.[5]

On the British side the Act of Union was carried by a good
majority, but there was resistance among the Irish. Daniel
O'Connell, "the uncrowned king of Ireland," even declared he
would sooner have the Penal Laws back than lose the national
parliament.[6] Of course, the act of Union itself was not
submitted to popular vote.

Between 1800 and 1829 the issue that gave unity to Irish
political life was that of Catholic emancipation. The circumstances surrounding the victory in 1829 did much to raise
O'Connell's influence and it merits a word for those not familiar
with his strategy.

Vesey Fitzgerald, a popular landlord, sought re-election to
Parliament. O'Connell decided to enter the contest. If elected,
he would refuse to take the oath which would exclude him
from Parliament. This would bring the Catholic question into
focus and a conclusion would have to be reached. Fitzgerald
withdrew from the contest and O'Connell was declared elected.[7] His triumph spoke for itself. Even the leaders who opposed
emancipation thought it wise to yield. In March, 1829, a bill
was introduced by Daniel O'Connell in the House of Commons
calling for Catholic emancipation; and in April, it received royal
assent having passed both houses. By the terms of the Act of
Emancipation, Roman Catholics were eligible for all offices of

state except regent, lord lieutenant and lord chancellor, and members of either house were not required to take "the oath of supremacy."[8]

It was during the period of Irish history described here that Catherine McAuley was born (1778).[9] Sometime later she entered upon a life devoted to relieving Ireland's poor and suffering people and to extend opportunities such as are afforded by education.

Catherine, the second daughter of James McGauley[10] and Elinor Conway, was born at Stormanstown House, some distance outside the city of Dublin, on September 29, 1778. James McGauley was a successful businessman, a builder and realtor who, according to the records, held considerable property.[11] Men of means were rather rare among Catholics, and he was a good Catholic, a man of strong convictions who left an indelible picture on the mind of his five-year-old daughter, Catherine, when death claimed him in July, 1783.[12]

Catherine McAuley seems to have retained a memory of her father as a man strong in faith who gathered poor children about him on Sundays to instill in their young minds the truths of faith.[13] Her love for the poor, her devotion to education, as well as her long struggle to maintain the faith against all odds point quite unmistakingly to the influence of her father.

Her mother, Elinor Conway, was gifted and beautiful, a Catholic too, who had won the heart of James McGauley, but she was not so deeply appreciative of her faith as was her husband, nor as well prepared to impart it to her children. She seems to reflect a rather long association with affluent friends or relatives, often bitter Protestants, in the Dublin society which was more occupied with the good things of this world than by eternal values.

Contrary to the opinions of some early biographers, Elinor did not totally neglect the faith of her children. They were prepared for the sacraments, and they were trained to follow the life of Christian virtue. And yet, the mother's worldly outlook and their strong Protestant exposure during their formative years were not calculated to mold them in the Catholic way of life.

Dr. Daniel Murray, the future Archbishop of Dublin, was assigned to the parish church of St. Paul's, Arran Quay, shortly after his ordination in 1792. Catherine received her first Holy Communion from his hands in St. Paul's parish church.[14] At that time, according to present day consensus, Catherine would have been fourteen years old, but the date of her birth is uncertain.

Father Savage states that it was also at the parish church of St. Paul's that Catherine was confirmed by Archbishop J.T. Troy whom Dr. Murray succeeded as Archbishop of the See of Dublin. Father Savage admits that the date is uncertain because in his papers Dr. Troy recorded only the numbers and not the names of those he confirmed. Catherine always showed a marked appreciation of the sacrament of Confirmation and the importance of the preparation for its reception.

After years of government effort to suppress Catholic worship and restrict Catholic education, it is not surprising to find families unable to guarantee their offspring an adequate knowledge of and the sufficient opportunity to practice their faith so that they could preserve their most precious heritage. This was particularly true where children were very young when bereft of their parents.

It will be remembered that the McAuley children were quite young when their father died and that he was the strength of this family. Catherine was then about five and her brother a mere infant.

When Mrs. McAuley died in 1798, two of her children, Mary and James, found a home with William Armstrong, a Protestant relative of their mother. Catherine, however, accepted an invitation to live at the home of Owen Conway, her mother's brother,[15] a practicing surgeon. The Conway home proved a very happy choice because Ann Conway, her cousin, was very companionable, and it was she who introduced Catherine to Reverend Andrew Lubé,[16] the curate at St. Mary's on Liffey Street. Father Lubé instructed Catherine in Catholic doctrine and encouraged her in her doubts and difficulties. Although Catherine seems to have been of a different stamp than her sister, Mary, her stay at the Conway home may well have served to explain why at this point in their lives Catherine was especially favored by the Holy Spirit. According to Ann Conway, Father Lubé's direction for the next ten years contributed more than any other factor to the preservation of Catherine's faith, at times sorely tried.

Within a short time, however, Owen Conway suffered a severe reversal of fortune, which reduced him almost to penury. Catherine then felt that she should not add to her uncle's plight, and at the offer of William Armstrong she joined her sister and brother in 1801. During her stay at the Conway home, she had received a lasting appreciation of the Catholic faith and a first-hand experience of what it meant to be poor.

William Armstrong was good to Catherine, but he was a rigid Dublin Protestant and was intolerant of those who did not share his views.[17] Catherine was, at this time, not equal to Mr. Armstrong or his friends in adult debate, but she was better equipped than Mary and James who, under his influence, became a prey for Protestant proselytism. In the all-too-frequent theological debate, or even at table talk, Catholic dogma was held up to ridicule. Catherine realized she lacked sufficient training to meet the controversies and although she yielded no ground, she remained silent when she could not disprove the argument.

Her uncertain and tortured mind led her to consult Reverend Thomas Betagh, S.J., at that time parish priest at St. Michael's in Dublin. Catherine found him very understanding and well able to clear up her difficulties. Father Betagh, S.J., also guided her reading and opened to her an inexhaustible treasure of faith. Meanwhile, Catherine was strengthened by the life-giving food, the Holy Eucharist.

It was at the home of the Armstrongs that Catherine met Mr. and Mrs. William Callaghan who came to be quite impressed by Catherine McAuley, and finally proposed that she make her home with them. She accepted their offer in 1803 when they occupied apartments in the Apothecaries' Hall on Mary Street.[18] Mr. Callaghan had a recognized reputation in the field of drugs and served on both the teaching and administrative staffs at the Hall.

Less than a year after Catherine went to live with the Callaghans, Mary, her sister, married William Macauley in St. Mark's Protestant Church, Dublin. His father was a successful merchant but William was not yet established in his career as a physician. He is not listed in the Dublin Directory until 1807 and did not receive his appointment to the Royal Hospital, Kilmainham, before 1819.

Catherine's only brother, James William McAuley, like his uncle, Owen Conway, and her brother-in-law, William Macauley, also chose a medical career.

When the Callaghans secured the Coolock property, on April 26, 1809, Catherine moved with them to this suburban estate.

Here she found that the Callaghans, though quiet in their tastes, were hospitable people, and not infrequently she invited her relatives and friends to Coolock House.

Although the Callaghans disapproved of Catherine's religion, they did not interfere with her belief nor with her attendance at Mass in the village church. True, they could not fully share her sympathy for the poor, yet they readily provided Catherine with money as well as food and clothing to distribute to the needy. Gradually Catherine won the respect and then the love of this good couple who came to appreciate her sterling worth.

Meanwhile, her sister, Mary, and James, her brother, had become Protestants, but Catherine did not write them off. She kept in close contact with them and the rising generation.

During her stay at Coolock, Catherine, in the summer of 1821, adopted Ann Conway Byrn's frail infant daughter, Theresa. Ann died on August 9, 1822, leaving three children besides the baby.

Catherine weighed each need as it presented itself. Her stay at Coolock was fruitful in the service of others and marked by rare happiness and peace. The bonds between her and the Callaghans grew stronger until Mrs. Callaghan, with feminine intuition, began to see that the remarkable force of her character was due to the strength of her religious convictions and she was finally drawn to mention the subject of religion. Just exactly what words she used is anyone's conjecture, but she opened the question and Catherine readily responded, careful not to intrude her own belief but only too happy to say what her religion meant to her. What deterred Mrs. Callaghan from embracing the Catholic faith was the fear of displeasing her husband and at the same time of jeopardizing Catherine's position. Catherine readily dismissed any thought of her own prospects and advised her to follow her own conscience. Mrs. Callaghan finally consented to see a priest.[19]

Sister M. Raymond Byrn tells us that not long afterward Mr. Callaghan agreed to see Father Joseph Nugent, who devoted himself to Mr. Callaghan and was instrumental in receiving him into the Church the day before his death, November 10, 1822.

In the three years that followed the death of Mrs. Callaghan, Mr. Callaghan came to appreciate Catherine not only for what she had meant to his wife during her long illness; but he also observed how much she did to make him comfortable and able to adjust to his great loss. His appreciation continued to grow

18

and one day he asked her what she would do when he was gone. She spoke to him, quite frankly, of a plan to devote herself to the unfortunate, especially to the protection of young girls by teaching them to support themselves and by guiding them in truly Christian living. He asked her what amount of money would provide for her project and was surprised at her estimate. Perhaps it was this conversation that led to his generous legacy when he made his will on January 27, 1822.

Mr. Callaghan had long been impressed by Catherine's good judgment, her generosity in helping the unfortunate and her economy in the use of money. Thoughtfully, he made provision in his will by various bequests to all who had claims upon him, but he made Catherine McAuley his principal beneficiary. At first he named as residuary legatees Catherine McAuley and Mary Anne Powell,[20] but a codicil of the same date dissolved this phase of his will, and he named Catherine McAuley as the "sole residuary legatee of all my estate and effects, real or personal, subject to the specific legacies mentioned in the will." Mr. Powell, Mary Anne Powell's husband, had made an unfortunate statement which reached Mr. Callaghan and provoked the change.

It would be difficult to evaluate the worth of the estate Catherine inherited in terms of the American equivalent of today.[21] Of course, there was litigation over Mr. Callaghan's will, but the will was so carefully drawn that while the procedure delayed matters, the legal action stands as a testimony of affirmation to Mr. Callaghan's decision. Thus he played a major role in providing the means for initiating the Institute of the Sisters of Mercy, which has since come to encircle the globe.

Even before the legal difficulties were settled, Catherine, assured of a fair income, began plans for the Dublin house. Father Michael Blake, whom she had consulted, selected a site on the corner of Baggot and Herbert Streets. It was in Archbishop Murray's parish. The property chosen belonged to the Earl of Pembroke. It was leased on June 22, 1824, at the annual rent of sixty pounds for 150 years.[22]. Dr. Blake laid the first stone before going to Rome in August, 1824. This good priest was concinced that Catherine McAuley was destined for a very special work in the Church and he publicly said so.

While the building was under construction, Catherine wisely visited the best schools and busied herself in the study of teaching methods. She also made a visit to France to observe methods and although she left no record of her stay there, she was doubtless enriched by the experience.

At this time her almost constant companion was Miss Frances Tighe. Although the latter was already interested in religious life and was drawn to enter the Presentation Convent, she decided to lend assistance to the Baggot Street project at least for awhile.

In May, 1825, Catherine learned of the illness of Father Nugent. He had been sick for some days before she heard of it. She found him in a sad state of neglect and stayed with him until he died, on May 30. Catherine lost in him a sincere friend and a capable adviser. She may well have made a mental observation that perhaps his death might have been averted had professional nursing been more available.

While the building was in progress on Baggot Street, Catherine continued to reside at Coolock House. At no time in her life was Catherine so evidently led by the Spirit as during the early years in which she was working on the Baggot Street project. Nothing was further from her thoughts than that she was laying the foundation for a religious institute that would spread throughout the English speaking world and devote itself to works of mercy. In fact, she seemed really adverse to nuns, with a strong prejudice born of her Protestant environment in Ireland in the early nineteenth century. Yet in this respect, too, Catherine was led by the Spirit. As far as she could see, there was no reason for her to entertain such a thought for which she had no attraction.

During these years, her sister, Mary, had kept in touch with Catherine, visiting Coolock House and bringing Catherine to her home; but there was definitely a lack of common ground between the sisters. With the passing of time it became evident that Mary's life was seriously threatened by tuberculosis and that she sorely needed the consolation of religion. The Macauley residence on Military Road afforded no opportunity for a heart to heart talk. Such a chance finally did come when Dr. Macauley agreed to move his wife to the mountains at Stillorgan for relief. Catherine lost no time in arranging a visit with Mary and having a serious talk with her sister before it was too late.[23] This meeting opened the way for Mary to return to the Church. Father John McCormick, of Booterstown, was able to effect a reconciliation and administered the last sacraments in July, 1827.

Mary took her daughter, Mary Teresa, into her confidence and earnestly recommended that she follow her aunt's guidance. Little Mary Teresa so loved her aunt that she did not find it difficult to meet the request.

Mary Macauley died early in August, 1827. To take care of her sister's five children, Catherine agreed to stay on at the doctor's home on Military Road.

Provision was made that Miss Anna Marie Doyle and Catherine Byrn would live at Baggot Street. At the same time, it was decided to open here what became the Institute of Our Lady of Mercy on September 24, 1827.[24] Catherine herself would arrive that day, and it was only a coincidence that she had chosen the feast of Our Lady of Mercy, of which she became aware only after she had sent her letter.

Catherine McAuley, Anne Marie Doyle, and Catherine Byrn conducted the admissions on September 24, 1827, when two departments were opened at the center. There was a heavy registration at the poor school but only two applicants for the working girls' residence. The personnel in the school were mainly Dublin socialites, attracted by Miss McAuley's invitation to temporary service, and with the leisure to devote themselves to a good cause. After the project got underway, an employment agency was added in 1827, and that same year the Baggot Street Social Center opened its doors to needy widows and homeless orphans.

Despite her legacy, Catherine saw that the growing work would far exceed her resources were it not supplemented by other means. She therefore wrote letters of appeal which drew some evidence of resentment and more than a stir of opposition. And yet, she did get encouraging support in a subsequent letter of appeal signed by the Archbishop of Dublin, Daniel Murray, and in the bazaar held in 1828, which netted three thousand pounds, contributed chiefly by Protestants, Catherine's own connections and the truly charitable who were moved to help the unfortunate. From another quarter, she was persecuted by good people who misinterpreted her efforts as a move to compete with the work of Mother M. Augustine Aikenhead, foundress of the Irish Sisters of Charity.

In these early years, she drew much strength from the support of Reverend Edward Armstrong. But it was not for long, for on Ascension Day, 1828, Father Armstrong was called

21

by God in death. It was this priest whose dying advice to Catherine is often quoted by her biographers: "Do not place your confidence in any man, but in God alone."

After Mary's death, Catherine continued to live for about ten months at the home of Dr. William Macauley on Military Road. Nor did he object to her bringing the children with her on her visits to Baggot Street. Although happy that the children found in her another mother, he thought it his duty to counteract her religious influence by attacks on the Catholic position. He even went so far as to remark that his wife detested the Catholic religion and would be pained if any of them should embrace it. It was then that Catherine finally revealed to him that Mary had returned to her Catholic faith before she died. This was a hard blow to William but, contrary to early accounts, his resentment was short-lived. When Catherine decided it was time to take up permanent residence at Baggot Street, in June, 1828, it was he who suggested that she take his two daughters to live with her so that she might direct their education. He wisely thought that the military circles in which he moved were ill-suited for young girls without the care of their mother or aunt.

About six months later, on January 25, 1829, he died after a short illness. Catherine did everything she could for him but was unable to win him to her point of view. His remarks at the time of his death indicated the sincerity of his religious position: "You know the prejudice in which I was reared. I desire to belong to the Church of Jesus Christ, whatever that is."[2][5] The provision he made for his children confirms this sincerity. They shared equally in his estate and he left them free to select either Catherine or their Uncle, Dr. James Macauley, as their guardian. The latter was a Protestant and the choice of guardian would doubtless imply their choice of religion. All five chose Catherine.

The girls were glad to go to Baggot Street, and the three boys were enrolled at a prep-school of Carlow College. This same year Catherine decided to sell the Coolock estate. Her plan necessitated that she make provision for the children for whom she had agreed to care. There were Mary Macauley and Catherine, children of her sister; Teresa Byrn, her godchild whom she had adopted at birth; and two other homeless children, Ellen Corrigan and Ann Rice. For these Catherine opened a second dormitory at Baggot Street and hired a governess.

22

Miss Georgina Moore, a convert of five years, came to serve as governess. Little did she dream that she was taking a step toward being listed among the first Sisters of Mercy professed at Baggot Street. Of course, even Catherine McAuley had no such plans as yet. Catherine committed her thoughts at this time to writing in a letter to the Very Reverend Francis L'Estrange, O.C.D., announcing that she intended to train a corps of Catholic social workers to assist in the work of the education of children, the preparation of young women for employment and the care of the sick.[26]

As the work began to develop she asked the Archbishop for permission to dedicate the undertaking to Our Lady of Mercy and on September 24, 1828, the Archbishop granted her wish and the institution became known as the House of Mercy.[27]

It was not long before members of the clergy and laity began to question her style of life. True, her group rose early and followed a program which in religious life would then be called an horarium. They even adopted a rather sombre type of dress and sometimes playfully called each other, "Sister." And yet, much of the daily round of prayer and work resulted from a desire to make the most of time, and the simple dress was adopted to eliminate expense in order that they might do more for the poor.

What really brought the matter of life-style into focus was the difficulty faced in getting a chaplain so that large numbers would not have to go out to Mass and the sacraments. From Dr. Armstrong's death until Dr. Blake's return home from Rome, the Carmelites on Clarendon Street had received them at daily Mass and served the needs of the center. Dr. Armstrong's successor, also administrator of St. Andrew's, was the Rev. Matthias Kelly. He viewed Catherine and her project as a unique experiment, lay inspired, and also led by a woman. He saw it as an affront to Mother Mary Augustine Aikenhead, foundress of the Irish Sisters of Charity.

At this juncture, Dr. Blake returned from Rome. He immediately set about getting daily Mass at St. Mary's, Baggot Street. He and the Carmelites agreed, and Dr. Blake as chancellor pressed the matter with the Archbishop.

On June 4, 1829, St. Mary's Chapel in the House of Mercy was dedicated by Archbishop Daniel Murray. Dr. Blake was the speaker on the occasion. It was at this time that he said it was his fixed belief that Catherine McAuley was a chosen instrument in a divine plan and that anyone who opposed her would summon divine disfavor. Archbishop Murray appointed Rev. Daniel Burke, O.F.M., chaplain and advised Miss McAuley to erect tribunes in the chapel of Our Lady of Mercy so that Catholics of the vicinity might attend Mass there.

Meanwhile, Dr. Blake began to implement his plan for a change in status for the Institute of Our Lady of Mercy. He urged Catherine to study the advantages that would be derived from a more recognized status in the Church. Of course, Father Blake knew that all the socialites would not make religious, but he also believed that the recognizable features of a religious life would draw very desirable members. Father had even suggested that Catherine examine the Rules of Religious Congregations in the Dublin area.

Daily Mass in the house seemed to initiate a new pattern of living. Quite naturally all arose at the same hour and assembled for morning prayer, meditation, and for attendance at Mass, which was followed by breakfast. The allotment of duties determined the activities from nine until four, when the group made an examen. After dinner there was a visit to the Blessed Sacrament, and an evening rosary. It would be but an easy step to introduce the Office.

There was also some evidence of instability among the volunteer workers as "the socialites" decided to come and go; and there were reports, too, of the hesitation of some who would have liked to devote themselves to works of mercy but in a life of greater stability. Catherine herself was one of the first to see the weaknesses of the present setup but she still had an aversion to convent life.

It was during this era of uncertainty that Father Matthias Kelly decided to visit Catherine McAuley, for he had learned of her interest in the Rules for religious women. Miss McAuley received him and he asked to be shown around the place. While she conducted him through the House of Mercy, he stated the purpose of his visit, which gave her the impression that he was sent by the Archbishop.[28] He said that he understood the institution was to be assigned to the Sisters of Charity, but that she and her helpers would be allowed a few rooms to continue their work among the poor of the parish. Catherine informed him that she had already put the house completely under the direction of Archbishop Murray and that he was free to do with it as he wished.

After his departure, she sat down and wrote to the Archbishop, accepting whatever plan he had, as it had been represented as his wish. The Archbishop paid Catherine a prompt visit to learn what her letter meant, and he recognized in her submission that "the Finger of God was here." He told her that he had no intention to change the plan of her project, but he did say, referring to the title, Sisters of Mercy, "I had no idea of a convent starting up of itself in this way." She was stunned that she seemed to be founding a convent, and an irregular one at that! And yet, she had taken no step without direction and the Archbishop's sanction.

Again she turned to Dr. Blake. He who had envisioned the course of events was not so disturbed. He had tried to prepare her for what seemed to be God's plan for her. Then he turned to the Archbishop to rescue her and her associates from a very uncomfortable position. The deciding factor in the solution of the problem was Dr. Murray's insistence that Catherine either return to secular life or originate a religious institute. Here, too, she was led by the Spirit and she readily obeyed.

Of the Rules examined, the group favored that of the Presentation Sisters. The Archbishop offered full cooperation and proposed a plan to ease the transition. To spare her the difficulties of a novitiate among strangers, he suggested that two professed religious, whose rule she might choose, be sent to the Dublin house so that she and the Sisters might serve their novitiate under them. Thus, she would not have to be away from her infant establishment, and she might continue with the management of the temporal affairs. Catherine saw several reasons why this would be unwise, and it was decided that if permission were obtained from the superior of the Presentation Convent, George's Hill, she and two of the little community would serve their novitiate there.

On September 8, 1830, Catherine McAuley, Anne Marie Doyle, one of the first residents at Baggot Street since September 24, 1827, and Elizabeth Harley, one of the last to join them on October 30, 1829, crossed the city to the Presentation Convent.[29]

The House of Mercy had made a good start during the initial three years, 1827-1830. The records show that the schools were crowded, that a residence of working girls had been established and that soon after, an employment agency was created. The sick were visited in the local hospitals and in their homes;

25

orphans were befriended, and provision was made for the many needy who sought aid.

In the absence of Catherine McAuley, Mary Anne Delaney was appointed to take charge and Frances Warde was assigned to manage the household affairs. The would-be Sisters, completely devoted to the works of mercy, numbered twelve. The "socialites" were dismissed, not only because they were unpredictable but also because they had little appreciation of the importance of time. A few persons were not accepted either because they lacked a sense of dedication or had proven unsuitable for such a life.

Meanwhile, convent life held no more attraction for Catherine McAuley at close range than she had envisioned it would. Because of the many things repugnant to her feelings, she found it very difficult to spend 460 days at George's Hill, and were it not for the fact that the foundation of the Institute was at stake, she might have surrendered to nature and returned to Baggot Street.

The ceremony of Reception, or Clothing, was to be held on December 8, 1830, but was deferred one day to accommodate Archbishop Murray who would officiate. Sister Catherine asked that the Sisters be permitted to retain their baptismal names, prefixing Mary—in this way our Blessed Lady would be their personal as well as the community patroness. For the novitiate period, the three novices wore Presentation dress, and the evolution of the Mercy habit was temporarily postponed.

The period of the novitiate brought the expected trials, but they were nothing compared with the anxiety that Sister M. Catherine had concerning her "Sisters" at Baggot Street. One, Caroline Murphy, did not live even to enjoy Catherine's homecoming. Great, too, was her concern for Mary Teresa Macauley, her niece, who seems to have almost hemorrhaged to death.

At length, on December 12, 1831, the ceremony of profession took place at the Presentation convent, George's Hill, and Archbishop Daniel Murray received their vows according to the Presentation Rule, with certain modifications. Each Sister received a silver ring. The ring of the foundress was inscribed on the inside: *Fiat Voluntas Tua*, and on the outside, *Ad majorem Dei Gloriam*.[30] This ceremony date marks the founding of the Sisters of Mercy. Dr. Michael Blake preached the sermon.

The next day, Dr. Daniel Murray visited the Mercy Convent,

St. Mary's, Baggot Street, and formally appointed Catherine the Mother Superior.

Shortly after Mother Catherine's return to Baggot Street, the first seven faithful followers were clothed in the habit of the Sisters of Mercy, on January 23, 1832; again, the Archbishop presided. Mother McAuley decided to keep the first ceremony private, and the following dressed as postulants:

Catherine Byrn	Sister M. Josephine
Mary Teresa Macauley	Sister M. Joseph Teresa
Frances Warde	Sister M. Frances Teresa
Margaret Dunne	Sister M. Angela Teresa
Mary Anne Delaney	Sister Magdalen de Pazzi
Georgina Moore	Sister M. Clare
Anne Carroll	Sister M. Agnes.

The Archbishop also approved of the Sisters reciting in English the Little Office of the Blessed Virgin Mary. Later, when Dr. Paul Cullen succeeded Dr. Daniel Murray in 1851, permission was given for the Office to be recited in Latin.

When the foundress asked Dr. Murray what Rule she was to follow while the Rule for the Sisters of Mercy was being completed, he stated that the chapter on "Union and Charity" in the Presentation Rule would suffice.

In the early years of the Institute, Mother McAuley took the responsibility of devoting herself to the formation of the young Sisters, and the notes of many of them attest to the inspiration and encouragement which Mother McAuley's conferences provided.

In the spring of 1832, Mother Catherine lost her novitiate and profession companion, Sister M. Elizabeth Harley. She was the first professed Sister of Mercy to die, on April 26, 1832.

Scarcely had the foundress recovered from the loss when she received a letter from the local Board of Health requesting the cooperation of the Sisters in combating the dreaded cholera in Dublin. Many victims of the disease were dying. She obtained the Archbishop's permission, and she and her Sister helpers, using every precaution against infection, readily devoted themselves to the work.[31]

On January 24, 1833, the first Baggot Street profession took place. The Archbishop presided at the religious profession of

Sister M. Francis Teresa Warde, Sister M. Angela Teresa Dunne, Sister M. Magdalen de Pazzi Delaney, and Sister M. Clare Moore. The first Sister of Mercy professed at Baggot Street was Sister Mary Francis Teresa Warde, often referred to as the American foundress.

Dr. Michael Blake was consecrated Bishop of Dromore on March 17, 1833. At this time Canon Walter Meyler replaced Dr. Blake as Vicar General to the Archbishop. It might be noted that the new appointee was somewhat influenced by Canon Kelly with whom he lived at St. Mary's, Liffey Street, and that he had better success when he demanded that the chapel on Baggot Street be closed to the public.

And yet, in spite of this opposition, the illness or death of some of the finest of the Sisters, and the frequent need of funds, the work of the Sisters of Mercy prospered. Bishops were beginning to beg for Sisters, and Mother McAuley was very generous. She usually gave a professed Sister and novice near profession and offered the services of others as well. A ceremony, held in the church not long after the foundation, introduced the Sisters to the townspeople and explained their way of life and the nature of their work. Some Sisters entered specifically for a given mission but as a rule only two from Baggot Street remained on the mission. The foundress herself usually accompanied the pioneers and remained for a month or six weeks on the new foundation. On some occasions she remained longer, such as when she offered to train a postulant (Susan Egan). She loved to explain the life of a Sister of Mercy, with its spirit of contemplation and labor, about which she would write more fully when she was less pressed.

At this time she was also engaged in the compilation of the Rule. Early in 1832 she had been given the assistance of Reverend Miles Gaffney in drafting the first proposals, using the Rule of St. Augustine as adapted by the Presentation Sisters. By January, 1833, two original chapters had been submitted to the Archbishop of Dublin, on the visitation of the sick and the protection of young women.

When rumors began to circulate that there was no approval of Catherine and her work, Dr. Murray agreed to submit what had been done and to petition for Papal approval of the special object of the Institute. In a letter dated March 24, 1835,[32] he received word from cardinal Fransoni that the Holy Father had given cordial approval of the works of the Institute and the establishment of the organization, but he did add that His Holiness had decided that it was not opportune that those admitted make solemn vows.

Encouraged by this turn of events, Catherine McAuley and her able assistant, Mother M. Clare Moore, carefully examined the Presentation Rule once more and modified it as was thought best. Subsequently some of the modifications were reversed by the Archbishop before he gave his approval to the Rule. He explained that his motive was not disapproval of the changes suggested, but that he acted out of a spirit of caution. He judged that the closer the Rule remained to the Presentation original, the more certain it was of a definitive approval by Rome. The main changes were concerned with the distinctive work of the Institute and the removal of any obstacle to the visitations required by the works of mercy. Catherine also included a characteristic paragraph in whcih she outlined her ideal of deportment and religious modesty such as becomes persons consecrated to God.

Archbishop Murray wrote a formal approval on the last page of the manuscript on January 23, 1837. After a period of trial of the Rule, it was approved and sent with letters of commendation from all the Bishops in whose dioceses the Sisters of Mercy had, by then, made foundations.

The Original Foundations—1835-1841

When most women would feel that their life work was over, Catherine McAuley, now in her fifty-seventh year, began the most remarkable phase of her career, the spread of the works of mercy by the Sisters of her Institute. True, she left it to other Sisters to carry her project to the distant lands of Canada, America, Australia, New Zealand, South America, and even Africa. Yet, to send forth fourteen missions before her death in 1841 was a phenomenal achievement in six years.

We are fortunate to have this phase of her story so well documented, thanks to a valuable and extensive collection of her letters covering this period.[33]

Worried by the frequent illness and in some cases death of her Sisters, she sought means to guard the health of the zealous young Sisters. It may even seem strange that this very factor prompted her to open her first mission, a house away from the city, close to the sea, to serve as a rest haven for delicate Sisters. Both Father Redmond O'Hanlon, O.C.D., and Father Daniel Burke, O.F.M., supported the doctor's views favoring a change of air, and this obviated any hesitancy Catherine may have had. Funds for the purchase of Sussex House, Kingstown, were provided by the wealthy widow of Dr. McCann.

[34] Kingstown, St. Patrick Convent—March 24, 1835

On March 24, 1835, Mother Catherine and some of her Sisters took possession of St. Patrick's Convent in Kingstown, subsequently called Dun Laoghaire. Here Catherine appointed her companion of novitiate days, Mother Mary Anne Doyle, as the acting superior. This was the first of two [35] branch houses established by the foundress. Such a house depended on the Motherhouse and the superior of the branch house had the same authority as the Mother Assistant. The area was just beginning to develop. It had been a fishing village until the landing of George IV, who gave it the name Kingstown. By 1841 the population numbered about seven thousand. It was within easy reach of Dublin by the Dublin-Kingstown Railway, which began to operate in 1834. At first the active work of the little community was limited to the visitation of the sick poor, but soon the zeal of the Sisters prompted them to provide a school for girls. Catherine offered to give the coach house, the stables and part of the garden for the proposed school, but she was not able to meet all the costs. If the school were to be maintained, the expenses would have to be met by the parish.

A misunderstanding concerning the school led to the withdrawal of her Sisters in November, 1838. Catherine's letter to Mother M. Theresa White, the superior in Kingstown, on November 1, 1838, clearly shows how concerned she was for the Kingstown people, but that she needed to be firm with the pastor whose views were subject to change. She says:

I would rather be cold and hungry than that the poor in Kingstown or elsewhere should be deprived of any consolation in my power to afford. But in the present case, we have done all that belonged to us to do, and even more than circumstances justified.

In the eighteen months between the departure of the Sisters, in November, 1838, and their return in April, 1840, Father Bartholomew Sheridan invited them back and withdrew his offer two or three times. When they did return they did so at the request of Dr. Murray, Archbishop of Dublin.

The school population soon came to number about two hundred, and the Sisters also found in the town ample scope for their zeal in other works of mercy.

Tullamore, St. Joseph's Convent—April 21, 1836

Tullamore, about sixty miles from Dublin, was the first foundation of the Institute outside the Dublin Diocese. Mother Catherine was attracted by the picture of destitution then in Tullamore. To the joy of the pastor, Father James Rafferty, Catherine said, "If we don't take Tullamore no other group will." Trusting in God's providence, she accepted the offer with the approval of Dr. Murray, the Archbishop, and the blessing of Dr. Cantwell, Bishop of Meath.

The founding party, composed of Mother Mary Anne Doyle, the superior, and Sister M. Teresa Purcell, a novice within six week of profession, was temporarily assisted by Catherine's niece, Sister M. Agnes McAuley, and by Sister M. Clare Moore.

The community was formally erected on April 23, 1836, by Dr. Cantwell, who confirmed Mother Mary Anne Doyle as mother superior. Catherine remained with the Sisters for about six weeks and during her stay she prepared Sister M. Teresa Purcell for profession. These precious conferences were carefully recorded by Sister M. Teresa and are preserved in Tullamore.

The Sisters visited the sick, instructed adults, and soon were able to conduct a school; for Dr. O'Rafferty determined to build both a school and a convent. Sometime later, when Catherine McAuley saw the new convent and school, she remarked that this foundation was a grand tribute to religion.

After Mother Catherine returned from Tullamore she showed an increased determination to develop the schools and devote some time to visitations, but she was soon making plans for another foundation.

Charleville, St. Joseph's Convent—October 29, 1836

Reverend Thomas Croke visited Mother Catherine at Baggot Street and so impressed her with the needs of his parish that she promised him to make an attempt. Two previous efforts had failed and the prospects were not too bright.

Father Croke's parish was in Charleville, a small town in the northwest of County Cork, near the Limerick border. One of his parishioners, Miss Mary Clanchy, offered to give a house and the sum of five-hundred pounds toward the foundation. Catherine knew the income from this would be inadequate, but she was prepared to trust providence. What they had would be sufficient to make a start.

About this time, a good flow of postulants to Baggot Street insured that the community there could afford to give up some of its members to form a nucleus for Charleville.

The foundation party set out for Charleville on October 29, 1836. It was an exhausting trip but Mother Catherine decided to break it at Tullamore, both to cheer Mother Mary Anne's community and to give some rest to the travelers. Father Thomas Croke was there to welcome them as they stepped off the canal boat. He had come from Charleville to accompany them on the second stage of their journey. At midnight they boarded another packet to continue the slow ride to Limerick, where they arrived in late afternoon.

The next day, a twenty-mile drive by stagecoach brought them to Charleville, a town beautifully situated, with a view of the Ballyhoura Mountains and the Glen of Aherlow. Miss Clanchy's house, however, was not as inviting as the scenery. It was small, quite damp, and some distance from the school in which the Sisters would teach. Father Croke's attitude, at this time cold and reserved, was not reassuring and gave little promise of his future loyalty and generosity or of his deep satisfaction in having the Sisters for his school.

Dr. Bartholomew Crotty, Bishop of Cloyne, arrived the next day to give them his blessing and to install Sister M. Angela Dunne as mother superior. Although Mother M. Angela had none of the encouraging drive of Mother Catherine, she was determined to make the most of what she had and she did; for Charleville, despite its difficulties, developed into one of the finest convents and schools of the Institute.

During the first hard winter, Mother Catherine had Charleville as a chronic worry. The work was taxing, and the convent location too damp. There was practically no middle class and consequently little assurance of resources for the Sisters and the poor. Miss Mary Clanchy, who had become Mrs. French, could hardly be expected to guarantee further support of the venture. Then, too, subjects are also scarce where there is no strong middle class.

Catherine's greatest concern was the health of her Sisters. She leaned trustingly for support and guidance on her heavenly Father whose interests she sought to meet. A niece of the benefactor finally became Sister M. Angela Clanchy of the Charleville Sisters of Mercy, and the family consistently contributed to the works of mercy in Charleville.

Carlow, St. Leo's Convent—April 11, 1837

As early as 1834, the president of Carlow College, Dr. Andrew Fitzgerald, O.P., had suggested that Catherine McAuley make a foundation in Carlow; and during a visit to Baggot Street he had renewed his request. It will be remembered that following the death of Dr. Macauley and his wife, Mary, Catherine had sent the boys to school in Carlow. Catherine here found a strong friend in Dr. Andrew Fitzgerald. She was always most grateful for what he did for her boys, Mary's sons, and from time to time she heard from him, as in a letter dated August 4, 1839, which commended her on her plans for a mission to England (Bermondsey).

In 1836, Dr. Edward Nolan, Bishop of Carlow, received a legacy of seven thousand pounds from a hard-working Carlow man, Michael Nowlan, who kept a delft shop there. Dr. Nolan decided the legacy could serve no better purpose than to bring the Sisters of Mercy to Carlow for the benefit the town.

On April 10, 1837, Dr. Nolan introduced the Sisters of Mercy to Carlow. Mother Catherine chose Sister M. Francis Warde as the first superior for the Carlow foundation.

By September 24, 1840, the new convent and school were completed as well as a House of Mercy. The building program was made possible chiefly by the generosity of Michael Nowlan's brother who gave three thousand pounds for the purpose.

This was the first mission south of Dublin, and the new convent, St. Leo's, was the first building erected as a Convent of Mercy.[36] Carlow itself proved most pleasant, and no other foundation progressed so rapidly. Not only was provision made for the children of the town, but the new St. Leo's also offered a school of secondary education for the girls of the middle class.[37] Dr. Nolan had requested that the Sisters establish a pension or boarding school for these girls, and this work has continued even to this day. The foundress not only approved it but stated that it was from schools such as this that one got the best novices. Of course, in true Mercy tradition, the Carlow Sisters were also employed in the care of the poor, the visitation of the sick, adult education, and the education of small boys and girls.

In her brief religious life, Catherine McAuley actually founded more pension schools than Houses of Mercy. The latter required more funds than were available, and the need was not really great in the smaller towns.

It was in Carlow that Reverend James Maher introduced Catherine McAuley to his nephew, Dr. Paul Cullen, the future Cardinal. Not long after, the rector of the Irish College in Rome spoke in her behalf when His Holiness approved the Institute and confirmed the Rule and Constitutions of the Sisters of Mercy.

Cork, No. 4 Rutland Street—July 6, 1837-1852
St. Marie of the Isle—1852-to date

Dr. John Murphy, Bishop of Cork, was very desirous to have Sisters of Mercy for his diocese, but Mother McAuley kept him waiting because the Presentation Sisters, the Ursulines, and the Irish Sisters of Charity were already there. Cork, however, with its population almost six-sevenths Catholic, offered an inviting field for the works of the Sisters of Mercy.

This bishop's request was heeded sooner than was expected when Miss Barbara Gould offered a house for the McAuley foundation on Rutland Street together with a gift of two thousand pounds.

Mother McAuley chose Sister M. Clare Moore to head the venture. This appointment was the first of a series in which Mother M. Clare proved to be one of the ablest superiors in the early history of the Institute.

The contrast in Cork between the poor and the rich was not as marked at it was in Dublin. The city of Cork was filled with business houses and there was ample evidence of heavy exchange in butter, beef and livestock for export; and breweries and distilleries provided another prosperous industry. Labor was well paid and Mother Catherine wrote, "Among the very lowest classes on Sundays I saw very few rags." The evidence of faith was very strong and the churches were packed.

The day after their arrival, the Sisters began the visiting of the sick and needy. To their great joy, the community welcomed within two weeks their first postulant, Miss Margaret O'Connell.

A message from Baggot Street soon marred Catherine's intense joy when word came requesting her to come to the bedside of her dying niece, Sister M. Anne Agnes, her sister's youngest daughter and her own namesake, Catherine Macauley. Sister M. Anne Agnes did not linger long. She died peacefully on August 7, 1837.

Catherine loved her family and suffered much because of them and for them, but she had such a deep love for Christ that she never allowed herself time for misspent grief. She had hurriedly left Cork when she felt her niece's death was imminent, but she was just as prompt to return to straighten out details and give Mother M. Clare the support she needed.

It was through the liberality of the people of Cork that a House of Mercy was established, and it became the favorite charity of Dr. Murphy.

While Mother Catherine was in Cork she left Mother M. de Pazzi Delaney in charge of the Baggot Street community. She was the last of the first seven to remain at the parent house. She seems to have had a dread of responsibility, and she had no great enthusiasm for foundations, but, as assistant, it fell to her charge to take command during Catherine's absence. In reply to a plea to return to Baggot Street from Cork, Catherine wrote to Mother de Pazzi:

It would have been useless for me to take such a long journey if I did not remain until Sister M. Clare was fixed in her new office; and I know you feel very anxious about her and would not wish me to leave her too soon. She continues extremely timid. . .She promises to overcome this soon. She is in excellent health, thank God, and looks remarkably well. I am quite surprised to find no remarks made as to her youth in any quarters. . . .[38]

Mother M. Clare developed into an able superior and remained in this office until her death thirty-seven years later, but not in the same convent. It was she who guided the early years of the Bermondsey foundation, the first to be established outside Ireland. Although rather exacting in her younger years, she possessed a mature judgment that fitted her for her office, and she learned to combine kindness with devotion to duty.

Booterstown, St. Anne's—July 26, 1838

On July 26, 1838, at Booterstown on Dublin Bay, St. Anne's Convent was established as another branch of the Baggot Street convent. It was supposed to take the place of the house at Kingstown, when it closed in 1838. The Booterstown house was established, as was the place in Kingstown, as a rest haven, and was ready for occupancy in the summer of 1838 when it was dedicated to St. Anne on her feast day, July 26. Located halfway between Dublin and Kingstown, Booterstown was truly a garden spot of beautiful trees and flowers, and a mere step out the gate would afford a fine view of Dublin Bay.

The chief benefactor of Booterstown was Mrs. Verschoyle, the Catholic wife of one of Lord Fitzwilliams' agents. She was now deceased, but had done a great deal of charity for the Catholic poor. Having observed the work of the Sisters of Mercy in Kingstown, a committee of men, entrusted with the management of her charities, decided they would be better handled by religious. With this plan in mind they procured a house and approached Mother Catherine and her Sisters to staff the convent at Booterstown.

Because a number of subjects had recently entered in Carlow, Catherine decided that she might withdraw Sister M. Ursula Frayne from there in order to take charge of Booterstown. Sister M. Ursula was to be one of the pioneers to go to Newfoundland in 1842. In 1845, she would found a convent in Perth, Australia, and in 1857, still another in Melbourne.

The original plan of a health haven at Booterstown continued without change but the work itself increased very much. To the nursing of the sick and the visiting of the poor were soon added a national school, St. Anne's Children's Home, where orphans were cared for, and later, an industrial school for girls.

Limerick, St. Mary's Convent—September 24, 1838

Mother Catherine was not allowed to forget her promise of a foundation in Limerick as soon as she could spare Sisters. With this in mind, the Bishop of Limerick, Dr. John Ryan, sent his Vicar-General, Dr. Patrick Hogan, to Dublin in August, 1838, to conclude the negotiations.

The success of foundations led to more and more invitations, and it became increasingly difficult to supply an experienced Sister to head each new establishment. It must be remembered that the Institute was not yet ten years old, and that Limerick would be the eighth foundation. Writers of this time frequently quote a remark of Mother Catherine to the effect that heads were lacking to supply the need. It might be more to the point to stress how many of these early members were exceptional young women, deeply spiritual, of solid character, capable of adapting to the demands of their office and of succeeding in a phenomenal manner. Quite a few became superiors when they were still under thirty and were but a few years beyond novitiate days. Of course, they were a living tribute to the power of example and training of Mother McAuley.

For the Limerick foundation, Mother Catherine chose Mother Elizabeth Moore, and to assist her, as two permanent companions, Sister M. Vincent Hartnett, a novice from Limerick, and Sister Eliza Liston, a postulant. The former became one of Catherine's earliest biographers, and to her especially do we turn if we want more than the facts of Catherine's life and times. As a religious who lived close to Mother McAuley, she studied the deeper side of Mother Catherine's spirituality.

Mother Catherine herself led the foundation party. They left Dublin by packet on the morning of September 8, 1838, and reached Cork by nightfall.

After a few days in Cork, Catherine and the Limerick Sisters set out for Charleville. The Charleville foundation had been a great cause of anxiety to Catherine. Father Croke, the pastor, knew that if the foundation were to survive, he must provide a more suitable dwelling for the Sisters. He had even stated that if he were obliged to go to England and beg for them, they should not feel any loss from Miss Clanchy's marriage. Catherine felt it was "strong language from a rather cold character."[3][9] She was also able to give them some of her own confidence in the providence of God. The first stone of the new convent was laid on September 24, and she left the Charleville Sisters quite happy when the group departed for Limerick on the same day.

About twenty-five years before, Dr. Young, the Bishop, had brought three Sisters from the Poor Clare Convent, North King Street, Dublin, to open a school for the Limerick poor. In due time a chapel was added to the original house provided by the Bishop. Part of the property was girded by a wall of what was once an old Dominican priory and as a result, the house became known as Peter's Cell. The school had met with little success and the community of that time, 1830, was forced to disband. Two lay Sisters had clung to the old place, and with the aid of some good ladies had kept up a small school.

When Dr. Ryan asked Mother McAuley to come to Limerick, these two sought to join the new community. The Poor Clares had prepared the house for Catherine, and the latter was pleased with what she found. She wrote to Mother M. Teresa White, at Kingstown on October 12, 1838:

> . . .We have found much more here than we had expected. A very nice old convent enclosed by the walls of an Abbey—a beautiful ruin!. . .A very nice chapel and choir, good garden and extensive school-rooms. . . .The house is surrounded by trees and walking ground and all enclosed by fine old walls lined with ivy. It is capable of being made a valuable institution if God grants His blessings to our exertions. . . .[40]

Much of the material help was provided by a most generous benefactor, Miss Helena Heffernan, who inherited the estates of her brother, one at Ardagh and the other at Raheenagh.[41] These were given to the new community, and by her generosity the donor removed the pressing financial worries that usually attended a foundation. Then, too, the bishop and other Limerick people were very kind in equipping the convent.

And yet the Sisters were not without their problems and difficulties. Although Mother M. Elizabeth Moore had eagerly accepted her office with all its demands, when responsibilities fell upon her she was fearful and hesitant. Mother Catherine admitted that Sister was "a faint-hearted soldier," but added, "she is greatly liked and when the alarms are over and there are but few in the house, I expect all will go well."

Because of the failure of previous communities to take root in Limerick, at first, postulants were slow to make the venture. Within six weeks, however, four postulants came, which good fortune was attributed to Sister Ellen Potter's zeal for Limerick. Her local interests and connections promoted the object, too.

The worth of the Poor Clare lay Sisters did not escape Mother Catherine. During her three-month stay she had ample time to observe their religious character and she found them very desirable subjects. They were then admitted to profession in the congregation and raised to the status of choir Sisters.[42]

Sister M. Vincent Hartnett, the novice, was professed about a month after her arrival in Limerick, and she was very appreciative of the advantage of a pre-profession retreat by the foundress, of whom she has left us her impressions:

> ...In the midst of important and pressing occupations our venerated foundress was never seen in a hurry. She seemed to have nothing to attend to but the one matter in which she was occupied and she performed that with the utmost quiet of manner and without the least impulsiveness. . . .

On November 9, 1838, the House of Mercy was opened, and Mother Catherine began to look forward to returning to Baggot Street. Before her return she was able to see the Limerick community humming with long-needed works of mercy. This community continued to prosper and was eventually able to send out foundations of its own. In 1844, Limerick established a convent in Kinsale, from which, ten years later, eight Sisters of Mercy would set sail for San Francisco.[43]

In 1839, after a rather lengthy stay in Rome, Monsignor Nicholas Wiseman returned to England. He had been very conscious of the stir of Catholic activity at home. As rector of the English College in Rome, he had made many contacts and was aware of the Catholic Renaissance in the British Isles and of its desire to restore the dignity and beauty of Catholic worship through architecture, and the development of church music and the liturgy. John Augustus Pugin, a brilliant young Protestant, had found his way into the Roman Catholic Church and was soon employed in supervising the erection of a number of church buildings. Among them, perhaps the finest was the Birmingham Cathedral, the first Catholic cathedral in England since the Protestant Revolt.

Dr. Thomas Griffiths, Vicar Apostolic of the London District, had sent Father Peter Butler to look after the Bermondsey Catholics on the south side of the Thames, below the Tower Bridge, then one of the poorest and most crowded parts of London. Father Butler knew at first hand the problems of these people. Few priests, however, had greater success in attracting converts from the influential classes than this humble priest, who looked upon himself as the workingman's patron. He compelled the attention of all by his sincerity and unselfishness. He recognized that the success of his work depended upon the establishment of a church to replace the one in the back lane so ill-suited to divine worship. And he needed helpers to assist him in teaching the children and in caring for the sick. Thanks to the Countess Montesquieu, he was able to begin work on a good Gothic church, which was dedicated to the Most Holy Trinity in 1836. It, too, was designed by Pugin.

When his new church was completed, Father Butler turned the old building into a school. He attempted to gather a group of ladies to staff it, but this proved to be harder than building the church. A number were drawn to work but many did not have a sufficient spirit of sacrifice to stay with it, for the work was laborious and not so rewarding as they had expected. Finally, with the approval of the Bishop, Dr. Griffiths, Father Butler sought the assistance of the Sisters of Mercy, Baggot Street, Ireland. They seemed best fitted to meet his needs, and negotiations were begun promptly for a foundation. Two English women, Miss Elizabeth Agnew and Miss Maria Taylor, were sent to Cork in May, 1838, to serve their novitiate.

While Miss Agnew, now Sister M. Clare, and Miss Taylor, now Sister M. Augustine, were making their novitiate, Dr. Thomas Griffiths and Father Peter Butler had gone ahead with plans for the new convent that would house the Sisters on their return to England. They, too, commissioned John Augustus Pugin, the architect, to design the Bermondsey convent.

Sometime before their profession on August 13, 1839, Mother Catherine went to Cork to give them a suitable course of instruction and to instill in them the ideals of a Sister of Mercy.

As the building would not be ready before November, 1839, Mother Catherine decided to spend the intervening months taking the Bermondsey Sisters on a tour of the convents already founded in order to give them a better idea of the works of the Institute.

Meanwhile, on September 24, 1839, Mother M. Francis Warde led the first foundation from Carlow. The latter was a flourishing convent and ready to extend its apostolate.

Naas, St. Mary Convent—September 24, 1839

Mother M. Josephine Trenor, who had entered Baggot Street April 5, 1836, and who as a novice had gone on the Carlow foundation, was chosen as the first superior of the Naas convent, County Kildare.

At this time, Naas had a military barracks, and proselytism was carried on quite boldly. Soldiers were compelled to march to the Protestant service on Sundays and remain to the end. Conditions were such—so foreign to an Irish heart—that it was hard to really like the place. There was heavy work to be done and few to do it. Mother Josephine devoted herself to what was evidently God's will for her. When her term was up, however, she returned to Carlow where she died in 1856. Were she not listed in the necrology of the Naas convent, there would be little evidence that she was ever Mother in Naas.

A foundation was sent from Naas, in 1851, to Little Rock, Arkansas, U.S.A., but her name is not associated with this venture.[44]

As a branch house of Carlow, the Naas convent served a town of about four thousand. It lies about twenty miles southwest of Dublin on the road to Carlow. Much earlier, it had been the seat of the kings of Leinster. Today, with the westward movement of wealthy Arabs, it is no surprise to find a rather regal house and stud farm, belonging to the Ali Khan, in the neighborhood.

Bermondsey, Most Holy Trinity Convent—November 21, 1839

On November 18, 1839, Mother Catherine and the founding party for the Bermondsey mission left Kingstown aboard the *Queen Victoria*, bound for Liverpool.

The day after their arrival, Dr. Thomas Griffiths, Bishop of the London District, visited the Sisters and gave them a warm welcome.

Within a week, six ladies who had already been engaged in teaching and social work in the old chapel-school entered the

41

new community as postulants. What with preparing them for their reception and caring for the poor in whose midst the Convent of Bermondsey stood, Mother Catherine had little time to think of herself. Her poor health, none the better for her trip and stay in the damp, drafty unfinished convent, was further aggravated by her concern for the young community and by the news of the death of her nephew, Robert.

In a letter to Mother M. Elizabeth Moore, St. Mary Convent, Limerick, dated December 17, 1839, Catherine described the Bermondsey reception of the six postulants:

...On the morning of the ceremony the church (the Most Holy Trinity) which accommodates four thousand, was crowded to excess. Tickets had been circulated by the Bishop's direction and none that we would call poor was invited. The Seats next to the sanctuary were filled with nobility; the Countess of Newburgh, the Countess Constantia Clifford, Lady Bedington, Dowager Countess Newburgh, Lady Petre, and Misses Canning, Mrs. Weld, Mrs. Maxwell—you will be surprised that I remember all these titles, but they are the particular friends of Sister Agnew and familiar visitors. Some were the immediate family of one of our postulants, Lady Barbara Eyre.

At eleven o'clock, a grand High Mass commenced; the organ and choir are considered very fine. After Mass the hymn, *O Gloriosa*, was entoned and we advanced from the entrance leading to our convent. The Bishop wished the ceremony to be last, lest any of the high persons should be late. . . .

Procession: Sister M. Teresa carrying an immense cross; Sister M. Cecilia Marmion, Sister M. Clare Agnew, Sister M. Augustine Taylor, one by one to make the most of a few; Mother M. Clare and her valuable assistant, "Friend Catherine," with their six postulants following. All were admitted to the Sanctuary. The Altar is the highest I have even seen, nine steps and two platforms. The Bishop was at the top in very rich episcopal dress. Mother Catherine had to go up and down eighteen times, three times with each. . .

There were thirty-six priests. The sermon was delivered by Dr. McGuire, who explained the nature of the
Institute and the spiritual and corporal works of
mercy. You would think the Bishop performed the
ceremony every month; he did not make a mistake
and pronounced every word audibly. . . .[45]

On January 13, 1840, Catherine McAuley, accompanied by
Sister M. Cecilia Marmion and Sister M. Teresa White, left
Bermondsey, arriving at Baggot Street the next day. Her trip to
Bermondsey was not only tiring, but some of those closest to
her believed it was the beginning of the end. However,
Catherine did not feel that her work was done.

About two weeks after her return from London she wrote to
Mother M. Francis Warde:

> . . .I received your letter in London. As to what you
> said of the application to Rome, I did exactly what
> was marked out for me, a petition from the Mother-
> house—a memorial from the Archbishop of Dublin
> praying a confirmation of the Rule to which his
> approbation was attached—and letters of recommen-
> dation from the Bishops in whose dioceses branches
> of the Order were established. This has been most
> fully executed; the letters were as favorable as could
> be. . . .[46]

Soon her mind reverted to Bermondsey. The newly established
foundation never seemed to be far from her thoughts:

> . . .I do not know how my poor Sister M. Clare will
> be disposed of. She is superior in London until the
> 22nd of August. On that day Sister Agnew takes her
> place. I am sure they will all be anxious to keep her,
> if Doctor Murphy (Bishop of Cork) consents. The
> Bishop of London said he never saw such maturity in
> so young a person, that she had judgment on her
> countenance. She is, thank God, perfectly indifferent
> where or how she will be placed. . . .

Shortly after her return from Bermondsey, Mother Catherine
again faced requests for foundations. Very Reverend Peter Daly,

parish priest of Galway, had requested a community of Sisters and had received a tentative promise, which prompted her to make the necessary preparations.

Meanwhile, Rt. Rev. Dr. Thomas Walsh, Vicar Apostolic, Midland District, Birmingham, England, wrote to finalize the prospects of a foundation for Birmingham. The details of his earlier proposal are made clear in his letter to Catherine of February 1st, 1840:[47]

Dear Madam:

I had the honor of being introduced to you at Bermondsey Convent and of having an interesting conversation with you on the Holy Order of the Sisters of Mercy. I intimated on the occasion that it was in contemplation to establish ere long Sisters of Mercy in Birmingham. . . .

The Earl of Shrewsbury has already offered two thousand pounds, the interest of which, one hundred pounds per annum, it is proposed to devote to the support of the Sisters, which will no doubt be increased by contributions. Mr. Hardman, a respectable Catholic. . .is desirous to build and furnish a small convent for the Sisters of Mercy. He wished to know what would be required for the buidings to make them comfortable. The convent would be adjoining St. Peter's Catholic Chapel and spacious schoolrooms. . . .

May I expect that when everything is ready for their reception you will kindly allow two or three members of your community to devote themselves to the works of mercy in Birmingham and to commence the establishment of a branch of your order in this town?

Were two respectable ladies from this country sent to the novitiate on Baggot Street, would they be received and on what terms? Would they be allowed to prepare themselves for the convent in Birmingham as Miss Agnew and Miss Taylor were permitted to do?. . .

Despite the promises made to Father Daly for Galway after Easter, Catherine did not hesitate to make arrangements for the Birmingham project, and Dr. Walsh decided to send a group of postulants to Baggot Street by the end of April.

In Catherine's letter to Dr. Walsh she readily agreed with his suggestions but stressed simplicity and service in the convent building. She asked for something plain, well-lighted, and durable that would not cost so much as a building ornately styled architecturally.

The five English postulants arrived in Dublin to make their novitiate for the Birmingham foundation on April 29, 1840, and three days later Mother M. Catherine set out with the foundation party for Galway.

Galway, St. Vincent Convent—May 2, 1840

Galway, with a population that has reached about twenty-five thousand today, is a seaport town on the northern shore of Galway Bay. It had long been an important port of Ireland and had witnessed a number of painful invasions. Ruined abbeys and traces of Anglo-Norman and Spanish architecture recall a fabled past that contrasts sharply with the modern progress of this coastal town with its mills, foundries and factories, which turn out such exports as woolen goods, polished marble, china, etc.

Sister M. Teresa White, a veteran of foundations, was entrusted with the mission, but Mother Catherine accompanied the group. Upon their arrival at Galway, the Sisters were welcomed by Dr. George J. Browne, the bishop, and their good pastor, Reverend Peter Daly.

Writing to Mother Francis on June 6, 1840,[48] Mother Catherine reported that four Galway postulants had entered and that there could be as many as fifteen in six weeks were it not for the financial condition placed upon the Galway foundation requiring a dowry sufficient to support a Sister. There was little money among the people.

In the meantime, Mother Catherine was receiving more requests for Sisters. The Vicar Apostolic of Newfoundland, Rt. Rev. Michael Anthony Fleming, caused her to turn her efforts westward across the Atlantic. On July 12, 1839, he came to Baggot Street to celebrate Holy Mass for the Sisters and later he begged her for a foundation for St. John's.[49] She agreed to prepare for it and a tentative date was set. But Mother Catherine was never to see Newfoundland.

Birmingham commanded her immediate attention, and at the expressed wish of Archbishop Murray of Dublin, she had promised that the Sisters would return to Kingstown in the spring in order to prepare children and grown-ups for Confirmation.

In the fall of 1840, she also received an urgent request from Dr. Griffith for two professed Sisters for Bermondsey. Catherine was not inclined to question the bishop's command even though she was shorthanded, and she prepared to send Sister M. de Sales White and Sister M. Francis Xavier O'Connell Word also came that Father Butler was already in Dublin waiting to escort the Sisters to Bermondsey.

Little did she know that she was sending them to face a crucial test. The Bermondsey community had been stricken with typhus, contracted while caring for a family in their district. The afflicted family recovered but two of the English Sisters died of the fever; Sister M. de Sales and Sister M. Xavier remained well however, and provided much needed assistance.

Wexford, St. Michael Convent—December 8, 1840

Wexford was one of the fourteen original foundations and one of the two from Carlow. It was an old town with a turbulent history dating back to the Viking invasions, and later was the center of the uprising in 1798.

In a letter of Mother M. Catherine as early as October 12, 1838,[50] the foundress recounts that a Wexford priest told a Cork priest that the Sisters of Mercy were going to Wexford immediately, indeed in a week. Catherine by way of suggestion said, "I think they will wait for me. I am so experienced now it would not be well to go without me." But they did go without her, although Mother M. Francis Warde consulted Mother McAuley on matters of importance.

It seems that Miss Julia Redmond of Lancaster Place, Wexford, had invited Father James Lacey, the parish priest of Wexford, to her reception. He took the occasion to mention to the bishop and to Mother Francis Warde his desire for a foundation. Since both seemed to give him every encourage-

46

ment, he promptly secured a place for the Sisters and made preparations for their coming. On the Feast of the Immaculate Conception, 1840, Sister M. Teresa Kelly and her little group began their work.

God blessed their undertaking by giving them the support of two good friends, Father Lacey and Mr. Richard Devereaux, a local merchant.

Wexford, in turn, sent out foundations to Ireland, England and Australia. Two rather recent foundations were sent to Florida, U.S.A.—Lake City in 1959 and De Land in 1962.[51]

It must have pleased Mother McAuley to see her Sisters ready to assume the responsibility of extending the works of mercy as their own foundations prospered. It was this trend that accounts for the unusual growth and spread of the Institute of the Sisters of Mercy throughout the world. And basic to this vitality was her choice of government whereby each new foundation became independent when it was able to stand on its own.

Birr, St. John's Convent—December 27, 1840

About this time, Father Theobald Matthew, O.F.M. Cap., the Apostle of Temperance, begged Catherine for nuns to bring both peace and union to the people of Birr. Father W. Crotty, one of the curates of Birr, had flouted the authority of the bishop, Dr. Patrick Kennedy of Killaloe, and had taken a number of the parish into a schism. The pastor, Dr. John Spain, had sought the help of Father Matthew. The latter recommended that he secure a foundation of Sisters of Mercy, and peace would soon be restored.

Catherine readily complied that her Sisters would do what they could. To expedite matters Dr. Spain proposed giving up his rectory to house the Sisters. Sister M. Aloysius Scott was chosen as superior for the difficult assignment. She had just recovered from a three months' illness and was still quite frail. The task contemplated was very different from anything for which the Sisters had been trained. Father Matthew had insisted that this apostolate required truly spiritual women, and they proved their worth. With a spirit of dedication supported by deep faith and confidence in God, the Sisters went from cottage to cottage winning the affection of the people. They knew that this was a case that would require what scripture calls "prayer and fasting," for they were dealing with the powers of darkness.

That winter was exceedingly cold, with plenty of snow and ice. Yet nothing prevented their moving among the people, trying by every means in their power to bring them back to the faith of their fathers. A letter from Catherine McAuley to Mother M. Cecilia Marmion in January, 1841, gives some details of their work:

> . . .Sister M. Rose and I walked a mile and a half through the snow to visit an unfortunate family, followers of Crotty. Our excuse for going uninvited was that they had a son twenty-six years of age killed by a fall from a horse and we came to offer our sympathy and consolation.

> We were pretty well received until a Crottyite arrived who probably saw us and dropped in. In all her little speeches, which she gave in profusion and looking deeply at me, she said, "We are all sinners." I bowed as low as Sister Vincent does dancing Sir Roger de Coverly.

> It was snowing greatly and she seemed resolved to wait till it would cease but found us disposed to wait her out. . . .

> Our lady retired and I did all I could to awaken the poor people to a sense of their state. They both promised to come to us, but I fear. . .it will take more than one visit. . . .[52]

Perseverance, kindness and the personal interest of the Sisters ultimately paid off. There was other evidence, too, that their efforts were to bear fruit. Within six months of their coming, more than four-hundred children were enrolled in the school of the Sisters. Father Matthew had insisted from the beginning that the Sisters of Mercy would reach the parents through the children in their school. Father Matthew's initial assumption appeared to be sustained. With the help of God, of course, the healing of the schism seemed in a large measure to be due to the efforts of the Sisters who gradually won over the Crottyites.

Later in the year, Catherine went to Birr to conduct a retreat for the Sisters to be received on May 20. The Bishop of Killaloe, Dr. Patrick Kennedy, presided at the ceremony, and Father Matthew spoke. It was evident that this was one way to express their gratitude for the successful efforts of the Sisters at Birr.

Mother Catherine did not live to see the final victory. Father Crotty admitted his error and, with due sincerity, he was fully reconciled.

Calls for Sisters continued to flow into Baggot Street from Liverpool, England, from Canada and even from the United States. Catherine had set in motion the great waves of mission activity, but her own work was about over.

Early in June, 1841, word reached Carlow that the Rule of the Sisters of Mercy had been finally confirmed in Rome. The news came to Father Maher from his nephew, the future Cardinal, Dr. Paul Cullen. As early as the sixth day of June, 1841, His Holiness Pope Gregory XVI, in an audience, had kindly confirmed the Rule and Constitutions and had approved the Institute unreservedly. The decree itself was issued later under the date of July 5, 1841. Finally, Cardinal Fransoni, the Prefect, sent the official communication from Rome to the Most Reverend Archbishop Daniel Murray of Dublin, on July 31, 1841.[53]

The "Bermondsey Manuscript"[54]

It was also in the summer of 1841 that the difficulties in Bermondsey came to light. Mother M. Clare Moore returned to Cork and Sister M. Clare Agnew succeeded her as superior in Bermondsey. The extreme views of the latter became more apparent when she assumed office.

Shortly after Mother M. Clare Moore left England, the new superior chose Sister M. de Sales Eyre (Lady Barbara) for the office of Mother Assistant. They had been friends and had moved in somewhat similar social circles, but it is to the credit of Sister M. de Sales that she was not entangled in the strange notions of Sister M. Clare Agnew. Despite her own personal struggle to maintain her vocation she was to the end loyal to the true spirit of the Institute. In fact, her life reads as the antithesis of that of Miss Agnew. Sister de Sales, at first, found it hard to give up *all*. She not only decided to relinquish all but she spent her life in heroic self-discipline and self-conquest, and died a humble Sister of Mercy.

Not long after Mother M. Clare Agnew took over the office of Superior in Bermondsey, she announced to the Sisters that they might choose between a life of action or contemplation. Those drawn to the service of the poor and the sick or education continued to engage in the works of mercy, while those who sought to pursue a life of contemplation spent more time in the chapel than the schedule of a Sister of Mercy was ever intended to provide. The new Reverend Mother also applied to the bishop for permission to establish Perpetual Adoration in the Bermondsey Convent. Since the Rule had already been confirmed, the bishop saw he had no power to give such a permission.

Finally, when Mother M. Clare Agnew found her position untenable she decided to withdraw to the Trappistines in Dorsetshire. The latter gesture was unsuccessful and she even sought to found an order of her own, which did not materialize.

If she had confined herself to her own fantasies it would have been serious enough, for she claimed her revelations were the source of her requests; she did, however, have some influence and she created a peculiar atmosphere of unrest among the Sisters. Her trouble seems to have arisen within herself and in her inability to adapt to religious life. Some Sisters were drawn to abandon the work of education, the care of the sick or social work, and to favor a life of contemplation. Of course, even some of those who would not go that far tended to lose the proper concept of a Sister of Mercy.

Two Sisters were alienated from each other and the congregation, before they left the Institute. Some of her views of religious life infected even the most promising members of the Bermondsey group until Mother McAuley recognized something of an alien spirit in Sister M. Clare Moore and Sister M. Cecilia Marmion, and she nipped this tendency in the bud.

After Sister M. Clare Agnew left the Institute, Sister M. Clare Moore was brought back to Bermondsey to serve as Superior, December 10, 1841, and this at the request of Bishop Thomas Griffiths, "to save the foundation." Much of the success in dealing with the Bermondsey situation should be credited to the integrity, maturity and loyalty of Mother M. Clare Moore.

One very good result of the trials in Bermondsey was the timely action of Mother McAuley, who suppressed the innovations that might have undermined the spirit and true aims of the Institute. Here Catherine saw the first threat of division in the congregation by a subtle attack on the spirit of the Institute itself and the very fundamentals that distinguish the nature of its life and work. She was quick to observe in the new spirit proposed under the guise of contemplative fervor, a pernicious move to neglect the salvation of others, an end and object of the Institute of Mercy.

In the *Bermondsey Manuscript*, Mother McAuley clearly delineates the spirit of the Institute and its two-fold aim:

> To devote our lives to the accomplishment of our own salvation and to promote the salvation of others is the end and object of our Order of Mercy. These two works are so linked together by our rule and observances that they reciprocally help each other. We should often reflect that our progress in the spiritual life consists in the faithful discharge of the duties belonging to our state, as regards both ourselves and our neighbor and we must consider the time and exertion which we employ for the relief and instruction of the poor and ignorant as most conducive to our advancement in perfection, and the time given to prayer and other pious exercises we must consider as employed to obtain the grace, strength and animation which alone could enable us to persevere in the meritorious obligations of our state; and if we were to neglect these means of obtaining Divine support we would deserve that God should stop the course of His graces, to make us sensible that all our efforts would be fruitless except we were continually renewed and replenished with His Divine Spirit. . .

Birmingham, England, St. Ethelreda's Convent—August 21, 1841

The Birmingham Convent, originally dedicated to St. Ethelreda but long known as the Convent of Our Lady of Mercy, Handsworth, was founded on August 21, 1841 at the request of the Most Reverend Thomas Walsh, Vicar Apostolic of the

Midlands District. The building itself was designed by Pugin but at the expressed wish of Mother McAuley it followed simple lines, well suited to a convent.

It was John Hardman, Esq. who gave the land, provided for the structure, and completely furnished the convent with its beautiful chapel. A second benefactor, John A. Talbot, the Sixteenth Earl of Shrewsbury, had really wanted to build it but he yielded to Mr. Hardman and agreed to endow the convent with a gift of two thousand pounds.

At the request of Bishop Walsh, Juliana Hardman and her three companions had gone to Baggot Street in 1840 to be trained under the aegis of the foundress for religious life and the duties of the Institute. Every effort was made to avoid the difficulties faced in Bermondsey, but it was soon evident that circumstances alter cases. Although some of the Birmingham community came from the "best of England's families," those interested in St. Ethelreda's Convent were not especially worldly and their love for the Church and her interest left nothing to be desired.

Meanwhile word had been sent to the Holy See as a follow-up on the petition for confirmation of the Institute and the Rule of the Congregation. This letter updated the development of the Institute in the intervening years. There were fourteen foundations at this time and 142 Sisters.[55]

Before she left for England, the official confirmation by the Holy See of the Institute of the Sisters of Mercy and their Rule and Constitutions had been received, and Catherine set out on her last mission pleased with the news. Now that her work was nearing its close she could well say, *"Nunc dimittis servam tuam."*

The four Sisters[56] professed on August 19, 1841 left for Birmingham the day after the ceremony in the company of Mother McAuley, Mother Cecilia Marmion and three novices.

They were received by Bishop (later Cardinal) Nicholas Wiseman, co-adjutor of Bishop Walsh. With a good group of Birmingham clergy they proceeded to the chapel where Dr. Wiseman, in full pontifical robes, recited the *Te Deum* after which he spoke for a few minutes and concluded with a blessing upon the Sisters and their work.

Catherine remained about a month at Birmingham to give the Sisters every needed encouragement. On September 6, 1841, Bishop Walsh affirmed the appointment of Sister M. Juliana

Hardman, the first superior of the new community. Mother Catherine felt it wise to appoint an English woman, and she had no reason to regret her decision.

She took Sister M. Juliana with her to visit her father who, although very ill, seemed so happy to see how things were turning out that he had a temporary recovery. As yet the Sisters had no school and they gave themselves to the charitable and benevolent works he had initiated. Great was his pleasure to see their zeal and enthusiasm as they devoted themselves to the care of the orphans, the visitation of the sick and the education of adults. In a relatively short time they saw the fruits of their efforts in the growing numbers of good practical Catholics.

Catherine had brought Sister M. Cecilia Marmion with her to Birmingham because she had been Sister M. Juliana's novice mistress, and she would be a valuable support while the young Sister gained experience. Sister M. Cecilia was to be home by Christmas.

During her stay in Birmingham, Mother Catherine tried to conceal her physical condition; doubtless, she did not realize how serious it was. The trip home was difficult and she arrived exhausted.

In Liverpool, she met Dr. Thomas Youens who brought her to the site where he proposed to build a new Mercy convent. Sister M. Francis Warde had some interest in the Liverpool foundation; perhaps she felt Mother Catherine was not equal to it. It was in reference to the Liverpool foundation that Mother McAuley characterized her efforts as "pious anxiety." Be that as it may, it was quite evident that the English bishops were convinced they wanted Sisters trained at the Baggot Street house. In reference to Liverpool, Mother Catherine made this quite clear on August 3, 1841 in a letter to Sister M. Teresa White in Galway:

> I have had a writing business about the Liverpool foundation, but Dr. Youens, a most pious, respectable English clergyman has been making some arrangements for it in Carlow, as he knows Mr. Maher. Dr. Brown, the bishop, wishes to treat with the Motherhouse and I fear my poor Sister M. Francis will be disappointed as she had such genuine ardor and a kind of real innocent pious anxiety to be engaged in such works. I am sorry and still hope she

may be chosen, hence, I have manifested all the indifference that Mr. Daly admires so much. . .ever praying that God may produce the effect He most desires. . . .[57]

Bishop George Hilary Brown[58] arranged with Dr. Thomas Youens to proceed, as did Dr. Thomas Walsh of Birmingham, to have English subjects prepared in the Motherhouse, Dublin.

The day after the Feast of Our Lady of Mercy, the foundress returned from England and dispatched a few letters to her Sisters. There was more than an intimation of death for she wrote, "Pray fervently that God may grant me the grace of a holy penitential preparation and the grace of a happy death."

On Tuesday, October 12, 1841, just about a month before her death, Catherine wrote Mother M. Francis Warde the last personal letter extant.[59] Then she turned to put all her affairs in order. Her last extant letter was a business letter to the attorney, Charles Cavanagh,[60] concerning a small legacy left to her for Baggot Street. Having done what a faithful steward could do she placed everything in the hands of God.

Mother Catherine's Death

Like so many of her family, Mother Catherine McAuley died of pulmonary tuberculosis. For some time she felt the hand of death upon her, but she did not quit until God made His will clear to her.

It must have taken an heroic effort to arrange, plan and execute all the details of her last foundation, St. Ethelreda's, Birmingham. Even on the journey home she seemed to be planning the next foundation in Liverpool. And yet she was not so absorbed that she did not recognize the summons, for in the fall of 1841 she seems to have given her chief attention to the business of preparing for death.

Mother M. Clare Augustine Moore has given a rather specific account of Catherine's last days in November, 1841.

An abscess had formed internally; her debility was most painful so that to walk from room to room fatigued her. She coughed incessantly, her appetite was gone, and she could not sleep. The highest medical advice was procured, but it was useless, and she knew it. She took all that was ordered, however, and submitted to the little alleviations in the way of diet which the Sisters presented her, though a foul taste with which she was constantly afflicted prevented any comfort from them. This was perhaps the reason she accepted them. . . .

Besides the internal abscess she had a hideous ulcer on the lower part of her back. . .which she consented to let the Sister (Teresa Carter) who slept in the infirmary dress. . . .[61]

On Monday, November 8, Mother Catherine was anointed and on the following day, Sister M. Ursula Frayne was directed to notify all the superiors of their convents that Reverend Mother M. Catherine was considered beyond recovery. In the early morning of November 10, Mother Catherine's abscess ruptured and according to Dr. Stokes, this served as the forerunner of her death.

Before Mass on Thursday morning, Mother Catherine greeted each Sister as she passed by her bed with a fitting remark or special exhortation. Then the foundress, quite like herself, said it would be a comfort to see the Sisters in their church cloaks since they had not worn them for her anointing on Monday. At 8:30, Mass was offered in the infirmary, with Mother Catherine surrounded by her Sisters.

During the day, Dr. James Macauley, with his wife and daughters, arrived. They were her closest relatives then living. Later Dean Meyler called, and also Dr. Walsh from Kingstown. Finally, Dean Gaffney and her faithful Carmelite friend, Reverend Redmond O'Hanlon, came. These two priests had been a strong support for her in life.

At five p.m. she asked for the blessed candle and taking it in her hand she posed, ready to go forth to meet her Bridegroom. She waited, however, for three hours and breathed her last about eight p.m., November 11, 1841.

From Thursday until Monday, November 15, she lay in state in the convent chapel. Archbishop Daniel Murray of Dublin, unable to perform the solemn rites for his dear friend, had asked Bishop Kinsella to represent him, both in consecrating the burial plot and officiating at the solemn high Mass.

Dr. Miles Gaffney, Dean of Maynooth, who had worked closely with Catherine McAuley in the compilation of the Constitutions of the Sisters of Mercy, very pertinently chose to add these lines from St. Matthew's Gospel to his eulogy on the occasion of her death:

> . . .Few ever left this world that could with greater confidence expect to hear from the lips of the Divine Redeemer: "Come ye blessed of my Father, possess the kingdom prepared for you. For I was hungry and you gave Me to eat; I was thirsty and you gave Me to drink; I was a stranger and you took Me in; naked and you covered Me; sick and you visited Me; I was in prison and you came to Me. As much as you did it to one of these, my least brethren, you did it to Me."[62]

PART II—SHOOTS AND OFFSHOOTS

Chapter 2

THE CALL OF THE FAR WEST[1]

Although Catherine McAuley was inspired to devote herself to the needs of the poor, the sick and the ignorant of Ireland, her spirit of mercy knew no national limits to her generosity. In fact, even before her death she was entertaining calls from overseas. Just two years later Sister M. Francis Warde, one of the first seven professed at Baggot Street, set out for America to open a convent of Mercy at Pittsburgh (1843).

By mid-century, gold had been discovered in California and thousands had poured into San Francisco, which served as a port of entry, a base of supplies, and finally, as the financial center of the American West. Mindful of the needs of his growing flock, the Most Reverend Joseph Sadoc Alemany, the first Archbishop of San Francisco, sent Reverend Hugh Gallagher to Ireland in the summer of 1854 so that he might get recruits from the relatively new Institute of the Sisters of Mercy, already widely known for its social service work as well as for its interest in education.

In Kinsale, Father Gallagher, with the permission of Bishop William Delaney, presented his plea to Mother M. Francis Bridgeman, superior of St. Joseph's Convent. Almost the entire community expressed readiness to go but the bishop would allow only five professed to undertake what seemed a rather wild venture. Mother Francis entered generously into the project but only after Father Gallagher gave her convincing assurance that the spirit and Rule of the Institute would be well respected. Five professed Sisters and three novices were chosen from twenty-nine volunteers and they were given about six weeks to get ready.

Into what sort of place were they preparing to set forth?

California—Historical Background

The history of California and of San Francisco in particular is full of variety, color and human interest. Yet there was a long period following the Spanish discovery when little happened to change this land of promise into the cynosure of world-wide interest. Between the discoveries of Juan Rodriguez Cabrillo in 1542, two centuries elapsed before Spanish activity initiated by Jose de Galvez drew California into the orbit of Spanish influence.[2] In 1769, Don Gaspar de Portola and Fray Junipero Serra opened a new era in California history. The former, as the first governor, was commissioned to establish royal presidios and promote permanent settlement; the latter, as guardian of the mission system, initiated a chain of twenty-one missions with the founding of Mission San Diego de Alcala, July 16, 1769.

When the Spanish came, they brought their culture to California as is evident in the place names, missions, architecture, and fruits of the field. To them California owes an era of romanticism and an appreciation of the beautiful, such as marked their picturesque homes and their ever recurrent fiestas. But they were not apostles of change.

The chief agents of transformation and development of California's potential were the Americans who began a steady infiltration during the Mexican period[3], especially after the secularization of the missions.[4] The Anglo-Saxons were activists who contributed a new drive, characterized by evidence of ambition, courage, thrift, as well as a very materialistic turn of mind.

As late as July, 1846, Yerba Buena counted just a few hundred people, but that very month things began to happen that would soon draw the attention of the world. Early in the morning of July 9, 1846, Captain John B. Montgomery, Commander of the U.S.S. *Portsmouth*, landed at the foot of Clay Street and marched his men to the plaza which came to be known by the name of his ship. Here he raised the American flag by order of Commodore John D. Sloat who had hoisted the Stars and Stripes over the customs house in Monterey just two days before. Of course, California had not yet been ceded to the United States. Sloat's action merely indicated occupation, but by the Treaty of Guadalupe Hidalgo, February 2, 1848, which followed the Mexican War, the transfer of California was complete.

Even before this, a move had been made to change the name of this sleepy town, which swung like a hammock between Rincon Point and Telegraph Hill. On January 30, 1847, the *California Star* carried the following proclamation:

Whereas the local name of Yerba Buena as applied to the settlement or town of San Francisco is unknown beyond the district, and has been applied from the local name of the cove on which the town was built; therefore to prevent confusion and mistakes in public documents, and that the town may have the advantage of the name given on the public map; it is hereby ordained that the name of San Francisco shall hereafter be used in all official communications and public documents or records appertaining to the town.

Washington A. Barlett
Chief Magistrate

Published by order
J.G.T. Dunleavy
Municipal Clerk

It was the discovery of gold by James Marshall, on January 24, 1848,[5] in the tail-race of the sawmill at Coloma that changed the course of history in California; and the excitement precipitated a mad rush that drew thousands to the gold fields from all parts of the world.

By the beginning of 1849, San Francisco's population had reached two thousand. Before the year was out it was estimated at between 20,000 and 25,000. It was this phenomenal growth during the gold rush and the attendant increase in the criminal element due to the absence of law in the period of transition from Mexican to American rule, that prompted Brigadier General Bennett Riley to call the Constitutional Convention which assembled at Colton Hall, Monterey, on September 1, 1849. The Californians, however, did not wait for admission into the Union to start operating as a state. After approval of the constitution by the election of November 1849, the first legislature met at San Jose, in December, and on the twentieth, Peter H. Burnett was sworn in as the first constitutional governor.

But the creation of state government did not establish the hoped-for security. As 40,000 Argonauts funneled through San Francisco on the way to the mines, the burdens that fell to the municipal government were staggering. In 1848 San Francisco was a frontier village with but two hotels and two incomplete wharves. That year saw a decline in population as her citizenry took off for the mines. Two subsequent developments reversed the exodus: 1) the fact that farsighted people saw possible fortunes in meeting the miners' needs; and 2) San Francisco became the logical financial center to handle the miners' gold. Even before the year was out business began to flourish in San Francisco. Prices and wages skyrocketed but no amount of stretching could accommodate the motley throng, many of whom sought only temporary accommodation. There is little doubt, however, that the flood of wealth was a major cause of the rise of San Francisco as the greatest port on the Pacific. But meanwhile, the sudden wealth of California initiated one of the most chaotic periods ever experienced in any port of the world. By land and sea men poured in—gentlemen, villains, sophisticated adventurers, Australian convicts, merchants, traders and none too few of the unscrupulous and unprincipled who hoped to fleece those who sought an honest share of the golden opportunity.

Meanwhile popular tribunals arose in San Francisco in 1849 due to the lack of local law enforcement, and a citizens' court tried and banished a number of those convicted. The First Vigilance Committee, however, was not formed until 1851. Its first victim, John Jenkins, arraigned on the charge of safe-stealing, was promptly found guilty and hanged from the veranda of the City Hotel. Before it disbanded, the First Vigilance Committee hanged three malefactors and banished more than two dozen. Summary action gave the criminal element some cause to pause, and many fled the city or went into hiding.

Within five years after the adjournment of the First Vigilance Committee in September, 1851, the Second Vigilance Committee was formed, on May 15, 1856, following the assassination of James King of William, editor of the *Evening Bulletin*, who had launched a vigorous campaign for better government.

Although the Second Vigilance Committee is generally reported to have dispensed justice with a fair respect for decent procedures, the fact that it had usurped the authority and functions of regular government aroused opposition from many of the law-abiding citizens of San Francisco. After operating for only three months, the Second Vigilance Committee was permanently disbanded on August 21, and the work of the vigilantes came to an end.[6]

Mother M. Baptist Russell and her companions experienced the era of the Second Vigilance Committee. Fort Gunnybags, headquarters of the committee, was a two-story building on Sacramento, between Davis and Front Streets. It was the center of action for some eight to nine thousand volunteers and was distinguished by a cannon mounted on the roof and a breastwork of sand bags, either to inspire respect for its self-appointed authority or fear in those who threatened the common good. The town was overcrowded, ill-planned and without adequate sanitation facilities. There were as yet no cobblestone roads, just endless sand hills, which were gradually cut down as the plank boards were extended out Mission Road. The wharves were being extended in the opposite direction, following the fill-in below Front and First Streets, but there was as yet no Ferry Building, much less bay bridges. Even the cable cars did not come until September, 1873.

From this sketchy picture, it can be seen that the Sisters came to San Francisco in its turbulent infancy, when government was poor and municipal services correspondingly so. The Sisters saw the city grow and played an important part in the development of its health and educational services as well as in the care of the poor, the neglected and the aged. By mid-century, San Francisco was a city of promise, of golden adventure, but she sadly needed the humanizing ministrations of the Sisters of Mercy.

The San Francisco Foundation—December 8, 1854

In the bleak dawn of December 8, 1854, eight figures swathed in black descended the gangway of the *Cortez* which had dropped anchor in San Francisco Bay about 2:00 a.m. on the Feast of the Immaculate Conception. Most of the motley crowd aboard, gold seekers, wild with excitement and impatient to shoulder their way to fortune, had quickly cleared the ship. By 1854, easy gold was already in decline but each ship that touched dock to pour out its human cargo gave evidence that there were still many who had to come to see for themselves.

Having sized up their companions aboard the *Cortez*, the Sisters decided it would not be seemly to venture into the city until morning and so bided their time until 5:00 a.m.[7]

They were quite unobtrusive as they followed in the footsteps of Reverend Hugh Gallagher toward the two carriages that were to take them to St. Patrick's on Market between Second and Third. As they drove along, Sister M. de Sales reached into her pocket and tossed a miraculous medal into the mire, placing the California mission of the Sisters of Mercy under the protection of Our Lady. Later they were to learn that on that very day, Pope Pius IX had pronounced the dogma of the Immaculate Conception, a truth of special significance to American Catholics.[8] Their ride was long enough for them to realize how grateful to God they were that they had arrived safely and that they had had the strong support of a seasoned traveler, Father Hugh Gallagher.

In the little wooden church, St. Patrick's on Market, Father Gallagher offered the Holy Sacrifice of the Mass, a truly fitting manner in which to begin the California apostolate. Although the Sisters could not have known what lay ahead, theirs was a fervent thanksgiving and a total abandonment to Divine Providence. After Mass they were graciously conducted next door to the Convent of the Daughters of Charity.[9]

That very afternoon, the Most Reverend Archbishop, Joseph Sadoc Alemany, called to extend a warm welcome and to promise that he would return to offer Mass on December 12, in order to formally initiate the apostolate of the Sisters of Mercy in San Francisco. By happy coincidence the date chosen marked the foundation day of the Institute of the Sisters of Mercy by Mother M. Catherine McAuley. That the Archbishop made a deep impression on Mother M. Baptist Russell we learn from a letter to Ireland in which she said, "We have a saint for an Archbishop."[10]

The history of the Sisters of Mercy appears to move with that of the Church in California. As the first Bishop of California after the Mexican War, Alemany had been appointed to the See of Monterey in 1850. His vast diocese extended from Oregon to the Mexican border, from the Pacific eastward, to include all of California and Nevada, most of Utah, and part of Arizona in the extreme south. True, it was not heavily populated, but his flock was widely scattered and transportation was most primitive. When the First Plenary Council met in Baltimore on

May 9, 1852, he found sympathy in his fellow bishops who favored a division of the diocese. In a brief dated Rome, July 29, 1853, he was appointed first Archbishop of the new See of San Francisco. The archdiocese had its limits established: on the north the Oregon border; on the east, the Colorado River; on the south, the limits of the town of San Jose; and on the west, the Pacific Ocean.[11]

When the Sisters arrived in San Francisco, three months had elapsed since they had left their convent in Kinsale. To recount this momentous event, Reverend Matthew Russell, S.J., gives but a curt paragraph in his book, *The Three Sisters of Lord Russell of Killowen:*

> As Mother M. Baptist is now leaving Kinsale forever, we transcribe the page of the convent register which relates to her:
>
> Sister Katherine Russell, in religion Sister Mary Baptist Joseph, daughter of Arthur and Margaret Russell, of Newry, County Down. Born in 1829. Entered the Convent of Our Lady of Mercy, St. Joseph's, Kinsale, on 24 November, 1848. Received the holy habit 7 July, 1849. Made her religious profession 2 August, 1851. Offered for the California Mission on which she was sent as Mother Superior on September 8, 1854.[12]

The facts are here but they leave much to be desired if we would really know Mother Baptist Russell. Who was she? And why was she, the youngest of the group, chosen as Superior for the California mission?

As early as the thirteenth century, the Russell family had settled in County Down, at Killough, a seaport about five miles southeast of St. Patrick's grave. They were a people of faith who stood firm during the trying times of Henry VIII, of the Tudors and of the Stuarts who followed. Furthermore, they kept the faith all through the crushing era known among the Irish as the "penal days."

Doubtless due to limited opportunities for Catholic lads, Arthur Russell joined the merchant service and rose to be captain of his own ship in a lively trade with Norway. It was probably with an eye to marriage that he decided to give up the sea and settle at Newry, where he bought the Southwork Brewery.

Katherine Russell, the third child of Arthur Russell and Margaret Mullan Hamill, was born April 18, 1829, at Newry, a town beautifully set in a valley where the Glanrye winds its course to Carlingford Bay. At this time, with its commercial advantages, it was considered a rival of Belfast.

Katherine came into this world shortly after the long fight for Catholic emancipation had scored its first victory with the success of the Catholic Relief Act of 1829. It is Reverend Matthew Russell, S.J., her younger brother, who tells us that when the tiny child was brought to her mother, she called her her "first free-born child."

Before her marriage to Arthur Russell, Katherine's mother had been married at a very early age to John Hamill, a successful merchant who left her a widow, with the responsibility of rearing three sons and three daughters when she was not yet thirty. Five years later she married Arthur Russell. This second union was also blessed with six children, four girls and two boys. Perhaps the fact that all were children of the same mother, and that she was the woman she was, explains the strong bond and enduring interest of all the members of the household.

Matthew Russell, S.J., speaking of his sister Katherine, says, "She was a very sensible, healthy child, not unpleasantly precocious but very bright and good." He adds that at an "unusually early age Kate was presented for the sacrament of Confirmation to the new Bishop, Dr. Michael Blake, but that. . .she still had some years to wait before she was allowed to make her First Communion, which she received in the Old Chapel of Killowen in the year 1841, the same day that the oldest of her brothers was confirmed."

Between Katherine's Confirmation at Newry and her first Communion in Killowen, her life had taken several turns. Her father's health gave the family deep concern and, hopeful that he would improve in a warmer climate, plans were made to lease the brewery and go to France, where the girls would also profit by special educational advantages. Suddenly, however, their preparations were halted by the serious illness of Katherine's eldest sister, Mary. On June 28, 1838, the day of Queen Victoria's coronation, a fever claimed the precious thirteen-year-old child. While the rest of the British Isles celebrated the gala day, the Russell family kept a lonely vigil over the corpse.

All thought of going to France was given up and, while the family cast about for a small farm by the sea where it was hoped Mr. Russell might regain his health, they spent some months in a quaint little house in Rostrevor. It was here they were on the "night of the Big Wind," as the Irish call the terrific storm that hit England and Ireland on January 6, 1839. Rostrevor was a woodsy place and the fury of the storm wrought a memorable havoc.

That year they purchased a beautiful estate, Seafield, at Killowen, its large old-fashioned house well situated on sixteen acres, stretching downward to the sea. To accommodate the Russells, another wing had to be added, and a bit of refurbishing made it the home of Katherine Russell's dreams. Here she was to live the happiest years of her "days in the world."

Only a short walk away was Old Chapel; it had no other name. Here Katherine received her first Holy Communion and here, too, she grew in loving intimacy with the Divine Presence; for all who write about her remark how intense was her devotion to the Blessed Sacrament.

Life in Killowen was a happy life—exhilarating romps in the open country; challenging the steep Mourne Mountain between the Slieve Ban and the Croagh Shee for a breathless view of the rolling meadows and white capped sea; or, in the warm summer, enjoying the sparkling waters of Carlingford Lough. Yet it was not so idyllic that the Russell family was not schooled to a life that was real and earnest. A large family may add to the fun and zest of living, but it also furnishes ample opportunity for give and take, for the development of the social virtues of human understanding, sympathy, sharing, generosity, and self-control—just to mention a few.

The fall of each year found the Russell children busy at school under the direction of a very capable governess, Miss Margaret O'Connor; and from early morning until dinnertime, the large parlor at Seafield was as formal as any classroom. The curriculum probably consisted of English, with special stress on the use of the mother tongue, and an appreciation of the great classics; French, then considered a necessary cultural accomplishment; botany, often given a practical turn by a tour of the fields; natural philosophy, not the abstruse principles of metaphysics but the observable processes of nature, which we today call physical science; the history of Greece, Rome, and England, which served to show them the development of Western civilization, because from such origins they were heirs of the ages; and, of course, music and art, so that they might cultivate the talents God gave them and appreciate the special gifts of others.

Theirs was a very disciplined life, marked by a proper balance of work and play, wholesome pleasures, happy family gatherings, and a wise development of truly Christian living.

In 1844, the two eldest girls were sent to Belfast to school that they might broaden the scope of their education. However, the May following they were called home to the death-bed of their father who died on the twenty-ninth of that month. Seafield was a sad and lonely place that summer.

It was also the year when there appeared the first evidence of the awful potato blight that brought such misery and desolation to Ireland from 1846 to 1850.

With the death of Mr. Russell came another change in the Russell family. It was decided to abandon their place at Killowen and return to their home in Newry, in December, 1845. This adjustment helped somewhat to allay the pain of loss, as a new life began in the dear old town. So, too, did the demands of the poor and suffering victims of the famine provide the Russells with an opportunity to spend themelves in alleviating the sorrows of others. The blight on the potato crop was truly devastating, a terrific blow to the Irish economy and to the life of the nation.

The cause of the famine—the blight—was a natural calamity, like an earthquake, flood or the like, but the disaster originated in the ordering of human affairs that condemned so many to a lifelong dependence on a single crop, and a perishable one at that. The primitive state of the Irish economy and the disaster itself had deep roots in Irish history—Irish poverty was the sequel to years of penal laws that deprived the Irish of their heritage and that fastened landlordism, the curse of an agricultural economy, on them. For these absentee owners cared little or nothing about their estates so long as they yielded a maximum income.

Probably as many as a million perished in the famine years, and some authorities estimate the emigration during the decade at two million. It would be impossible to say how many died of starvation. Death stalked the land and many died of disease.

Malnutrition and a series of very harsh winters lowered the resistance of the people. Writers speak of "famine fever," which is not a medical term but may be taken as an indication of the serious diseases that followed in the wake of the famine.

Local communities, like Killowen and Newry, organized their own forces; for in such places the aid of the crown was less likely to penetrate, but so too was there less likelihood of contagion or poverty.

And yet, Mrs. Russell and Katherine found ample scope for an apostolate of charity. The former was chosen president of the relief organization in Newry, and Kate was a responsive and untiring member of the team. Reverend Matthew Russell, S.J., gives us a pen picture of their activities during these days of famine and death-dealing disease:

> . . .Between visiting the sick and poor in their homes in order to give any assistance needed and collecting from door to door the weekly subscriptions of those who were a little better off, Katherine found time to prepare her share of the clothing which was distributed to the poor. In fact, during the crisis, she was totally devoted to what was to be the work of her life.[13]

Before the ordeal was over, she was convinced that hers was a vocation to serve God in His less fortunate creatures, the poor and the sick; and early in 1848 she sought her mother's permission to consecrate her life to God in the religious state.

So fertile has Ireland been in the production of religious vocations that we are likely to think that religious communities were numerous at that time. As in so many phases of Irish life, where freedom of religion was so long proscribed and even education stifled by the penal laws by which the English fought to keep the Irish in subservience, there was relatively little evidence of religious life in Ireland before the Catholic emancipation. Some managed to keep up a stealthy existence. In 1830, the Poor Clares had founded a convent at Newry, but it was some years before the Sisters of Mercy would come to Newry. Katherine Russell first turned toward the Sisters of Charity, founded by Mary Aikenhead, but her own mother's interest in the new Mercy Institute, founded by Mother M. Catherine McAuley, together with the predilection of Dr.

Michael Blake, her bishop, whom she consulted, paved the way for her final admission into the Institute of Mercy. Since her father's death, Dr. Charles Russell, D.D., of Maynooth, had been the guardian of Arthur Russell's children, and his advice too was solicited. Perhaps his strong friendship for Reverend Denis Murphy, parish priest of Kinsale, caused him to counsel her to choose the distant Mercy Convent, at Kinsale, which had been founded only four years before (1844). Mrs. Russell paid a visit to Kinsale and was much impressed by the remarkable Superior, Mother Francis Bridgeman, and by the work of her convent among the poor.

In November, 1848, Katherine entered her new convent home in Kinsale. For this nineteen-year-old postulant there was no violent change in her life, although the pangs of parting with her family were indeed keenly felt.

She received the habit of a Sister of Mercy on July 7, 1849. The famine crisis had not yet passed. Cholera visited Ireland in December, 1848, and reached its peak in May, 1849. Sister M. Baptist, as we must henceforth call her, was allowed to tend the stricken creatures. Although a very young novice, she had already learned much about practical nursing from her mother. She was thoroughly sensible and healthy, and she evinced a remarkable skill in nursing and comforting the sick and the dying. Fear seemed almost unknown to her. She was quick to learn, quietly firm, and showed clear, calm judgment.

When the time came for Katherine's religious profession, it happened that Dr. Daniel Murphy, bishop of Hyderabad, was visiting his brother, Father Denis Murphy, pastor of Kinsale. Dr. Delaney, Bishop of Cork, deputed the visiting bishop to receive her vows on August 2, 1851.

Her early years in religion were spent in the classroom where she showed great promise in the instruction of the young. She had been solidly educated, and she proved particularly efficient in the schools. She was both gentle and firm, very self-disciplined and yet, for one still quite young, she commanded respect because of her understanding and sympathy.

Three years later she was chosen as superior for the California foundation which left Kinsale on September 8, 1854. Although there are several accounts of this momentous adventure, it seems fitting to limit the story to the facts as related by Mother M. Baptist Russell who speaks from experience and was leader of the group.

It was in the spring of 1854 that Archbishop Alemany sent Reverend Hugh P. Gallaher to Europe on diocesan business and with the commision to visit Ireland in order to seek recruits from the Sisters of Mercy for his very needy vineyard. On July 28, 1854, he arrived in Kinsale and stated his case to Mother M. Francis Bridgeman as fully as time would permit—he was obliged to return to Dublin that same day.

The "Discreets"[14] of the convent lost no time in a matter of such urgency and resolved that it would be wise to commit to writing the conditions under which the community would agree to affiliate. To seek Divine direction, a novena was undertaken immediately, and the Sisters were informed that no one would be sent to so distant a mission who did not, after due reflection, offer herself for it. Furthermore, the Sisters were cautioned against letting themselves be influenced by any other motive than the desire to accomplish the Divine Will.

Meanwhile, at least six letters passed between Mother M. Francis Bridgeman and Father Gallagher.[15] By August 16, the mission was considered in some measure abandoned, but a letter of August 19 from Father Gallagher cleared up several difficulties and communications were resumed. Mother Francis Bridgeman's prompt return letter drew the following conclusive response from Father Gallagher.

Killygordon, August 21/54

Dear Reverend Mother,

I did not allow a single post to intervene since the receipt of yours of 19th inst. My visit to Scotland, about some missionaries, retarded the receipt of your last, which I forgot to give in explanation of apparent neglect.

Now to the points on which you say your action will "depend."

1st. We have *all* the objects of your Institute in our Mission—and these shall be the Sisters' primary duties.

2nd. I know of no authority nearer than Rome that might dare to modify your Holy Rule. It must consequently remain for you, *as it is.*

3rd. No duties shall be pressed on the Sisters but such as they shall cordially approve.

These answers I give without qualification and with the full knowledge that there is not, and will not be, any wish to interfere with those things.

I think the above meets the essential points in your admirable letter, except this that I am not expecting Sisters of Mercy from any other house.

Please say whether you can meet me in Dublin by the 16th prox. or whether you wish me to go for you to Kinsale; or whether it may be necessary to furnish your traveling expenses thence to Dublin, should I not go.

I will write today to your most excellent Bishop. I will not cease to make commemoration of you.

I am, dear Reverend Mother, yours sincerely in Christ,

(signed) H.P. Gallagher

P.S. You know we set out from Southhampton on the 13th of September.

Meanwhile, Dr. Delaney had left for England, but he had taken care before his departure to give Father Kellegher, the parish priest, the authority to make a selection in conjunction with the Superior. The pastor's great unwillingness to act made him keep this fact secret almost to the last moment, September 1.

On Sunday, September 3, the following Sisters were chosen: Sister M. Frances Benson, Sister M. Baptist Russell, Sister M. de Sales Reddan, Sister M. Bernard O'Dwyer, and Sister Mary Howley. Three novices who had earnestly begged to be sent were also approved: Sister M. Gabriel Brown, Sister M. Paul Beechinor, and Sister Martha McCarthy.

On the morning of September 8, the mission band left Kinsale, accompanied by Mother M. Francis Bridgeman and Sister M. Aquin Russell. Upon arriving in Dublin, they were informed that the California party was so large that they could not secure passage on the *Arctic* and were obliged to await the sailing of the next ship.

The *Canada* sailed from Liverpool on September 23. Ships were then neither as comfortable nor as safe as the liners of a later day, but Mother Baptist is silent concerning the events of the passage except to say that they reached New York in safety on Friday, October 6, when they heard of the unhappy fate of the *Arctic*.[16] That there was a delay of almost a month before they resumed their journey is evident from the dates of her journal entries concerning sailing, but the only interim event she describes is the conference given by Father Isaac Hecker, who had been ordained a Redemptorist priest only five years before (1849). He had not yet been tested in the crucible of misunderstanding, which prepared him for his great work as founder of the Paulists.

It is Mother Austin Carroll[17] who tells us that at Cork they were joined by five Presentation Sisters, who had accepted the Sacramento mission when Father Gallagher had found it impossible to get a second group of Sisters of Mercy. It is she too who said that because Father Gallagher was obliged to delay his trip, and the Sisters of Mercy did not wish to make the perilous voyage to California without him, they remained with the Sisters of Mercy on Houston Street, New York, until November 13. The presentation Sisters went on and therefore arrived in San Francisco before them.

On November 13, the *Star of the West* left New York for the isthmus.[18] On this trip, the Sisters enjoyed the company of four Notre Dame Sisters and several Jesuits. By the twentieth, they had passed Cuba, arriving at San Juan del Norte on November 23, a trip of ten days. Here they got into a river boat, about eight o'clock in the morning, November 24, and at 2:00 p.m. they had reached the Castilian Rapids. Again there was transfer of bag and baggage to a Lake Steamer, the *Virgin Maria*, to cross Lake Nicaragua, the largest lake in Central America and the most beautiful phase of the journey. On their arrival, they transferred to what Mother Baptist called a "covered wagon" to cross the Isthmus of Nicaragua, perhaps the most dangerous part of the trip. The Cordilleras are a continuation of the mountain chain that extends from Alaska to the tip of the continent. The mountains are high, volcanic, sometimes jagged, and sometimes wooded, and the roads were as primitive as any in 1854. They reached San Juan del Sur at 5:00 p.m. and although the ship would not sail until morning, Father Gallagher advised that they board the *Cortez* at 6:00 p.m., November 25.[19]

The thirteen days up the Pacific were uneventful; the

71

quarters were cramped and the company rather rough. Mother Baptist and her Sisters, although strangers in a strange land, were glad to anchor in San Francisco Bay on December 8, 1854, and prepared to make this city their home.[20]

It was soon evident that the Sisters were not entirely welcome in California, as this excerpt from the *Christian Advocate* clearly illustrates:[21]

CARRIED PAST THEIR POST

The large company of European priests and nuns who arrived yesterday morning by the *Cortez* should obtain heavy damages from the Nicaragua Steamship Company for bringing them *past their port.*

The ignorance, debasement, licentiousness, and bigotry of the people of Acapulco is certainly not more than paralleled in any other part of Mexico or in any quarter of the city of Rome. Though it has been for so many years the metropolis of the Roman Catholic possessions on the Pacific, it *still* needs their ecclesiastical labors. That port opens up also a wide field which they have hitherto cultivated with great success—we refer to Mexico and the regions south of it extending from Guymas to Chagres. We trust these ladies and gentlemen may be able to return without delay to their proper destination particularly as the institutions of our Protestant and Republican country are known to be obnoxious to their sentiments and tastes. In case they do not commence suit against the Nicaragua Company for damages in bringing them here, we think it the duty of the Attorney General of California at once to institute proceedings in behalf of this State. . . .

The Sisters were advised to disregard such invectives, but some of their friends rallied to their support. The following is the spontaneous reply of Captain Cropper to a similar communication sent to one of the city papers by one of the passengers. The purport of the letter can be gleaned from the

72

captain's reply:

...I feel myself called upon to notice the article alluded to and to pronounce it the most disgusting, detestable calumny I have ever known or heard. The Fathers and Sisters in question are Catholics, and on board the *Cortez* their seats at table were next to me, and I may say that at all times they were constantly under my eye and observation.

Their religious exercises were performed not only on Sunday, but every day by themselves, without intruding on others; and in regard to "hard drinking," I cannot imagine how any person could be so very base a slanderer as to prefer such a charge against them. The extreme propriety of their deportment, their unobtrusiveness and the gentle, ladylike manners of the Sisters, and perfect correctness of the Fathers, should have shielded them from so gross an outrage.

Thomas B. Cropper
Commander of Steamer *Cortez*

San Francisco, January 18, 1855.[22]

It will be remembered that bigotry in the United States had reached such proportions in the 'fifties that it became crystallized in the Know-Nothing Party, known also as the American Party. California even succeeded in electing a Know-Nothing governor, J. Neely Johnson, in 1856.[23]

As early as December twentieth, Archbishop Alemany made arrangements with the hospital committee to have the Sisters visit the County Hospital and assist in the care of the sick. On January 1, 1855, the annals note that the Sisters renewed their vows in the private chapel of the Sisters of Charity and on the same day visited the County Hospital on Stockton near Broadway for the first time. This institution was then known as the State Marine and County Hospital. It was in order to be near this hospital that Mother M. Baptist rented a small house on Vallejo, about the 600 block, and on January 3, 1855, the group left their kind friends on Market Street to open the first Convent of the Sisters of Mercy in California.[24]

Chapter 3

ST. MARY'S HOSPITAL, STOCKTON STREET, SAN FRANCISCO
Founded July 27, 1857[1]

Anyone familiar with medical practice today must indeed be surprised to learn that in 1857 Mother M. Baptist Russell, when only twenty-eight years of age, and having been but three years in America, undertook to establish St. Mary's Hospital, San Francisco. She had no degree in hospital administration, no formal training as a nurse, and the problems that faced her were enormous. And yet, Mother M. Baptist brought to her projected apostolate a compassionate heart, loving concern for the sick and suffering, experience in practical nursing which expressed itself in the care and comfort of the patient, and what is also important, recognized business ability. We must remember, moreover, that medical science and the training of nurses and hospital management were, for the most part, developments of the late nineteenth and early twentieth centuries. St. Mary's Hospital was born and grew to its present stature along with the development of medical practice in California.

In the era of the gold rush, the profession of medicine had its quota of adventurers who poured into the state and ranged from savant to crook, some with little qualification to practice medecine. Not until 1876 did relief come in the form of the Medical Practice Act. passed by the Twenty-first California Legislative Session of 1875-1876. This is not to say that there were not outstanding men in the field of medicine who figured in the early years of California's history, to say nothing of thyunsung heroes of the medical profession of superior character and resourcefulness who rode the saddle up the mountain trails, often through the snows, to serve the sick in pioneer communities.

sured by the limitations of the doctor in the diagnosis and treatment of disease. In 1800, he did not have a clinical thermometer, a stethescope, or the X-ray, much less sphygmomanometer[2] or an electrocardiograph. But before these diagnostic aids were to come, there was need for the development of medical science.

Dr. Henry Harris has given us a good picture not only of health conditions in early California, but of the progress of medical practice and the story of California's early hospitals. Speaking of the latter, he says:

> ...The first public building provided with state funds and built on state owned land was located on Stockton Street, San Francisco. This was known as the State Marine Hospital. ...In 1851 San Francisco tied in with the State Marine Hospital agreeing to pay the state $30,000 annually for the care of the indigent sick. It was, however, considered superfluous when Congress appropriated funds for establishing the United States Marine Hospital in San Francisco. ...[3]

Therefore, a legislative act in July, 1855, abandoned the policy of state general hospitals, and the State of California proposed to sell the State Marine Hospital in San Francisco. On August 17, 1855, the Sisters of Mercy purchased the old brick building on Stockton between Broadway and Vallejo, and the County Board of Supervisors agreed to pay the Sisters five-hundred dollars a month for the rent of the same until a new County Hospital at Greenwick and Jones Street would be completed.[4]

With the arrival of the S.S. *Uncle Sam*, on October 5, 1855, the cholera epidemic visited San Francisco, and the Sisters offered their services to attend the victims in the County Hospital as the State Marine Hospital was now called.[5]

Impressed by the Sisters' compassion and efficiency in caring for the plague stricken, the County Board of Supervisors voted to hand over the management of the County Hospital to the Sisters on October 16, 1855.[6]

This proved a very unfortunate experience, for the Board of Supervisors, even under contract, sought to impose upon the Sisters by refusing to meet their obligations.

In March, 1857, Mother Russell notified the board that the Sisters could not shoulder the burden of caring for the city's patients, unaided:

Gentlemen:

> ...It is now nine months since we have received any money from the Treasury and you must be aware of

the immense outlay necessary to carry on a hospital such as this averaging one hundred and forty patients; it cannot therefore be a matter of surprise that we should be obliged to give up the contract. We would indeed be very anxious to accommodate the authorities especially in the present state of the city funds but it is utterly impossible to hold out longer and we feel every just mind will exonerate us from all blame when they consider what a sum it requires daily to supply food, medicine, attendance, fuel, etc. for such a number.

We are therefore obliged for the reasons given to decline entering on another month except on the following terms:

1. That the Board engage to cash on the first day of each month two of the audited bills now in our possession beginning with the one for July last.
2. That the terms for the monthly contract henceforth be $2800.00 in audited bills.

If these terms cannot be granted you will please consider the contract with us at end on the first day of April, from which date no new patients will be admitted, and the City and County will be charged for those remaining at the rate of one dollar each per day.

Respectfully,
Sister M. Baptist Russell
Superior of the Sisters of Mercy[7]

By April first, the Board of Supervisors had taken no steps to clear their obligations and Mother Russell was compelled to terminate the contract by refusing to take any County patients.

On July 19, 1857, the last of the County patients were moved to the municipal hospital.

St. Mary's Hospital, Stockton Street

When the contract was revoked, the Sisters of Mercy took

down the old County Hospital sign and replaced it with "St. Mary's Hospital, on July 27, 1857.[8] Arrangements were made with Dr. A.J. Bowie and Dr. I.P. Whitney to serve as attendant physicians when the hospital reopened under the patronage of Our Lady. Each was to serve alternate months with the understanding they were liable to be called at any time.

On the morning of July 28, 1857, the Stockton Street hospital received the startling report that Mother M. de Sales Reddan was dying. She had accompanied Mother M. Baptist Russell to Sacramento to conclude arrangements for a new branch at the state capital. An attack of influenza, followed by a series of complications, rendered her speechless and almost unconscious on the twenty-eighth, when she was anointed by Reverend Joseph Gallagher. Despite the efforts of the medical staff, she died at 11:30 a.m. on July 28, 1857. This was, indeed, a great cross for Mother M. Baptist Russell to bear following as it did the day of the opening of St. Mary's Hospital and during the arrangements for the establishment of the first branch house of the Sisters of Mercy in California in Sacramento. Here first Superior was to have been Mother M. de Sales. She had been one of the original eight and the first Sister of Mercy to die in California. Aged fifty-four when she volunteered for the California mission, she provided strong support for the young superior, Mother M. Baptist Russell. Her long years of dedication to the service of God and man, her understanding heart and her deep spirituality offer some explanation of the tremendous loss sustained by many in San Francisco who knew but three years.

A letter from Sister Mary Frances Benson to her Sisters in Kinsale gives us a pen picture of life at St. Mary's Hospital in 1859.[9]

> St. Mary's Hospital
> Stockton Street
> San Francisco
> July 4, 1859

> ...You will perhaps be interested in a few words about this great country. Great it is and wonderful but also great in wickedness.... You may grow old and descend to the grave without even imagining there could be such depravity in human hearts as the American nuns have to deplore and work against....

A word now about our St. Mary's Hospital. Within its precincts are included the Convent, the House of Mercy, Orphanage, Magdalen Asylum and Office for procuring situations for servants or as they call them here, "help." To describe the multitudes that have found shelter under the roof of St. Mary's since we took possession of it, would be a difficult task. . . .

During the time we had the County patients, we had under our care persons from every country of the world and all religions, too. . . .We have had perpetrators of all crimes under advice, instruction or care. In truth, St. Mary's has been for more than four years a very world in itself.

Within it has been the continual administration of every Sacrament (except Holy Orders)—Baptism of infants and grown persons; Confirmation of children, adults and converts; first Communion and last Communions, confessions and general confessions, anointings and marriages;—reconciliations of husbands and wives, rescuing unfortunate creatures from self-destruction and exhorting to contrition those already fallen. These with other works of mercy, too numerous to relate in this hurried letter have been our occupations or that of the Archbishop or priest as the case has required. . .

We now have a half orphanage; we had in it one hundred sixty-two children but the Archbishop thought we had not sufficient accommodation for ourselves and them; and last winter when we had a good deal of sickness among the Sisters, he advised Mother to cease admitting any more and to dispose of the others the best way we could. Then came wailing and lamentations on the part of the parents. Many of the children, although they had one parent living, were worse off than those who had neither mother or father. . . .

In the House of Mercy we have had up to this time about six-hundred young women. We also have what in Ireland would be called a "Widow's House" and in it are several very old women. . . .

In the Office, for procuring situations for servant girls, four hundred forty-eight have been supplied with places.

In the Magdalen Asylum we have twenty-one penitents; some of those did not enter the Asylum but coming sick into the Hospital were converted there. A few died in very holy dispositions. . . .

We visit the jail continually and find there many sad cases. We prepared two prisoners for execution; the last was hanged three weeks ago. He was a well-known robber and terror of the country. . . .When the Sisters went to visit him, the jailer would not open the door of his cell unless he had two men with him; they were in much terror of Bill and were astonished that we were not afraid of being admitted to so desperate a creature. At first we thought him very hardened and so he was; for it was very difficult to bring him to any feeling of repentance until the trial was over and the sentence passed. Even then he said, "He would never give it to the Yankees to laugh at him hanging mid-air." During the trial Mother Gabriel's brother was in court and he described him as being a most ferocious looking man, with the fire of anger and desperation flashing from his eyes. He was the same on receiving the sentence; no one pitied him. . . . Well, we visited him frequently; we were locked in with him and though savage with others, the poor fellow was gentle with us. He said he would give his life for the Sisters. On conversing with him we found he had never received his First Communion and had been to confession but once in his life. Our great aim was to keep him from destroying himself. By constantly visiting him and giving him books to read we succeeded, under God, in touching his heart. The tiger became like a lamb; made a general confession and received his first Holy Communion. He was confirmed by the Archbishop and invested

79

with the scapular. He gave up all conversation save with the priest and the Sisters and said he did not wish to see anyone but those who would speak to him of religion. As the time for execution drew near, we visited him every day and generally found him engaged in prayer. . . .

On the scaffold his demeanor surprised everyone and the change wrought in him was the subject of conversation everywhere; even the Anti-Catholic newspapers expressed their astonishment. . . .

Describing this same case these lines came from the daily press:

The deputy sheriff Ellis read the sentence of the court which directed the sheriff to execute the death penalty upon the prisoner. The prisoner listened with respectful attention and when the reading was concluded he bowed his head as if assenting to its justice. He then advanced toward the front of the scaffold and kneeling down pressed the crucifix to his lips and said in a distinct voice:

O God, forgive all the sins I have ever committed; I pray God to forgive me; I forgive all who have wronged me; God be with you all. Pray for me. God bless you; goodbye.

Mother M. Baptist Russell drew to her hospital some of the finest men in the medical profession of that day. Dr. Henry Gibbons (1808-1884), who had been a professor of medicine at the Philadelphia Medical College before coming to California in 1850, was one of St. Mary's early friends. Soon after his arrival, cholera appeared in San Francisco and he set up a lazaretto on Broadway for the isolation of the victims. He offered to serve those stricken by the dread disease and even slept at the hospital. In one instance, in his medical writings he refers to the Sisters of Mercy whom he observed at their posts of duty during the epidemic and commends them for "their lack of cant and proselytism in the County Hospital in San Francisco." He also rallied to their defense when they were under fire during the bitter *Bulletin* campaign against the County Hospital in 1856.

Dr. Gibbons was outstanding in his contribution to medical practice, professional journalism and medical organization.

Dr. Richard Beverly Cole, a contemporary of Dr. Gibbons, also has a unique record in California's medical annals. Dr. Cole's professional status grew with the years. He was dean of the Toland-U.C. School, 1873-1881, and president of the American Medical Association in 1895. He, too, "extolled the Sisters of Mercy for their bravery during the smallpox epidemic of 1868."

Speaking of Dr. Elias Cooper, Dr. Harris, in *California Medical Story*, has this to say:

> . . .His heart's desires were beginning to be realized in 1860. There was less aggression about him. Conciliation showed itself in many ways: the praise given to the entire visiting staff (including Toland) of St. Mary's Hospital where much good teaching was carried on. . . .[10]

Dr. Hugh Toland (1806-1880) was long a member of St. Mary's staff and a notable donor to California medicine, having founded the Toland Medical School, which he created at the cost of seventy-five thousand dollars, and then transferred to the University of California, in 1873.

Dr. Levi Cooper Lane (1830-1902) served long and well on the St. Mary's staff, as chief surgeon. Of him, Dr. Harris says:

> Lane was the most brilliant medical scholar in the West, its leading surgeon and teacher of surgery and its largest medical donor. The intellectual excellence of his mind was unquestioned and with its power was linked a high morality, qualities expressed in his great love of medicine. . . .
>
> His local fellows knew of these many qualities and bestowed on him leadership and such distinctions as they had to give. . . .[11]

This by no means exhausts the list of outstanding men of the medical profession who were associated with St. Mary's in the early years. But these few references support the contention that St. Mary's Hospital served as a laboratory for medical teaching and played a real part in early California medical history.

St. Mary's Hospital pioneered for four years, July 27, 1857 to November 11, 1861, on Stockton Street, in the heart of old San Francisco; but the brick building, which pre-dated the gold rush, was beginning to show its age. The wet weather brought evidence of leaks, serious ones in five or six rooms. The Archbishop suggested some repairs, not to exceed one thousand dollars. After the inspection of an architect, who voiced some fears regarding its safety, it was thought wiser not to waste the money on the renovation. Moreover, the Stockton Street venture had been looked upon as an interim hospital, to be maintained only until the Sisters could acquire a well constructed building in a good location. In fact, we read in a letter of the Archbishop, dated May 1, 1857,[12] that Mother M. Baptist Russell had already secured a desirable piece of property at the corner of First and Bryant Streets, on Rincon Hill. Today it would be hard to point out the location because it is completely effaced by the San Francisco Bay Bridge, the western approach of which is anchored in the hill.

The Archbishop was not slow to see the necessity of an up-to-date Catholic hospital in San Francisco, but in the late 'fifties, the struggling archdiocese was not ready to give much tangible support to the undertaking. Because the whole archdiocese would profit by adequate health care, Archbishop Alemany deputed Reverend Michael King to tour the gold country bearing this letter recommending the cause:

> Pastoral Residence
> Corner of Dupont & California Street
> May 1, 1857

Reverend dear Sir:

> In order to carry out the charitable objects of their Institute the Sisters of Mercy have already purchased a hundred vara lot in a good location of this city where they propose to erect a large well-constructed hospital. ... Such a hospital must prove to be of great practical utility and efficient charity to the whole community of the State but in a particular manner to those in the mines who are so often

exposed to the danger of falling victims to some sad accident or disease who having perhaps no relatives or friends from whom they might receive aid, would find in such an institution relief and comfort in their distress. . . .

I therefore recommend to you the noble undertaking and request you to travel the interior of the State, exhorting all charitable persons to make some generous effort toward the erection of Mercy Hospital. I also request the local pastors to afford you every facility and assistance on the mission so important for the general good.

With the best wishes to you and all benefactors, I remain truly in Christ,

(signed)
J.S. Alemany,
Archbishop of San Francisco[13]

Records[14] state that Father King visited Mokelumne Hill, Grass Valley, Nevada City, and some less familiar places. Despite his efforts, he raised only $2,956 in four weeks, when he was forced to give up the work. Mother M. Baptist, however, was not dissuaded from her intent. She turned to Divine Providence, which never failed her. Had He not only recently enabled her to clear the thirteen-thousand-dollar debt on the Stockton Street property? She initiated a public novena on December 8, 1858, the anniversary of her arrival in California and stated plainly that the purpose of this concerted prayer was to acquire the means to build the new hospital.

Little by little things began to happen. On May 9, 1859, the Ladies' Fair at Musical Hall realized nearly ten thousand dollars. Several unexpected bequests raised the nest egg a few thousand more and on July 2, 1860, the Sisters' lot on the corner of Pine and Leavenworth was sold for four thousand dollars.[15]

Meanwhile, the grading was commenced at First and Bryant Streets on January 6, 1860. The Rincon Street property cost ten thousand dollars and the grading came to five thousand. By August first of the same year, the construction of the new St. Mary's was underway.[16]

On September 3, 1861, despite the gale that blew over Rincon Hill, Mother M. Baptist Russell assembled the builders and friends of St. Mary's at the corner of First and Bryant, to participate in laying the cornerstone of the new St. Mary's.

Provision for the Magdalens[17]

As early as 1856, Mother M. Baptist Russell befriended some wayward girls whose petition for shelter she could not reject. When the Sisters moved St. Mary's to Rincon Hill, they did not move the Magdalen group to the new location.

The Archbishop approved this decision and even loaned the Sisters a lot on the corner of Van Ness and Grove to erect a Temporary Magdalen Asylum. The following spring, March 3, 1862, eight penitents and the Sisters in charge of the work took possession of the new building. The California legislature, in 1861, made its first appropriation for the asylum, which had encouraged the Sisters to erect the building. From time to time the Sisters received additional funds—biennially, following a report to the legislature together with a letter requesting funds.

On February 15, 1865, the penitents were transferred from Hayes Valley to the new building in the Potrero district.

As the hospital neared completion, early in 1861, Mother M. Baptist Russell thought it would be wise to deal directly with English manufacturers of hospital supplies, and she asked her mother to contact the firms. With her usual thoroughness, the latter journeyed from one English town to another for the necessary equipment, sparing neither herself nor her purse until all the bales and crates were safely shipped to California. Reverend Matthew Russell, S.J., speaking of the incident says:

> To her too great exertions may be attributed the stroke of apoplexy which fell upon her soon after, and nearly proved fatal. She recovered, however, but she never was the same again. This was the perfecting grace that closed her energetic and most useful life. Her last six years were but a lingering death. . . .
>
> . . .Mrs. Arthur Russell was allowed, as a special benefactor of the Newry Convent of Mercy, to spend her last four years in a house on the convent

premises—the old convent. And so it came to pass. . . her happy and peaceful deathbed was surrounded by the nuns she loved and among them, two of her daughters. May God reward this valiant woman![18]

On October 25, 1861, eighty iron beds, ordered from New York, arrived, and in the same shipment were two crates of delftware as well as bales of blankets, sheeting, etc., from England and Ireland.

Chapter 4

ST. MARY'S HOSPITAL—RINCON HILL, SAN FRANCISCO
November 11, 1861

The annals state that twenty-seven patients and about half the Sisters took posssession of the new hospital on Monday, November 11. That evening about 5:30 p.m. the Rincon Hill convent was blessed by the Very Reverend James Croke, Vicar General.

On November 30, 1861, M. William Lee, M.D., took up his duties as resident physician in the new hospital. He was a graduate of the Royal College of Surgeons, in Ireland, and for some time had been a member of the medical staff of the English Navy.

Word was received on December 9 of the flood conditions in Sacramento, and the Sisters were happy to provide for a number of refugees on Stockton Street, the government assisting with food, blankets and clothing.

Several of the daily papers of December, 1861, carried advertisements of the rates charged by the "elegant and up-to-date St. Mary's Hospital":

St. Mary's Hospital
First & Bryant Streets

Terms payable in advance for board and medicine.

Wards	$10.00 per week
Double rooms	$15.00 per week
Private rooms	$20.00 per week

Liquors and washing extra. Confinement $10. extra.

Money refunded in case person leaves before the expiration of the month.

The new hospital, facing Bryant, with a frontage of 123 feet was a four-story brick structure with a spacious mansard attic occupying the length of the building and a finished basement. This "elegant and useful building" was one of the most substantial and imposing buildings of its kind at that time.

The chapel on the east side, facing First, was dedicated on Sunday, January 5, 1862, and in the presence of Archbishop Alemany, who presided at the ceremonies, Rev. James Bouchard was the speaker of the day.[1]

Of course, St. Mary's Hospital, in 1862, had not reached completion. It expanded to meet the growing needs of the city, and the city was indeed growing. Because the building housed the novitiate, the tiny chapel dedicated in 1862 soon proved too small to take care of the numbers who wished to witness the Ceremony of Reception or Profession; and by 1879 a new chapel, which could accommodate several hundred, was blessed by Archbishop Alemany on the Feast of Our Lady of Mercy, September 24.

It was not until the last decade of Mother M. Baptist Russell's life that St. Mary's Hospital on Rincon Hill acquired its final, memorable proportions. The grading of the new west wing was begun in July, 1890. There was no doubt that the hospital had reached its capacity, and insistent demands necessitated the building program. Again the annalist tells us that money on hand was short, and a prayer to Divine Providence after all choir exercises indicated that Mother Baptist was placing her entire dependence on God to enable her to complete the project.

Early in August of 1891 the new west wing was completed and ready for occupancy. A shaft for the elevator, sixty-five feet in depth, presented some difficulty, as water began to fill it quickly; but despite the limitations of construction at that date, all was achieved without accident.

An interesting letter of Mother M. Baptist to her aunt, a Sister of Mercy in Dundalk, Ireland, describes St. Mary's on Rincon Hill as it neared completion:

St. Mary's Hospital
September 8, 1891

Everyone says the hospital is very perfect. There is every convenience that could be imagined; electric bells and lights, speaking tubes, a passenger elevator, chutes for soiled linen, letters, dust, etc. The three long corridors are two hundred feet long with large triple windows at each end; there are thirty-five private rooms, about a dozen of which are double and there are eighteen wards, but none large—the largest accommodating only twelve. The bathrooms, water closets, lavatories are all nicely tiled, both floors and walls, to the height of six feet; the basins, slabs, etc., are marble. The house is heated throughout by steam. But the grandest part of all is the mansard story, in which the operating rooms are situated. There are two antiseptic rooms, the ceiling, walls and floor are tiled, the basins and slabs marble, and they are so constructed that the whole can be hosed out and the water flows to one corner and runs off down a marble gutter. The operating tables are heavy plate glass in nickel-plated frames. The ophthalmic and electric rooms are furnished in hard wood. There is a large washing-room off which these rooms all open.

We have better and more ample accommodation than formerly, fine offices for the Superior and Bursar, which we needed much. All this, of course, has increased our debt. Yet I have no doubt but that with the blessing of God we shall pay it off in due time. We have an elegant suite of offices—a dining room, drug store and a private parlor for the doctors on the first floor; also parlors and a very neat mortuary chapel from which funerals take place without being obliged as formerly to go from the hall door. Altogether, our place is now very complete. . . .[2]

When St. Mary's Hospital opened its doors on November 12, 1861, the United States had already plunged into the bloodiest war in its history, a Civil War that threatened to disrupt the nation.

It was the sixties, too, that saw the advent of the silver era. By 1862 the Comstock Lode gave evidence of such richness that San Francisco was caught in a fever of speculation. This stimulated the growth of the city. Speaking on this very subject, in the 'sixties, John S. Hittell gives honorable mention to St. Mary's Hospital:

> In the year ending 1861, fourteen hundred and fifty-three buidings were completed or commenced including St. Mary's Hospital on Rincon Hill, Grace Cathedral, the Lick House and the Occidental Hotel.[3]

Silver mining, like quartz mining, required more elaborate machinery and a heavy investment of capital. San Francisco was the most logical money mart to finance the sale of shares. It was during the 'sixties, therefore, that the San Francisco Stock Exchange Board was founded, on September 8, 1862.[4] Here, men bought and sold, with all the excitement of the game, the stocks that made Virginia City famous as fortunes rose and fell.

To this era also belong the development of transportation and communication: On April 14, 1860,[5] San Francisco welcomed the first rider of the Pony Express from St. Joseph's, Missouri. In his bag, letters had been carried two thousand miles in ten and a half days, at five dollars an ounce. During this same decade, the San Francisco Market Street Railway made its initial run, on July 4, 1860, followed, about a dozen years later, by San Francisco's unique contribution to local transportation. A.S. Hallidie,[6] a San Francisco wire rope manufacturer, started what would prove to be the successful operation of the San Francisco cable cars, on Clay Street from Kearny to Jones, in September, 1873.

The outbreak of the Civil War interrupted the Butterfield Overland Stage in Confederate territory. It was for this reason that Ben Holliday established the new Overland Stage, under government contract at one million dollars a year, to maintain the mail service. Despite the impression given by "Westerns," Ben Holliday's Overland Stage was rather soon nosed out by the transcontinental railroad, which was initiated when President Abraham Lincoln gave his signature to the Pacific Railroad Bill on July 1, 1862, and completed when the Union Pacific finally met the Central Pacific at Promontory Point, Utah, May 10, 1869. Long before the road was finished, however, San Francisco's enthusiasm for the railroad had cooled, to be followed by strong opposition. This is why those who framed the Constitution of 1879 put tight restrictions on the State

Legislature and established the Railroad Commission to deal with the "Octopus."[7]

In the sixties and seventies, Rincon Hill was indeed an imposing location; the Sisters of Mercy owned eight acres, rising a hundred feet above sea level with a fine view of the bay and the Contra Costa Hills beyond. The hospital occupied the southern half of the block bounded by First, Bryant, Rincon Place, and Harrison Streets. Beyond Bryant there was a rather abrupt drop to the bay. This was South Beach, where small craft were repaired. Later the tideland was filled in and even before the 1906 earthquake and fire that caused the hospital to be abandoned, shipdocks had already been built to berth Pacific mail steamers. It was here, too, that the *Modoc* was moored to aid in the evacuation of the hospital when it was threatened by the fire of 1906.

The northern half of the hill was site of a number of fine residences: the home of Henry T. Scott, president of the Union Iron Works and later of the Pacific Telephone Company; also that of the Lorillards, the tobacco family. Some business concerns began to locate on the northern slope; e.g., Schillings, dealers in spices and coffee, and Lachman and Bundschu, the vintners. Farther west was the Schmidt Lithography plant, the original clock tower of which may still be seen at the western approach to the San Francisco Bay Bridge.

But as business moved in, fine families looked for new quarters, away from the noise and odors that began to claim attention. Some moved to South Park, an exclusive residential district to the southwest of Third Street, between Brannan and Bryant. Here Lord George Gordon, an Englishman who arrived from London in 1850, had secured a subdivision which he sought to transform into a park-like garden resembling Berkeley Square in London. The residences placed around the central plot were occupied at one time or another by such people as Henry Miller—the cattle king; Dr. Peter Smith; Peter Burnett— California's first governor; Peder Sather—who gave his name to the Sather Gate at the entrance to the University of California and to Sather Tower, popularly known as the Campanile; the Donohues; the Folsoms; James D. Phelan; and Gertrude Atherton—who wrote *A Daughter of the Vine*, the story of Lord Gordon's daughter.

In the early seventies, San Francisco was riding the crest of a wave of prosperity. Silver mining speculation, combined with

89

the business depression in the East and the completion of the transcontinental railroad, lured many to the west coast.

Stocks continued to rise and fall and interest remained high, at least until 1874. Then followed a reaction, and the city felt a serious depression as the market value of stocks declined. Again, men faced the reality of hard times. Of course, man blamed his plight on any available scapegoat rather than blame his own wild speculation in the boom times. "The Chinese must go," became the cry of the Sand-Lot party. The California Constitution of 1879 was supposed to cure the ills to which the state was heir.

About this time, Benjamin E. Lloyd wrote *Lights and Shadows in San Francisco.* A small excerpt from his book gives us some idea of the image already created by St. Mary's on Rincon Hill, an impression quite the reverse of the unfavorable press received in the fifties.

> Perhaps the best conducted and most appropriately arranged private hospital in the city is St. Mary's at the corner of Bryant and First Streets. It was built in 1861 and is under the care of the Sisters of Mercy. It is very commodious and every internal arrangement is conducive to comfort. It provides accommodations for one hundred and eight patients and is generally full.[8]

St. Mary's on Rincon Hill served as a dynamo from which a number of apostolic services radiated to meet the needs of the city. The hospital itself furnished the best available care for the sick of that day, but there were many whom the hospital would never reach had not the Sisters gone out in the streets and alleys of the city to seek out the sick poor. Mother M. Baptist did not merely delegate the work to others; she went herself, laden with food, other provisions, clean bedding, etc. Sometimes it meant cleaning the horrible abode, bathing the patient, caring for the children, supplying medication, and preparing food for the family. Unostentatiously, she sometimes paid the overdue rent or resolved some other problem that faced the distraught mother and father.

The hospital from the first was also the Motherhouse and novitiate, and many of the young Sisters received their first training in social service under the direction of Mother Russell whom they accompanied on her errands of mercy.

The Smallpox Epidemic—1868

In 1868 San Francisco was again visited by a severe medical crisis, smallpox of an unusually malignant type. The state did not as yet have a board of health, and while San Francisco had created a city Health Board in 1865, public health services had made little progress. San Francisco, the largest city on the west coast and chief port facing the Orient, was a perfect breeding ground for disease. The first smallpox case was reported in March, a few more cases appeared in April. By June, 153 cases had been verified and fatalities were mounting. Dr. Isaac Rowell, a member of the San Francisco Board of Health, made this report.

> The like of the epidemic has never been known. Previously, smallpox was much dreaded for the deformity likely to result rather than from a fear of fatal termination. But not so from this epidemic as may be inferred by comparing the mortuary record with the number of cases reported. Marked peculiarities characterize this plague. Death often follows before any well-defined variolous eruptions make their appearance. The cases that result fatally in the primary or secondary stage are generally accompanied by delirium and sometimes with maniacal ravings. . . .Remedies previously demonstrated as proper and efficacious in certain stages of the disease have proved of little avail. . . .[9]

To stem the tide of the disease, the Board of Supervisors, in May, 1868, hurried erected a Variola Hospital six miles outside the city. Of course, they hoped to prevent the spread of the disease by issuing an order that all victims be isolated. And yet, much as the citizens feared the disease, they dreaded the "Pest House" more. We read in the *Daily Bulletin*, August 5, 1868, an account that speaks for itself:

> The hospital is a new building situated about six miles from San Francisco between the Ocean House and

the Cliff House, a little distance from the Almshouse at Laguna Honda. It is too far from the city, and the everlasting fogs and heavy winds make it a poor site for a hospital.

The house consists of four rooms 20' X 20' for sick people and two rooms for nurses, a kitchen and storeroom. The rooms were meant for six beds each, but at least twelve beds have been crowded in. There are no water closets in the establishment. The nurses are compelled to close the openings made for ventilation by nailing carpet to protect the patients from cold winds. Very few of the beds have sheets. There is no resident doctor. Dr. Garwood comes once a day, but as he is responsible besides for the County Hospital, County Jail and the Almshouse, he has between five and six hundred patients to attend.

It was impossible to provide adequate nursing service. Only those who had had the disease and were in desperate need of work would take the chance. The press was not slow to draw attention to the management of the lazaretto and the treatment received. The San Francisco *Call* carried these lines:

At ten o'clock every night the lights are extinguished and the patients left in darkness. The nurses retire and are not seen again until morning. In the meantime the sick are without attendance and their sufferings present a picture too terrible for contemplation. Their piteous cries for water and attentions which they are too weak to procure for themselves are heartrending. . . .[10]

Dr. Richard Beverly Cole, who at this time was serving on the Board of Supervisors, met the barrage of complaints with this report:

. . .I gave orders that there should be a relay of nurses, some taking the night watch. One nurse, the oldest one, tried it but he found that he was called on eternally and he could not stand it. I must say that I cannot command the kind of nurses we need. We have had to advertise. . . .[11]

The cry of distress reached the ears of the Sisters. By this time, Mother M. Baptist Russell had ceased to be Superior and had become Assistant to Mother M. Gabriel Brown. The Sisters were on retreat but no time was lost in getting permission from the Archbishop to offer their services. Sister M. Francis Benson, who was fired with zeal to aid the sufferers, wrote and obtained approval for the request to offer their services to manage the hospital. Only too readily did Archbishop Alemany reply:[12]

August 9, 1868

Dear Sister,

I am always ready to encourage the works of charity so that you may go to the sick in the Smallpox Hospital with the permission of the Reverend Mother and you may remain at the hospital at night provided two Sisters remain without separating save for a few minutes.

I am very glad you do all you can in that way.

Yours truly
(signed) J.S. Alemany

The Superior, Mother M. Gabriel Brown, interrupted her retreat to write the following letter to expedite matters.

Beverly Cole, M.D.
Sir:

It is one of the privileges of our Order of Mercy that we attend our poor fellow creatures in whatever form of disease it is the Divine Will to afflict them. Therefore, if the city authorities are willing to accept of our services, two of our Sisters will, D.V., go to the Pest House to take up their residence there until such time as Almighty God wills to deliver the city from this terrible malady. If the authorities are willing to accept our services we shall go on Monday, August 17. One small room is all we require. You know the accommodations of a Sister of Mercy are very simple. We have been vaccinated lately.

Wishing you every success in your work, I am

Yours in J.C.,
Sister M. Gabriel Brown
Superior, Sisters of Mercy[13]

On August 17 Mother M. Baptist Russell and Sister M. Francis Benson went to the smallpox hospital. Released from the burden of office as Mother Superior, the former took advantage of her private station to claim a post of danger during the epidemic, but the Archbishop soon heard she was there and ordered her to return "to headquarters where she was needed to direct the operations of others." Sister M. Bernard Dwyer was sent to replace her.

Sister M. Francis Benson, who assumed the responsibility of the smallpox project after Mother M. Baptist Russell withdrew, worked hard at her task. The weather was miserable and she caught a severe cold. Constrained by her companions to take care of herself, she took advantage of a few days of enforced rest to write to Kinsale. It is one of the best first-hand pictures of the Sisters' work at the so-called Pest House.

It is truly a horrible disease, so loathsome, so disgusting, so pitiable. Twice the number of patients with any other disease would not require the care and attendance of those afflicted with smallpox. Not one spot from the crown of the head to the sole of the foot, sound; the eyes of the greater number closed, and pus running from them down their cheeks; their throats so sore that to take a drink almost chokes them; the tongue sometimes so swollen that not a drop can pass down; the hands so sore that they are helpless and the odor so terrible that they themselves cry out: "Oh Sister, I cannot stand the smell."

The doctors say it is an unusually malignant type. It is strange that few Irish take it. The majority of the sufferers are Germans; the next in number, native Americans; a mixture of Danes, Russians, French, Spanish, Italians and Portuguese.

The greatest precautions are used to prevent the spread of the disease; stacks of beds, bedding, clothing, etc., are burned. . . .

Now I shall turn from the body to tell you something of the soul. The number baptized is truly consoling; also, the number of negligent Catholics who have been brought to make their peace with God. We did not think of keeping any list until lately. It is easy for us in most cases to get to their souls, because in this terrible disease they become humble. Those proud cannot but feel they are an object of disgust to their fellow creatures and even to themselves. They are abandoned by their nearest and dearest, and shunned as an object of terror. Therefore, when they see us joyfully attend them they are astonished and thankful, particularly as they know we do not receive any money for it. Another thing that gives us great freedom in dealing with them is that not a single minister of any other denomination ever enters the Pest House, as this hospital is commonly called.

On two occasions they were sent for. In the first instance, the messenger returned with word that the minister could not come as his family would be endangered. The second case was an American lady, pious in her own way and much troubled about dying unbaptized but with a good share of prejudice against Catholics. We were almost sure that the minister she sent for would come as he is an unmarried man, and especially, as people are beginning to make remarks throughout the city that no one but the priests and Sisters will put foot inside these doors. Well, our messenger returned with the answer that M. So-and-So could not come on account of his congregation who would desert him if he entered the Pest House. When poor Mrs. Clay saw what little dependence she could place in her cowardly shepherd, she was glad to have Father Hayes baptize her. . . .

> It is truly edifying to read the records of miracles of
> grace; sometimes hardened men in the final hour have
> turned their dying eyes on their Savior in complete
> surrender like the good thief. Much good has come
> out of this horrible scourge.[14]

In September, 1868, the old Pest House was vacated and the
patients moved to a newly built frame building not far from the
new municipal hospital on Potrero Avenue. During this month,
122 new cases were admitted into the hospital, but by October,
only eighty were received. The disease continued to rage
unabated, but the city authorities had been forced to repeal
their ordinance requiring that all victims go to the hospital.
Cases were quarantined in their own homes, which were marked
by a yellow flag to indicate the presence of the disease and serve
as a caution.

The Sisters went, every Sunday and holy day, to Mass at the
Magdalen Asylum in the same ambulance that two or three
times a day conveyed sufferers to the hospital. They were
careful to go no farther than the sacristy lest they bring the
contagion among the penitents. Their clothes were also washed
at the asylum, and the most zealous among the penitents vied
with each other for the honor of doing the chore. Yet not a
single case of smallpox occurred among the Sisters or penitents.[15]

On October 21, 1868, at about 7:45 a.m., the community
attending Mass were quite shaken during their devotions by a
violent earthquake that lasted for forty-two seconds. Later the
Sisters learned that the city suffered some loss of life and
property damage but neither Rincon Hill nor the Asylum on
Potrero Avenue were affected. Even the weakened patients were
not very much alarmed. The shock occurred just before the
Consecration of the Mass, but the priest did not even turn
around, although a few in the congregation did cry out for
mercy.

After breakfast the Sisters went out to see what service they
could render and were surprised at the scene of disaster.
Business had stopped; sidewalks had buckled and were strewn
with glass; some homes had been rendered uninhabitable,
especially in areas where buildings were erected on filled-in

ground. Four terribly crushed men were brought into the hospital, but all ultimately recovered.

At 10:30 another shock occurred, followed by several less severe tremors that kept the timid in a state of alarm. The U.S. Marine Hospital was rendered uninhabitable.

In December, 1868, Sister M. Francis Benson was recalled from the Pest House, her health having been completely broken by five months of arduous service. She was brought to the asylum and quarantined, although she had not succumbled to the dread disease. This precaution was considered wise lest she bring the plague to others. On January 2, 1869, Mother M. Baptist Russell was sent to take over the direction of the smallpox hospital on Potrero Avenue.

That same month, a report was directed to the San Francisco Medical Society by three physicians who had been deputed to inspect the institution and submit their opinions.

January 25, 1869

Gentlemen,

Pursuant to a request made at the last meeting of the society, the undersigned visited and inspected the Smallpox Hospital and submitted their report with the approbation of Doctor Cole and Doctor Miller and the Matron of the house, Sister Superior Mary Russell. We went through and inspected every hall, ward, bathroom and closet in the hospital, and also the kitchen, dining room and room for attendants. In the wards we made particular inquiry of patients as to how they were treated in respect to physicians, nursing and general care and how promptly their rational wishes were complied with. . . .Our visit being at meal time we had a good opportunity of examining also the quality of the food and the manner in which it was served. We feel competent to draw just and truthful conclusions in regard to the present management of the institution.

The location of the hospital could hardly be improved upon for isolation and good atmosphere. The buildings are crude and unfinished and, of necessity, very unprepossessing. Everything around the outside of the building is rough and repugnant as improvised conveniences generally are.

Fortunately, the interior is better cared for, and in everything pertaining to cleanliness, ventilation and attention, it seemed to us all that could be expected. Indeed, it is wonderful that an institution so unmercifully crowded with smallpox patients in all stages of putrefaction and exfoliation could be kept so free from a sickening and disagreeable odor so common in all cases of private practice. Had we gone through the hospital blindfolded, we would not be able to ascertain that it was a smallpox establishment. This was one of the most striking facts and speaks volumes of praise to the medical management of those devoted Sisters whose sublime charity shrinks not from such repulsive and perilous labors.

The greatest defect of the institution was the crowded condition of the wards. . .cots so close together that there was scarcely room for a chair between them and yet a deficiency of room for patients arriving.

If any member of the Society doubts the accuracy of our report, we would most cordially invite him to test the matter by a personal visit and inspection. There will be no difficulty in his doing so; for the most unqualified invitation was given to the profession at any time to visit and see what the Hospital was trying to do and had accomplished.

Respectfully submitted

John F. Morse, M.D.
Joseph Haine, M.D.
Henry Gibbons, M.D.[16]

While some registered complaints because the Sisters were in charge of the hospital, and bigotry still showed its ugly head, the press in general was lavish in its praise and gratitude to the

Sisters during the crisis. The daily papers readily published testimonials of patients giving their experiences. One such testimonial addressed to *The San Francisco Morning Call*, speaks for itself.

February 9, 1869

Editors:

Permit me through the medium of your paper to express my feelings with regard to the Smallpox Hospital. . . .

I was an inmate of the institution for many weeks and I thank the Supreme Being that I am one of the fortunates who walked instead of being carried out of it. From the depths of a grateful heart I thank Dr. Johnson for his kindness to me and to the other patients. No doctor could be more attentive. The nurses, too, were kind to me. What shall I say to express my sentiments regarding those Ladies (so heroic), those angels of mercy! There were three, and the work they did for their suffering fellow creatures no words can describe. I shall begin with the youngest, a noble specimen of God's work. There she might be seen from six o'clock in the morning till a late hour at night, going around the wards carrying a tray laden with medicine or beef tea, wine or eggnog; always with a kind look and smile that did more good than anything the doctor could order for our health.

The next, a Spanish lady, whose kind interest in the poor sufferers was manifested by her untiring attention going her rounds morning, noon and night, with her pot of oil in one hand and a little brush in the other. Well may we thank her that there is a bit of skin left on our poor faces.

The third was an old lady, a real lady in every sense of the word. Here words fail to describe her goodness and kindness to every one, no matter who they were. Oh, Mothers, whose sons have died in that hospital, if

99

you could see that blessed lady kneeling by the bedside of your darling as I have seen her in the dark hours of night helping the dying. . . .I have seen her perform blessed actions for the loathsome bodies of these poor sufferers. But the works were done for God, not for the praise of man. I could tell a great many more works of these holy ladies that made the Pest House a place of happiness even though it was a place of suffering; but another time, if I find you good enough to publish this.

I hear that the most worthy and kind lady, the Reverend Mother of St. Mary's Hospital, is now at the Pest House in place of one of the three I knew there. May God protect them all! They are real Sisters of Mercy and mothers of the afflicted.

A Grateful Heart[17]

By April 18, 1869, it was evident that the number of patients had steadily decreased and that two Sisters would be sufficient to provide the necessary care. The two remaining Sisters left the Pest House on May 27, 1869, having been detained the last week by the lingering death of Homer Jenkins, the last of eighty-two persons received into the Church during the epidemic. All but fifteen of the eighty-two had died of the disease. There remained only eighteen smallpox patients, all in the convalescent stage. A few days later, however, the whole crew of a French man-of-war—officers and all—arrived at the hospital; fortunately, all had the disease in a mild form. The Sisters continued to visit the institution from the asylum on Potrero for several weeks.

Although the Sisters had specifically stated that they expected no remuneration for their services, the Board of Supervisors resolved to petition the legislature for authority to grant the Sisters of Mercy the sum of five thousand dollars as a mark of San Francisco's gratitude for their nine months of devoted service. In response to this request, on March 10, 1870, the state legislature enacted the following measure:

Whereas the City and County of San Francisco is indebted to the Order of the Sisters of Mercy for the invaluable aid rendered by the Sisters of that Order in attending upon the sick at the smallpox hospital during the prevalence of the late epidemic, saving by their noble and self-sacrificing efforts many lives of our citizens; and whereas in addition to these services and as recognition on our part of the great pecuniary assistance rendered to the city by them inasmuch as they obviated the employment of nurses at a time when great expense was incurred; therefore,

Be it resolved: That in consideration of these services, the Board petitions the power to authorize and order paid the sum of $5000. to the Order of the Sisters of Mercy.

The People of the State of California, represented in the Senate and Assembly, do enact that this sum of $5000. be paid immediately.[18]

This was indeed acknowledgment by public officials that the Sisters had heroically answered the call of duty when the city was in need. The author cannot find any record in the original annals of the Sisters of Mercy, their chapter reports, etc., that the money was ever accepted. In fact, all references to the action of the county and state officials are in the public records.

Compassion for the Wayward and Imprisoned

Nor did the Sisters confine themselves to the care of the sick. One of the initial works of mercy undertaken by them in San Francisco was that pointed out by the Good Shepherd during His earthly career—the seeking out of lost sheep, concern for the broken reed, the wayward and the imprisoned.

In 1871, Mother Baptist Russell reached out to bring comfort and consolation to the unfortunate prisoners of San Quentin. Because women visitors were strictly prohibited at the prison, Mother applied directly to Governor Haight for an exception in their favor, and the following gracious response was received:[19]

State Capitol
Sacramento

Sister M. Baptist Russell

101

Dear Reverend Mother,

The Sisters of Mercy can visit the State Prison at San Quentin at their convenience. It would be best, probably, to have regular times for visits but you can confer as to this with the Warden.

April 11, 1871

Respectfully yours,
(signed)
H.H. Haight

For many years Mother M. Baptist Russell herself assumed the responsibility for the visitations twice a month to San Quentin. When she was no longer able to do so she was succeeded by a namesake, Sister M. Baptist Mogan.

While Mother M. Baptist Russell did not condone crime, she had a very compassionate heart for the erring. She was ever mindful of the dignity of the human person and the priceless value of a soul redeemed by the Most Precious Blood. This she imparted to her Sisters who ministered to those in prison, which explains, in some measure, their amazing success in disarming even the most obdurate. Of course they did not believe that their own efforts won spiritual victories. They simply made themselves Christ-like agents to serve, with God's ready grace, in bringing men back to God. Many a prisoner found new purpose in life because of the Sisters' encouragement; or in death, surrendered to his God in Whom he found a merciful Friend. Mother Russell sometimes went to great lengths to right wrongs or save a mother the crushing blow of learning that her son died a felon. The account of one such instance is offered here.

Among the prisoners of San Quentin in the early 'seventies was a young man, Alexander Walker, who had been sentenced to fifteen years imprisonment. He was a native of Prince Edward Island and evidently belonged to a good family. To the end he protested his innocence but could find no one to fight his case. At last his health gave way. It became evident that he was wasting away with tuberculosis. His physical sufferings, however, were slight compared to the anguish that his disgrace would bring upon his parents. Understanding that the Governor would release him if there were some guarantee he would be taken care of, Mother Baptist gave a written promise to care for him at St. Mary's Hospital. Weeks elapsed before the official documents were processed, and he died on the eve of the date set for his release. The warden notified Mother Russell of the facts, and she had his remains brought to St. Mary's Mortuary Chapel. The newspaper notice stating that his funeral service would take place at St. Mary's was sent to his parents who were spared the grief of knowing that their boy had died in a felon's cell.[20]

That the prisoners appreciated the Sisters' compassion and sincere concern for them is attested by an open letter sent by the inmates to the *Monitor* and published December 7, 1894.[21]

Editor of the *Monitor*
Dear Sir:

At the request of the Catholic prisoners confined here and by the kind permission of Captain J.C. Edgar, we beg leave to publicly express through your columns our heartfelt thanks to Mother Russell and the Sisters of Mercy under her charge at St. Mary's Hospital for the many and varied services rendered the unfortunate inmates of this prison. The influence of the Sisters upon the prisoners is next to that of a priest, and many a man has been made to see the light and find a cure for his despair in the kind words and Christian teaching of these good Sisters. Men in convict garb are still human beings, capable of reasoning and susceptible to the influence of what is good. Many of them, through the Sisters' visits, have been convinced of the error of their ways and fortified by grace, their complete reformation has been made possible.

The work of the Sisters of Mercy at San Quentin does not stop there. It reaches into the homes and hearts of relatives and friends. Many a discharged prisoner has been given aid to enable him to lead an honorable life. The prisoners want, by this letter, to make known their appreciation for the untiring zeal of the Sisters of Mercy on their behalf. We wish, also, to thank them for the three hundred books they have brought to us during the last few years.

Sincerely yours in behalf of the prisoners,

J. J. Howard
T. J. Whelan

The Rincon Hill Complex

St. Mary's Hospital, on First and Bryant Streets, San Francisco, dominated the eight-acre site with its seventy-two-foot frontage on Rincon Place. But additional buildings on Rincon Hill housed other works of Mercy.

St. Mary's Hall—1862

On March 15, 1862, St. Mary's Society undertook the erection of a hall, thirty by sixty feet, adjoining the hospital. It was to serve as an assembly hall for their weekly meetings. This organization had been formed on December 25, 1859. It was really the first confraternity in honor of Our Lady in San Francisco, but it is not to be confused with the sodalities of the Blessed Virgin, which later became associated with almost every parish. From the beginning it drew large numbers because it offered a well-planned spiritual program and opportunity for apostolic action, as well as other mutual benefits. When the hall was completed, St. Mary's Society had six hundred members in attendance at their first meeting in the new building. Reverend Michael King, who had acted as their chaplain from the beginning, proposed a rule which was readily adopted.[22]

Home for Aged Women—1872

Shortly after Mother Russell had opened the hospital on Rincon Hill, she began to plan more adequate quarters for the several elderly woman whom she had transferred from Stockton Street. As she expressed it, a separate building for them would provide a more suitable place for them than the hospital. The young women of St. Mary's Society became interested in the project, and at their meeting, Sunday, September 26, 1862, they proposed to forward the erection of a home for the aged women by contributing all of the more than one thousand dollars then in their treasury and, in addition, five-hundred dollars per year for four years. Archbishop Alemany was present at the meeting and heard the offer. He would not give his permission, however, for the raising of funds for such a project because he feared the public was too often called upon by existing institutions, and because he thought that by admitting young women to be employed in laundry and needlework, such an establishment could be made to pay for itself. The members of the society and the Archbishop took opposing views on the matter, and no agreement was reached when the meeting was adjourned. A letter to the Archbishop was addressed by Mother Russell rather soon thereafter.

> If I understand aright what your Lordship said on last Sunday, your idea is to establish an institution in which all females of good character whether young or old, healthy or infirm, can have a home for a shorter or longer period according to circumstances—the young and healthy to be employed at laundry work, sewing, etc., as a means of support for the establishment. The "House of Mercy" properly so-called is one of the chief objects of our Institute and is intended as a temporary home for healthy able-bodied women during the time that elapses between their leaving one situation and procuring another and to it is attached the Registry Office through which employment is provided for the inmates of the House of Mercy, as well as for all who attend the Office. The inmates of the House of Mercy are obliged on principle to rise very early, work hard, etc., in order to fit them for the hardships of service; but should there be among them persons not able to observe these regulations, jealousies, dissatisfaction, and more or less discord is created. This is one of the difficulties we have had to contend with all along. There being no home for aged and infirm females and no Alms House, we were obliged to throw all such on the House of Mercy. Some twenty or thirty I could name are fit subjects for the proposed "Mater Misericordiae" or House of Mercy.

Another and a strong reason for not uniting the two objects is that it would have the effect of depriving the Institute of the interest and charitable assistance of the benevolent; for servant girls have been, as a body, hitherto so independent and even impudent in this country that the Public have no sympathy for them and think them no object for charity. Many say even now that in providing a "Home" for them, we are only encouraging idleness and that if they had no such place to retire they would be satisfied to go any place and at low wages. Now, although this is the language of those who do not understand the system of the House of Mercy nor the real facts, it must not deter us from doing what is right for our poor, faithful and much abused girls. Still I think it is reason enough against connecting their name with the proposed establishment which in its other form will, I am sure, meet with the warmest sympathy of the people. Neither is it intended to rest entirely on the charity of the Public. In such institutions are found many who bring ample funds for their own support and often even more. Even at this moment we know nice old women, whose children are well off but who live so far away from church that the aged parent would be delighted to get into such an institution just for the advantage of getting to Holy Mass. . .and their friends or relatives would pay for them.[23]

Mother Russell's special concerns for the elderly is well attested by this and other letters of hers, and by the comments of her brother.

And yet, it was not until ten years later, January 30, 1872, when Archbishop Alemany came to St. Mary's Hospital on the canonical visitation, that Mother Russell's cherished dream, a home for the aged, won his approval. This building, on Rincon Hill, was to be a very simple two-story frame building adjoining the hospital. Within four years it housed ninety guests. A reporter from the *San Francisco Post* gives us this picture of the home on March 23, 1879:

We also visited the "Home for Aged Females" of

whom there are now ninety-six ranging from fifty to
ninety years of age. The majority are kept for sweet
charity's sake, but some had a little saved and now
had secured a haven wherein to end their days. It was
pleasant to see their air of good fellowship that
prevailed. Those who were in bed from physical
debility were tenderly waited on by the healthy. At
several of the bedroom doors we observed trays as
nicely appointed as you would see at a second-class
hotel.[24]

The name "Home for Aged and Infirm Females" was inscribed
above the door of the building, but there was a persistent effort
to change the name to the La Salette Home. Because both
names appear so often, and as the former was more frequently
used in the press, there has arisen some question as to whether
these names represented two different establishments. The
answer to the question is, "No." As His Grace had more than
once hesitated to give his approval to this good work, Sister M.
Francis Benson, the devoted advocate of the aged and infirm,
attributed his ready acquiesence on January 30, 1872, to Our
Lady because on that day there arrived from France the statue
of Our Lady of La Salette, the gift of a French girl, Jeanne
Padin, who attributed her cure of a serious malady to the
invocation of Our Blessed Lady. She also gave one hundred
dollars for the oratory in which the statue would be placed, and
the Archbishop consented to bestow his blessing.

The home for the aged on Rincon Hill was completed by July
2, 1872, and was blessed by Reverend J. McCullough. Eight
elderly women from the hospital and four additional guests
were the original occupants of the new home.

By 1881, the La Salette Home had become so crowded, and
the number of applicants who could not be admitted so great,
that it was considered necessary to look for property for a new
building. Several desirable sites were considered, but the Sisters
were not free to make their choice. The Archbishop, although
limited in funds, had acquired considerable property by various
bequests, and he insisted that a selection be made from the
archdiocesan property. Accordingly, two blocks at the base of
Calvary Hill, facing Masonic Avenue, were selected. Grading was
commenced in the spring of 1881 under the superintendence of
the Sisters' good friend, James Kelly.

On October 22, 1881, the following article appeared in the

Among the many benevolent institutions of San
Francisco there is none that commends itself more
strongly to the charitable instincts of the public than
the "Home for the Aged and Infirm Females"
founded by the Sisters of Mercy and connected with
their Convent, Hospital, Schools and House of Mercy
on Rincon Hill. . . .

In 1872 a large three-story frame house was erected
on the Hospital property, but this is now quite
inadequate to the wants of the inmates. The fact that
the Home now shelters one hundred twenty-five
women varying in age from fifty to ninety years while
it has fair accommodations for only eighty or
eighty-five will give a better idea of the need for
enlargement than any detailed description could
convey. Having no more space in the present location,
the Sisters have purchased two blocks at the intersec-
tion of Masonic Avenue and Turk Street at a cost of
$11,500. of which $10,000. has been paid. The work
of grading the sand hills of which this purchase
consists has been going on for some time and already
something like $10,000. has been spent on this, a
well, windmill and a tank of 45,000 gallons capacity.
As soon as the grading is completed the building will
be commenced; it will cost at least $60,000.

No work can be considered more worthy of general
sympathy than this; the Sisters rely on the well-
known liberality of the people to aid them in this
noble undertaking. . . .[25]

The projected building was to be as commodious and
convenient as possible. Besides kitchen, refectories, workrooms,
storerooms, it was to contain about one-hundred bedrooms and
four dormitories, with a capacity of three-hundred. The cost
was figured at eighty thousand dollars, one-quarter of which
had already been spent in preliminary work. And yet this was
one project that Mother M. Baptist Russell was not able to
realize.

In December, 1885, Mrs. Gibson, a wealthy San Francisco lady, left a bequest of some ninety thousand dollars for the erection of a home for elderly ladies. Every word of the will was in her own handwriting, and it was placed in a safe deposit vault four years previous to her death. However, the will was contested by her relatives, and Sister M. Francis Benson received only thirteen thousand dollars. It was in expectation of this major bequest that Sister M. Francis had caused the foundation for the new home on Masonic Avenue to be laid. Even plans for laying the cornerstone had been made, and the ceremony itself was well attended.[26]

Lack of funds that had seemed guaranteed continued to cause major setbacks in the building of the new home for the aged. In January, 1893, James D. Phelan gave five thousand dollars to Our Lady's Home, and with it Mother Baptist Russell, in May 1893, purchased a new site—eight acres on Bray Avenue,[27] Oakland. Mother Russell, who was determined that the three-hundred thousand dollars needed to build the new home would be raised, pushed the work with her usual trust in Divine Providence. From time to time kindly benefactors remembered the projected home, and there was, by 1895, about thirty-three thousand dollars in the treasury with which to begin the work. The foundation was progressing rapidly, at a cost of $16,500. Since March 15, 1883, the California legislature had agreed to give state aid for the maintenance of indigent aged in charitable institutions. However, the withdrawal of funds by the state legislature on February 28, 1895, put too great a strain on the community. Without it the Sisters could not assume the entire support of so many residents, and the Archbishop requested that work on the new building be suspended. In 1901 there seemed no prospect of building the home in Fruitvale,[28] but the earthquake and fire five years later paved the way for the new home, which was dedicated March 17, 1908.

The Mater Misericordiae or House of Mercy—1873

The Mater Misericordiae was a residence hall for unemployed girls or women, and in the last half of the nineteenth century there were many who made their way to the city seeking work and were unsuccessful. Strangers to the big town and to the pitfalls that beset the unwary in cheap boarding houses, and out of work, they were glad to secure a safe refuge with the Sisters. This was one of the earliest services offered by the Sisters of Mercy after they came to San Francisco. The annalist tells us that on February 2, 1855, a house adjoining our place on Vallejo Street was used for this purpose. By December 11, 1855, so many girls had been placed under the Sisters' care that the younger girls were assigned to a half-orphanage which also provided a day school and was entirely separate from the House of Mercy.

As the demand increased, the Sisters offered not only a residence for girls seeking employment and an agency, but also an industrial school to prepare them to earn a living. On February 2, 1873, the Archbishop gave permission to add a wing to the home and on September 24, 1873, Archbishop Alemany blessed the House of Mercy.

The work at 23½ Rincon Place soon caught the eye of a newspaper reporter who carried this story in the *San Francisco Post:*[29]

> The Sisters of Mercy who have charge of St. Mary's Hospital have established a Home for Working Girls. The latter, who have come from all parts of the United States and who are unable to procure employment, find in this Home a stopping place until they can get employment. If they are at all able, they pay what they can, if not, they earn it in the sewing room and laundry. The work rooms are in the lower story and present a busy scene. Some thirty girls seated around a large table in the center of the room were learning to cut and fit, etc. Along the sides of the room a like number were engaged in sewing and the hum of the sewing machines attested their industry. The rooms were well lighted and sunny. Most of the girls were making skirts, filling an order for Murphy, Grant and Company. . . .All were busy and happy. A wardrobe displayed ladies' wrappers, underwear, baby jackets, aprons, etc. . . .The youngest of the girls is thirteen. Many of the girls are orphans. Some of these have a half day school, working the rest of the day. Situations are obtained for those who wish it as soon as they are well taught.

> . . .No girls are permitted to enter the Home unless

they have an unsullied reputation.

Upstairs are two large dormitories; one containing twenty and the other fourteen single beds with neat white bedspreads. Printed rules are posted, one of which states that the girls may sew for themselves after 5:00 p.m.

On December 8, 1874, Reverend J. Prendergast wrote to Mother M. Baptist Russell at the request of the Archbishop, urging her to open a downtown employment office. In response to this petition an office was opened on February 2, 1875, at 324 Stockton Street.[30]

The following letter to Archbishop Alemany was a report requested by his excellency relative to the House of Mercy.

November 23, 1877

Most Reverend Father in Christ,

The House of Mercy and Intelligence Office were opened simultaneously February 2, 1855. We have always been more anxious to do good than to keep an accurate account of the same. So that the subjoined figures are much below the reality but they are what is found in the register.

From the date given above to the present time, one thousand six-hundred and sixty-four persons (1664) have been lodged and fed for a long or short period in the House of Mercy. The present average number in the Institution is forty-five (45) of whom about fifteen (15) are employed in needlework, as are also about the same number of outdoor apprentices not included in the above average. From the opening of the Intelligence Office until our removal to this building, a period of nearly seven years, over nine thousand were supplied with situations, but after our removal to this locality the number fell away considerably. The books are not at hand and so the precise number cannot be given but from February 2, 1876, to the present date, November 23, 1877, I find that two thousand five hundred and forty (2540) have been entered on the books of the Office, while during the same period nearly two thousand families have applied for help in one capacity or another.

As to the expense of the Office, all I can say is that it occupies the entire time of a Sister and two or three rooms have been devoted to it. Of course, during the nine months it was on the corner of Post and Stockton Streets, the salary of the lady employed was $100. a month, while the receipts were small in comparison. In fact, among the applicants at the Office we daily met many cases of pressing necessity and destitution.

Your Grace may recollect my mentioning the number of men we were feeding every day during the nine months. We ceased that distribution in July as we were running into debt and besides employment was more easily found than in the winter. Many individual cases, however, continue to come, besides at least twenty families to whom we give bread, soup, etc.

I need not say that we are never without charity cases in the hospital and among the sick we visit in their own homes.

Of course, Your Grace is aware that there are eighty old ladies in the Home for the Aged.

I believe this answers all your queries.

I remain most respectfully your obedient servant,

Sister M. Joseph O'Rourke, Superior[31]

This letter refers to the great distress that prevailed nationwide among the laboring classes during the winter and spring of 1876-1877, so great that it was necessary to erect a pavilion on the hospital grounds where hundreds of men, young and old, formed long lines to receive hot soup and bread from a boiler erected in the yard.[32] In order to supply employment,

Reverend Hugh Gallagher urged the supervisors to begin work on the grounds destined for public recreation. Others took up the plea, and Golden Gate Park, the pride of San Francisco, soon began to take shape.

The Archbishop, convinced that the financial burden of maintaining the soup kitchen should not fall on the Sisters of Mercy, ordered a collection to be taken up in the churches of San Francisco.

Again, in 1893, there was widespread unemployment and distress caused by the Panic of 1893 which wrought havoc among the laboring class. The vortex of the storm was Chicago, where grave disturbances took place as a result of the wage cuts by the Pullman Car Company. But the depression that befell the country was widespread. Social legislation was not yet on the books, and labor organization had not yet become effective.

This was the second time that the Sisters of Mercy sought to meet a condition of considerable distress among the laboring class. In October of 1893, about eighty came daily to St. Mary's for food; but before the end of the year the number had increased to five hundred. Seven hundred people were fed on Christmas day and over eight hundred loaves were distributed. Through the benevolence of a few friends, the hospital was able to continue this work until prosperity returned and with it, much needed employment.[33]

In March, 1894, Mother Baptist Russell, writing home, alludes to the situation in San Francisco:[34]

> I think I mentioned the crowd of unemployed men in this city for the last five months; 589 at our door for breakfast yesterday. We had to employ a second baker. Some good people send flour, coffee and sugar. This has been going on since October. About Christmas the number was over six hundred for a few days.

St. Aloysius Novitiate[35]

Early in November, 1876, the German Hospital on Brannan Street was totally destroyed by fire, but happily it was discovered soon enough that no lives were lost. St. Mary's offered to open her doors to its patients until the completion of the new hospital, for which they had ample funds. This offer

113

was accepted by a committee of the German Society, and between twenty and thirty patients were given accommodations. In order to take care of the unexpected addition, St. Mary's purchased a house and lot adjoining the hospital property, at a cost of eleven thousand dollars, to which the novitiate was moved. The new quarters was formally blessed and received the name St. Aloysius Novitiate. Since St. Mary's on Rincon Hill was the Motherhouse and Novitiate of the Sisters of Mercy, an important phase of its activity was the formation of young women for the life of a religious and the preparation of the young Sisters for the work of their apostolate. St. Aloysius Novitiate was a step forward in making special provision for them.

The Schools

For some time, in San Francisco, there was evidence of misunderstanding among friends as well as strangers in regard to the educational apostolate of the Sisters of Mercy. This would seem to have stemmed from those more familiar with the Sisters' hospital work than with their schools. Yet, from the first, education has had a unique position among the objects of the Institute. The fact is well attested by Mercy schools at all levels—elementary, secondary and collegiate—that dot the English-speaking world.

Mother M. Baptist Russell, however, appears to have been almost totally engrossed in social service and hospital work for her first sixteen years in San Francisco. This, it has been explained, was due to the urgent need for these services and the recurrent epidemics that the city seemed powerless to meet. Yet as early as July 4, 1856, when Mother M. Baptist was asked to specify the objects of the Institute, she did not hesitate to give first place to education in an article published in the *San Francisco Herald*.[36]

> The first object to which the religious of this Order are solemnly devoted is the instruction and education of the ignorant, rich and poor, young and old, without distinction of country or creed.

Mother M. Baptist herself was prepared for the teaching

114

apostolate, and her brother, Reverend Matthew Russell, S.J., stated so in a few bold strokes:

> . . .Sister M. Baptist. . .was from the first particularly efficient in the schools. She had been solidly educated and what she did not know she was quick to learn, while her quiet firmness, her clearness, and her calm judgment gave her great power in instructing the young. . . .[37]

Shortly after Mother Baptist arrived in San Francisco, she opened a night school for adults while the Sisters were still located on Vallejo Street. The following September 24, the Feast of Our Lady of Mercy, the Sisters undertook to teach the elementary school then located in the lower floor of St. Mary's Cathedral. It was in reference to this school that she made clear that the Sisters of Mercy would withdraw from the school if it were placed under the Board of Education. She was familiar with the bigotry and arbitrary conduct of government agencies toward church-sponsored schools, which far outweighed any benefits that might have accrued from state financing. It was the action of the state legislature in 1855, especially the amendment to the Ashley Act, that caused Mother Baptist to recall her teaching Sisters from the cathedral school, October 16, 1855. The senate-appended amendment stipulated that the financing of church-sponsored schools would be conditioned by two provisions: 1. that no religion be taught during regular school hours, and 2. that the teachers be under the authority of the state Board of Education. Mother M. Baptist Russell's firm stand on government control of her schools was not at the time well supported. Even Archbishop Alemany and Father Hugh Gallagher seemed to favor accepting the law's application to the Sisters' schools; but the prelate left her free to follow her own judgment. That her position was tenable is evidenced by the glorious development of the Catholic schools of California under a system totally independent of government control.

It was in response to a plea for schools in the capital city of Sacramento that Mother Baptist opened the first branch house in California, on October 2, 1857.[38]

Not long after the Sisters of Mercy began their apostolate on Rincon Hill, the Reverend F. Dalton, pastor of Grass Valley, Nevada County, in the vicariate of Marysville, applied for a foundation in the gold country. The proposition was not immediately accepted, and it is not hard to conjecture why. Transition to a new hospital put enough pressure on the community that was still struggling to take root in San Francisco. Furthermore, Grass Valley itself, while a booming town, had not yet reached its potential as a mining center; and because it was in the heart of rough mining camps, it was not likely to be a cynosure for a group of rather timid women.

On August 20, 1862, however, Mother M. Baptist, Sister M. Paul Beechinor and Sister M. Teresa King visited Grass Valley and returned after a few days, having given a conditional promise of a filiation. The foundation was made August 20, 1863, with Sister M. Teresa King as the first Superior.[39]

On February 10, 1864, Reverend J. Prendergast requested that Sisters of Mercy be permitted to teach in the new school at Mission Dolores. The project was readily accepted. Three-cornered negotiations followed between Mother Baptist, Father Prendergast and the Archbishop, which rather clouded than cleared the question at hand until the schools at the mission were dropped.

The Rincon Hill Schools—1871[40]

Finally, in 1871, the Sisters of Mercy focused their attention on education, Mother M. Baptist having recognized the need for Catholic schools in the Rincon Hill area. Although unable to provide any financial assistance, the Archbishop wholeheartedly endorsed the proposal. While there were several fund-raising projects and some generous contributions, it was the substantial gift of Reverend John McCullough, chaplain of St. Mary's Hospital, that made possible the fine school which was to become so dear to many in San Francisco.

Construction of the new school began on March 19, 1871. On the Feast of Corpus Christi, June 8, 1871, the completed building was dedicated by Archbishop Alemany. The secondary school was placed under the patronage of Our Lady of Mercy, the elementary school for girls, under the Guardian Angels, and the Boys' primary school, under that of St. Joseph. When school opened, June 12, 1871, there were thirty-nine girls and twenty-seven boys admitted the first day, but before the end of June there were 178 girls and forty-one boys. Needless to say,

116

the number continued to grow.

One Sister, whose recollections went back to 1871 when Our Lady of Mercy school opened, spoke of Mother Baptist as her religion teacher and of how she held her pupils spellbound:

> I never knew anyone who so closely portrayed the life of Our Lord. . . . The Bible stories she told in such a fascinating way and so earnestly that we were deeply impressed; and the Scriptural quotations were so often repeated in appropriate places, in the course of her instructions, that we learned them without any labor. In fact, it was the lesson we most loved.

Another Sister who attended Our Lady of Mercy Academy left this pen picture from her memory:

> The school was situated atop Rincon Hill overlooking the Bay. . . .It was the most popular school for girls in San Francisco at that time. Young people who attended it came from all parts of the city—North Beach, Hayes Valley, Sutro Heights and even from the peninsula. It owed its prominence to the fact that the school was incorporated by the State of California as an Academy and empowered to grant diplomas. Furthermore, the school comprised elementary, grammar and high school departments. These were under the care and instruction of the most efficient teachers. The curriculum of the high school was very progressive; science, French, Latin, math, history and English, as well as music. Drama or elocution was a special feature. The entertainments and closing exercises on "the Hill" drew people from the whole city.

In 1886, the statistics of Our Lady of Mercy's school indicated that the enrollment of Catholic students from July 1885, to January, 1886, was 431; of Protestants, four; total, 435.

One of the outstanding features of the academy was the sodality of Our Lady, which grew to phenomenal proportions; but when sodalities were established in the local parishes the girls were encouraged to join their own parish group.

About 7:00 p.m. on the evening of December 11, 1887, as

the Sisters were returning to the chapel after supper, a fire was discovered in the small chapel dedicated to Our Lady of Lourdes. An alarm was given and the fire department responded promptly, but the supply of water was not sufficient. The firemen had to get water from the bay, and this entailed time and labor. For awhile it seemed as if the whole block would be consumed, so rapidly did the fire spread.

The flames made quick work of the schools which were to the north of the chapel, for a high wind was blowing at the time. Very few of the school furnishings were saved, and these were badly damaged. The new chapel organ, which cost two thousand dollars, had been used only a few times. Although not burned, it was ruined by water. And yet, the Sisters had every reason to thank God that the fire had been as confined as it was. It did not reach the hospital, nor the home for the aged, and the firemen deserve great credit for their accomplishment.

After the fire, the children were formed into classes in every available space, pending the building of a new school. Our Lady of Mercy was not rebuilt, but another school, entrusted to the Sisters of Mercy, took care of many grade school pupils. This was the new parochial school, St. Brendan's,[4][1] on Fremont and Harrison Streets, built by Reverend John Nugent in 1892. It filled a real need for grammar school education for both the boys and girls of the parish.

About 1899, Sister M. Liguori McNamara opened a commercial department at St. Brendan's to give its graduates a two-year course which would provide a creditable business education. Many of those who entered the business world reflected the excellent training combined with character formation which made them an asset to the business offices of San Francisco.

On the death of Sister M. Liguori, on May 16, 1958, the following news copy appeared in the *Monitor* and in the *Southern Cross:*

> ...Sister M. Liguori McNamara was a zealous educator, probably the founder of the system of business education in the Catholic schools of the Archdiocese. She organized the first such department in old St. Brendan's School in 1899 and transferred it, pupils and all, to St. Peter's after the fire in 1906. There she served as teacher and superior for seventeen years and

won the love and respect of thousands of San Franciscans who benefited by her instruction and guidance. It was during her assignment at St. Peter's also that she worked with Father P.C. Yorke, assisting him in his eminent work for the faith and for Catholic Education. When the Department of Education was established with the late Father Ralph Hunt as its first Superintendent in 1915, Sister M. Liguori was appointed a member and secretary of the Scholastic Council formed to assist him in drawing up the first courses of study.

In a brief interval away from the educational field, Sister also served for six years as Superior and Administrator of Mercy Hospital, San Diego, and there she solicited funds and supervised the erection of the Mercy Hospital (1929-1966). Moreover, though many of her efforts were expended on gigantic projects, her power and real strength stemmed from her devotion and care for the poor and the sick. No matter where or in what field she labored, Sister M. Liguori was always the friend of those in need. . . .

Our Lady of Lourdes Academy—St. Anthony's Parish, Oakland—1877

In 1871, a new parish was erected in Oakland to provide for the parishioners east of Lake Merritt. The annals speak of it as a "small parish," perhaps due to the fact that about fifty families were in attendance at Sunday Mass in the temporary church. The parish, however, extended from Lake Merritt to San Leandro Creek, and from the estuary to the hills. Even Alameda was a mission of St. Anthony's parish. When Father William Gleeson, then pastor of Brooklyn Township, now called East Oakland, visited St. Mary's Hospital to present his cause to Mother M. Baptist Russell, he left no doubt that this was a pioneering apostolate with very little promise of financial aid. With the insistence of a real shepherd of souls, he depicted the need of reaching the parents through the children; and this accounts for his determination to build schools and develop Catholic education even before he reared the Church. With little delay, the Sisters accepted his proposal, and the house was

119

opened in East Oakland on July 2, 1877.

St. Peter's Academy, San Francisco—1878

The following year, 1878, after Reverend Thomas Gibney's request that they provide for the many children of St. Peter's parish, San Francisco, the Sisters of Mercy opened the school on Alabama Street. Reverend Thomas Gibney, a devoted friend of the community in Sacramento, had been transferred from that city a few years before to the San Francisco parish. Although the premises were still unfinished in the summer of 1878, the good pastor was anxious that the opening day coincide with that of the public schools. Therefore, on July 7, 1878, the Sisters welcomed a large attendance.

In the summer of 1881, the several schools conducted by the Sisters of Mercy were incorporated under the laws of the State of California and empowered to grant diplomas.

The Sisters had learned that it was wise to incorporate their own institute under the laws of California and thereby establish a legal entity for the handling of business affairs. Accordingly, at a meeting as early as March 2, 1868, they formed a corporation under the title "Sister of Mercy," San Francisco, California.

Government of the Community—1855-1898[42]

On January 18, 1855, Mother M. Baptist Russell was appointed, for six years, the first superior of the Sisters of Mercy, San Francisco, California. This appointment by Archbishop Alemany was due to the fact that there could be no election until seven professed Sisters constituted a regular chapter. Mother Russell was elected on May 16, 1861, by the chapter that had been convened for that purpose, and three years later, May 12, 1864, she was again elected for three years. Save for three triennials that occurred in 1867-1870, 1876-1879 and 1885-1888, she held the office of Mother Superior from the foundation in San Francisco until her death, August 6, 1898. In every instance she served as long as canon law allowed, and her Sisters so voted. She would not allow a dispensation to be sought because she said it implied that no one else in the community could fill her place.

It was during the second interval of Mother M. Baptist's relief from office (1876-1879) that she made her only trip to Ireland. She had two objectives sufficient to warrant making an appeal to Archbishop Alemany for such a venture. The growth of apostolic works demanded more recruits than were supplied in San Francisco in the last quarter of the nineteenth century, and further, Sister M. Columba Stokes' family was urging her to visit Ireland to settle amicably some family affairs. The family also offered to defray all expenses. It was known that His Excellency was opposed to Religious traveling without very good reason. Before giving permission he referred the case to his Vicar General, Reverend John J. Prendergast, and to Reverend J. Varsi, S.J., and he requested that these two learned and estimable men give their opinions to him in writing. Their decisions being favorable, the Archbishop sent his apporoval in the form of a Latin letter to all the bishops through whose diocese the Sisters might pass.

On November 12, 1878, Mother M. Baptist and Sister M. Columba left San Francisco by train for New York City. Stops were essential, for Sister M. Columba's health was not good, and she found the trip very trying. A stop was made at Omaha to afford a two-day rest as well as to secure Holy Mass on Sunday. The next sojourn was to Chicago. In both places the Sisters were warmly received. Mother Baptist used the opportunity to visit several of the institutions conducted by Sisters, that she might learn by the experience of others. At the Cincinnati Convent of Mercy, established from Kinsale in 1856, she enjoyed a delay of five days while renewing old friendships.

On December 10, 1878, our travelers sailed from New York and on Friday, December 21, they reached Queenstown. They proceeded at once to St. Joseph's Convent, Kinsale, where they received the heartiest welcome. However, here Sister M. Columba learned the sad news that her father had died on December 12.

After uniting with the Community of Kinsale in the year-end retreat, the travelers set out on January 2 for Tralee, where Sister's family resided, and here the Sisters made them feel very much at home. From Tralee they went to Killarney, Charleville and thence to Dublin, where they stayed a week before proceeding to Newry, where Sister M. Emmanuel, Mother M.

Baptist's sister, was superior.

By this time Sister M. Columba's health was a serious concern for Mother M. Baptist, and a physician ordered complete rest if she were to return to California. Reluctantly she relinquished the pleasure of seeing once more her two younger sisters who had been sent to the Academy of Notre Dame at Clapham, near London. Leaving her to the loving care of the Sisters at Newry, Mother M. Baptist, accompanied by Mother M. Emmanuel, left for Dublin enroute to England. The following is Mother M. Baptist's description of this journey:

> We left the Convent of Baggott Street at 6:15. The cars run out on the pier at Kingstown and so one has merely to step from them on to the steamer. Soon we were both seasick and so we were not sorry when a good natured sailor told us to look at the breakwater, a solid piece of granite masonry which runs out a mile and a half into the sea from Holyhead with a lighthouse at the point. The Express train was waiting and in a few minutes we were whirling along at a rapid pace with hot water at our feet which we appreciated doubly, as sea sickness makes one so chilly. The Isle of Anglesey is rocky and bare, but the people must be comfortable for I did not see one poor hut. I was on the lookout for Menai Straits and had just pointed them out to my companion—when all of a sudden we were in darkness. I found the train runs through a tunnel under the Straits, not over the well-known suspension bridge as I had expected. The scenery of North Wales is picturesque to the extreme. . . .

> From Derby where we spent ten days in order to gratify Mother M. Evangelist Benson, sister of Sister M. Francis Benson we proceeded to London, enjoying the hospitality of the Sisters in Blandfork Square, spending a few hours in the convent of Bermondsey which was founded by our holy foundress herself. After six days we returned to Ireland; spending a day enroute in Liverpool where our Sisters have a grand place including all the objects of the Institute.

> On reaching the convent where we left Sister M.

Columba, we found her evidently worse but full of confidence that she would rally once she was on the sea and she longed to get back to California.

We fixed the day of departure for April 18, and the intervening time was to be spent in Kinsale, being a sea port it was hoped this city would agree with her. We reached Kinsale Tuesday of Holy Week. By Easter it was evident she would never leave her bed. She was prepared for death and expired on the morning of April 19. She was just thirty-four years of age and had been in our community ten years and six months.[43]

Now that Mother M. Baptist was no longer obliged to calculate when Sister would be strong enough for the journey, she determined to leave on April 30. Arranging to get a young Sister to serve as a companion, she set sail with ten aspirants. An additional postulant joined them enroute, to whom was assigned the patron of the deceased Sister M. Columba. She was destined to be Mother M. Baptist's immediate successor, following her death in 1898.

This Sister, Sister M. Columba O'Kelly, gives this account of their meeting on their first journey together:

On Sunday, May 18, 1879, I first saw Mother Baptist Russell. Her first greeting was, "Oh, I know you!" She had seen two sisters of mine who were Sisters of Mercy in Tralee, and recognized me from them. She won my heart at once, inspiring an affection that lasted for twenty happy years that I spent with her.

This meeting was in Omaha, on her way back from Ireland, where my sisters had actually brought me into communication with her. The next day at noon I left Omaha with Mother Baptist and her companions. Her kindness and thoughtfulness in the cars were extreme—always thinking of others before herself, waiting on them, procuring little comforts for them. We did not feel the almost five days' travel. The dear Mother beguiled the time with incidents of her early life in California, or of her recent visit to Ireland and

England. Our party had a drawing room car all to itself and Reverend Mother asked each one of us to tell a story, to sing, or recite. . . .

When I addressed her as Reverend Mother, she said, "I am not Reverend Mother," but added with a sweet smile that I think won my heart, "but have a very good chance of being such on my return."

On Friday, May 23, we reached our destination to the great joy of all. Our dear Mother was delighted to be home again. So here I am ever since and every day of my life I thank God for having been allowed to associate with Mother Baptist so long and to have known her so intimately.[44]

The day following the Sisters' return to San Francisco, Mother M. Joseph O'Rourke resigned her office as Superior and on the octave of the Ascension, Mother Baptist Russell was elected for another six-year term.[45]

On December 8, the Feast of the Immaculate Conception, the Sisters celebrated the twenty-fifth anniversary of the arrival of the Sisters of Mercy in California. In remote preparation for the fiftieth anniversary of the foundation of the Institute an effort was made to take a census of the Institute of Mercy. Blanks were sent to the chief houses of the order requesting the statistics of the specific community and its filiations. To avoid repetition, forms were sent only to Superiors of Motherhouses, who were each asked to include in their reports the branch houses under their jurisdiction. The world-wide responses were to be sent to Baggott Street. It was also suggested that a follow-up sheet be sent every tenth year.

FORM OF REPORT (as reported)

Name: Convent of Our Lady of Mercy of Divine Providence
Location: San Francisco, California
Parenthouse: St. Joseph's, Kinsale, Ireland
Date of Foundation: December 8, 1854
First Superior: Sister M. Baptist Russell
Number Professed: 76 Novices: 6 Deceased: 16
Free Day Schools: 4   A.D.A.   1100

Select Day Schools:	0	0
Infant Boys:	1	45
Night Schools:	0	0
Boarding Schools:	1	No. of Inmates 20
Industrial Schools:	1	25
Hospitals:	1	98
Orphan Asylums:	0	0
Magdalen Asylums:	1	140
House of Mercy:	1	18
Juvenile Reformatories:	1	60
Home for Aged Men:	1	15
Home for Aged Females:	1	100
Home for Aged Widows:	0	0

Day Nurseries: 0 Summer average 0 Winter average 0

Night Refuges: 0

Public Institutions Visited: City and County Hospital, State Prison (San Quentin), County Jail, Boys' Industrial School and Jail. Had we leisure to visit them every public institution is open to us.

Extern Visitations: Number on Register for last year 120

Number and Location of Branch Houses: 5

St. Joseph's	Sacramento, California
Our Lady of Lourdes	East Oakland, California
Magdalen Asylum	Potrero Street, San Francisco
St. Peter's	Alabama Street, San Francisco
Home for Aged & Infirm	Rincon Place, San Francisco

Number of Affiliations: 1   Grass Valley, Nevada Country California

Charles Russell Visits San Francisco—1883

On August 14, 1883, Charles Russell, the elder of Mother Baptist's brothers, started from Liverpool to pay his first visit to America. He traveled in the company of Lord Coleridge, whom he was to succeed as Chief Justice of England, and Mr. James Bryce, M.P., who left some permanent impressions of America in his book, *American Commonwealth*. On this trip Charles Russell also jotted down his impressions, but these were meant to be shared only with the family.

Mother M. Baptist expected him to travel by the transcontinental as she did, and Mr. D.J. Oliver daily scanned the list of passengers to give Charles a suitable reception. The latter, however, came to San Francisco by boat. He crossed Canada by the Canadian Pacific and sailed down from Vancouver to San Francisco.

The following Tuesday, September 18, 1883, he made good his promise to the family and gave them a pen picture of San Francisco at that date:

> My impressions of yesterday evening of the beauty of this place were quite confirmed this morning. We arrived at the Palace Hotel and found it all ablaze and a band playing in the atrium or courtyard which was crowded. . . .

> "Frisco" is certainly beautifully situated and beautifully laid out. Sheltered from the West by the Southern arm of the Bay, it rests upon a succession of hills—many of them very steep—which seem to run almost in regular parallel lines.

> Though much smaller than Chicago, it is a much more taking city. There is also a great appearance of business activity. Altogether, after New York, it is the finest city I have seen here.

> I went early to St. Mary's Hospital, situated on Rincon Hill. I was being shown into a parlor when Kate approached—looking on the whole very well and strong and exactly as she looked when in Great Britain four years ago—not looking a day older.

> . . .On Rincon Hill they have a large hospital, work school and a home for aged women. They have altogether five branches here in Frisco and in Sacramento and have in charge several schools. They receive no aid from State funds, and no compensation for the important teaching services they render. Neither do any other of the Catholic schools. In this important particular Catholic schools are much better off in England.

. . .So far as I can gather, there is no place in the United States in which on the whole the Catholic body, or in other words, the Irish Catholic body, stands so well as in San Francisco in point of religious organization, education, mercantile, social and political position.

I spent all yesterday afternoon and the greater part of today with Kate. At St. Mary's Hospital, the children of their schools—bright, healthy, intelligent looking children they were—went through certain calisthenic and musical exercises, very pleasant to see and hear. As to the latter, I was rather surprised when the pianist who accompanied the singers struck up the English National Anthem of John Bull. "God save the Queen" here in a republican country! However, my surprise soon ceased for the song was an ode to America and which, as a national air, ranks close after "The Star-Spangled Banner."

I also went through the hospital wards. They are bright, cheery and wonderfully neat and clean. They have wards for the poor and also rooms for those who can pay for higher class accommodation. The patients are frequently Protestants—indeed, Kate says she knows the Protestant Bishop very well from the fact of his frequently coming to visit his co-religionists and subjects in the wards.

Later we drove, that is, Kate, Sister M. Aquin Martin, James Gartlin and myself, in the convent carriage and pair to the Penitents' Home and Reformatory at Potrero Avenue on the outskirts of the city.

The establishment at Potrero was most interesting, and it is worth noting that, as regards the inmates of the Reformatory school, these are committed to the care of the good Sisters by State authorities, who pay for each, or at least contribute to the support of each girl.

. . .One interesting spot and a sad one in some sort,

too, is the Sisters' graveyard at Potrero. Here on the bright hillside, under the shades of maple and cottonwood trees, rest one-half of that devoted band whom Kate led, now nearly thirty years ago, from the old world to the new, carrying the Cross with them.

I left poor Kate, very sad, poor soul, but greatly pleased at having had the old land brought closer to her by my presence.

God bless her and all her sisterhood, who promised to pray very steadily for me and mine. By the way, as Kate was the Reverend Mother, I was promptly dubbed "Uncle" but without the Reverend. . . .[46]

In his early years Charles Russell's practice was chiefly at the passage court at Liverpool. In the 'seventies his success as a Queen's Counselor won attention. He served as a Member of Parliament and as Attorney General in Gladstone's administration. In 1894 he was appointed Lord Chief Justice of England and as such took part in the Venezuelan Boundary Arbitration of 1899.[47]

The Most Reverend Patrick W. Riordan Succeeds Archbishop Joseph Sadoc Alemany—December 28, 1884

For thirty-four years the Most Reverend Joseph Sadoc Alemany, first Archbishop of San Francisco, had borne the burden and the heat of the extensive archdiocese in the far West. He rode hundreds of miles, often over rugged mountain roads in the rough mining country of California, to administer Confirmation and bring encouragement to the lonely priests of the mining camps.

With the passing of time the archdiocese was somewhat reduced in size, and there were many more workers to tend the vineyard of the Lord. And yet the even increasing duties of a developing archdiocese weighed heavily on the frail shoulders of the archbishop, and he was too faithful a shepherd to retain his post if he could not meet every obligation. On September 16, 1883, he was given a coadjutor, *cum jure successionis*, the Most Reverend Patrick William Riordan. His petition to retire to a

Dominican monastery finally granted, he resigned on December 28, 1884, and left San Francisco for Valencia, Spain, where he died on April 14, 1888.

Archbishop Patrick Wm. Riodan (1884-1914) was a prelate of a very different stamp. Yet, he too brought to the office of Archbishop of San Francisco qualities of mind and heart—intellectual acumen, organizational and business ability—which were demanded by a growing metropolis. The industrialization and commercial expansion of the San Francisco Bay region brought an increase of population which required more churches and more schools, as well as a seminary to prepare young men for the priesthood. Archbishop Riordan had a princely bearing and a keen mind, but he also had a sensitivity that enabled him to provide what he saw was needed without casting the slightest reflection on his saintly predecessor.

In May, 1886, the Archdiocese of Northern California was re-drawn, and Sacramento, instead of Grass Valley, was made the episcopal see for the upper part of the state. The Most Reverend Patrick Manogue, who had succeeded Bishop Eugene O'Connell, the first Bishop of Grass Valley, on May 16, 1886, became the first Bishop of Sacramento.[48] The Sisters in Sacramento were given their choice of returning to San Francisco, remaining permanently in the capital or staying until the Sacramento convent was able to replace them. Sister M. Vincent Phelan, who had spent most of her life in the capital, chose to remain permanently in Sacramento. Some Sisters volunteered to remain a few years until recruits for Sacramento were professed.

On February 11, 1888, word was received from Kinsale of the death of Mother M. Francis Bridgeman, the Superior who sent to San Francisco in 1854 the original band of eight, among them her own aunt, Sister M. de Sales Reddan. For more than thirty-four years Mother M. Francis Bridgeman had maintained a steady correspondence with Mother M. Baptist Russell. The Kinsale Superior was most solicitous for the well-being of the community in California and was ever ready to lend support—financial aid, guidance and encouragement—but she was especially concerned that the California Sisters adhere to the spirit and rule of Mother Catherine McAuley. This tie was very helpful to the young Superior in the early days.

Among other guests in the eighties was Mother Austin Carroll, Convent of Our Lady of Mercy, New Orleans, who arrived on July 24, 1888, at Rincon Hill with two companions from Louisiana. The object of her visit was to obtain material for the fourth volume of her well-known work, *Leaves From the Annals of the Sisters of Mercy.* The last chapter of Volume III and the first of Volume IV deal with the San Francisco foundation. They visited San Francisco, Sacramento and Grass Valley and on August 12, the New Orleans Sisters left Grass Valley for Ogden, homeward bound.

Despite many duties and failing health, Mother M. Baptist Russell was ever alert to the trends of the times, especially in matters of an educational nature. In July, 1893, she sent to each of the old Missions of California to acquire tiles for the museum on Rincon Hill. On each tile she had the children, under the Sister artist's direction, paint the picture of the mission church from which the tile had come and mark the date of the foundation of the mission. One set of these she kept, and the other she sent to Bishop John J. Keane of the Catholic University, Washington, D.C. The latter wrote a grateful note for the contribution to the museum of archeology.

On February 25, 1895, Sister M. Francis Benson, who had resided at the Magdalen Asylum, was called to her eternal reward. She was one of the original eight and had served in religion for a fruitful fifty years. Her mother had died when she was a child, and an aunt had generously devoted her life to rearing her sister's children as Catholics. The father, a retired British officer, was a Protestant but did not object to his daughters being raised in their mother's religion. One of her sisters entered the Kinsale convent and was sent as Superior of the foundation to Derby, England. Although older than Mother Baptist Russell, and naturally of an impetuous disposition, Sister M. Francis Benson was edifying in her submission and humility but needed to be restrained from taking too much labor upon herself. It was she who in 1859 organized at Rincon Hill and promoted the Society of St. Mary's, a sodality and also a mutual benefit organization. A few years later, 1868, she devoted herself to the sufferers in the smallpox epidemic. When constrained to take care of a heavy cold, she wrote a letter to Kinsale which gives us our best account of this awful scourge. She spent her life promoting the cause of the aged and infirm.

Catholic Education at the Close of the Century

At the end of summer, 1894, the first Catholic Teachers'

Institute of San Francisco was held at the Presentation Convent, Taylor Street. Mother M. Baptist Russell had some part in bringing about this important step in the development of Catholic education in the archdiocese. She had been much impressed by the enthusiastic account of Mrs. Alice Toomey who had recently attended summer school in Pittsburgh, Pennsylvania. Mother M. Baptist decided to approach the Archbishop to sanction a similar venture that promised far-reaching educational benefits. At a preliminary meeting, May 23, 1894, Sister Angeline of the Sisters of the Holy Names and Sister M. Elizabeth Burscough, Sister of Mercy, prepared a program for the convention which would be held September 20, 21 and 22, 1894. The daily attendance at this convention ranged from 120 to 150, representing ten different religious orders or institutes. The Archbishop presided at the opening meeting and, after expressing his appreciation of the efforts expended in such a convention, he added that he hoped it would be held annually. There were several position papers, followed by questions and discussion. Toward the end of the meeting, steps were taken to secure a commitment to act for the coming year.

The attendance at the second convention of religious teachers, November, 1895, was even more gratifying than that of the previous year. The Archbishop contacted the Superiors of twelve different religious groups to guarantee representation from their schools. Despite his apparent deep interest, the Archbishop was unable to attend the November meeting of 1895. Through the secretary, however, he addressed the convention:

> . . .The experience of last year has made evident that an annual meeting of the teachers of our schools will be productive of the very best results especially in introducing methods and stimulating the teachers to continued effort to keep their schools up to the high standard which is demanded today. I need not say to you that the Church's most important work in this, and indeed in every country, is the religious training of her children. They will be in mature years largely what our schools make of them; hence the importance of the work committed to our teachers—the formation in our pupils of a strong, robust, and

enlightened Catholic conscience and at the same time the imparting of such knowledge as will be needed in the pursuits of life. . . .

It is, in truth, a sublime calling and only those furnished with special gifts should be entrusted with it. This is especially true of the teaching of Religion which should be interwoven with the child's earliest intellectual life and presented in an attractive and systematic manner. . . .

May God bless your efforts in building up the Kingdom of Heaven in the hearts of our children.

Sincerely yours,

P.W. Riordan, Archibishop of San Francisco

At this meeting, officers for the ensuing year were chosen to act as an executive committee, with the power to arrange the time and place of meeting and prepare the program. The following Sisters were elected:

President,	Sister M. Lorenzo O'Malley, Sister of Mercy
Vice-President,	Sister Angeline, Holy Names
Secretary,	Sister M. Elizabeth Burscough, Sister of Mercy
Treasurer,	Sister M. Alice, Sister of Charity

Two committees were appointed: one to draw up standards for evaluation of pupils in the parochial schools; and another to simplify the Baltimore Catechism, which had been recognized as the authorized text and adopted. Teachers had found it unsatisfactory as a textbook for children. It was too abstract and in terms beyond the capacity of the very young. There had been no provision to adapt it to grade levels.

Reverend Peter C. Yorke[50] was named chairman of the committee to adapt the Baltimore Catechism to classroom use, and for several years he experimented with teachers and pupils. St. Peter's School, San Francisco, and Our Lady of Lourdes Academy, East Oakland, served as laboratories for testing his program.

Father Yorke often brought the teachers together in meetings to seek their criticism and suggestions. Again and again he revised, changed, and recast the series before sending them to the press. His first book appeared in 1898. Those for the other grades followed soon after, but much of the labor of years was wiped out by the fire of 1906. In 1908, he re-edited his series, *The Textbooks of Religion.* In these books he took care to retain the basics of the Baltimore Cathechism as the authoritative work of the American bishops, but he recognized the necessity of grading the material and of presenting it to fit the grade level. He used the approach which distinguishes between instruction in religion and religious education. He envisioned religious education as including not only an explanation of Church doctrine, both moral and dogmatic, but also and chiefly the exercise and development of the mind by action in religion. For this reason he urged the correlation of religion with other subjects, reinforcing the application of principle in every phase of human conduct. In this way he sought to cultivate a sympathetic attitude and motivated acceptance of the the ideals and aims of the Church. While his series retained what was basic in the Baltimore Cathechism, it was enriched and supported by Sacred Scripture, liturgy, church history, literature, and life.

The impact of his work reached Rome, and his efforts won the recognition of Pope Pius X in 1906, who conferred on him the degree of Doctor of Sacred Theology. He was especially at home in dealing with the deep mysteries of the faith and the complex problems of the Church; yet he never lost the common touch, and he was able to read the mind and heart of a child. The last five years of his life he was engaged in preparing a religion course for the high schools. It was not completed when death overtook him, April 1, 1925.[51]

St. Hilary's, Marin County—1899

Almost the last work of the San Francisco foundress was the acquisition of a rest haven in Marin County, long called St. Hilary's. For many years Mother M. Baptist felt the necessity of a place away from the city, yet easily accessible, to which she might send the Sisters for a few days' needed rest or change after long hours in hospital wards or closely packed classrooms.

Dr. Benjamin Lyford, whom Mother Baptist knew in his professional career, had retired from medical practice and led a rather secluded life on his estate, the rancho Corte de Madera del Presidio, in Marin County. Mother Russell had not seen him for several years. In 1897 he asked her to visit him for the purpose of choosing a summer residence, so essential to the good health of the community. He did not know, unless by mental telepathy, that this very thought was uppermost in her mind at the time. Accordingly, on May 27, 1897, the Sisters accepted the invitation and visited him at his place in Marin. It was beautifully situated on an inlet of the bay, a short distance from Tiburon. He asked Mother to bring some Sisters and occupy one of his furnished cottages. After the experience, if she should find it suitable, he would give her a lot; moreover she could select her own site.

Her impression was caught in an enthusiastic letter to Sister M. Euphrasia Sullivan from Bay View Cottage:

> Sister M. Baptist is enraptured with this place and truly for a summer resort for the Sisters, I doubt if it could be equaled. Not a sound but a cawing of the crows in the morning and evening. Yesterday a rabbit or a hare came into the kitchen, and, as we were sitting in the front of the house last evening a whole family of quail walked down the road within fifty feet of us. If we were only any way smart, we could trap plenty of game while here. It is a quiet and retired spot, free from fog, the air balmy and invigorating. It commands a magnificent view of the bay with San Francisco in the distance.[52]

From the time the Sisters alighted from the train at Reed's Station, they were surrounded by a wealth of stately eucalyptus trees and a profusion of California wild flowers as they followed a road that skirted the beach along the bay. Mother Baptist chose a site in the fall of that year, an eminence commanding a magnificent view of the bay. Soon work was commenced on a commodious frame building. And yet, before the Sisters could occupy the "convent by the Sea," Mother M. Baptist Russell had answered her final summons. In November, 1898, Sister M. Rose O'Brien wrote:

> Just think! After all Mother Baptist's preparations for the new house she never slept one night in it.[53]

In their sadness, the Sisters were in no hurry to arrange the blessing of St. Hilary's, which did not take place until May 13, 1899. Father Valentini, the Rector of Sausalito, performed the ceremony and said a few words. He recalled that he had met Mother Baptist thirty years before in the pest house during the smallpox epidemic.

Death Comes to Mother Baptist Russell—August 6, 1898

Like many pioneer women, Mother M. Baptist had been blessed with very good health; in fact up to the last two years of her life she seemed in excellent condition. And yet, as early as December, 1888, she wrote to her sister:

> I fear Sr. Mary Francis' letter may make you anxious about my health. I will tell you I have since had an examination and it is found that the first opinion of the doctor was not correct. My case is not so serious as feared and in the course of a month or so I will, please God, be all right. But he keeps me lying either on a lounge or in bed, and has ordered me lots of good things to take. . . . So my day has come.[55]

The day, however, was still some time in coming, almost ten years. In another letter dated January, 1898, she says of herself:

> . . .At present I am very well, but as those attacks have come back unexpectedly I cannot say I am all right. If it be God's will, I should like much to build the Home next summer. Pray for my intention.[56]

Finally on July 28, Sister M. Aquin Martin wrote to Mother's Irish kin:

> . . .We have prayed hard that God would leave her with us a few years longer, but He wants her and we must submit, however hard it may be for our poor hearts. She was a model of every Christian virtue, but above all, charity in word and deed. Her tongue now silent forever in this world, never wounded any-one. . . . How the poor will miss her.[57]

Only two days later, Mother Columba, her assistant, and soon to be successor, sent a report to Mother Emmanuel at Newry:

Our dear Mother is still with us but each day she is growing weaker. Her eyes are dark to this world. . . .She cannot see for the past few days. It is so sad not to hear her voice; and to know that she cannot hear us is inexpressibly sad.

Reverend Matthew Russell states the cause of her death more explicitly in a biography of Mother Baptist Russell:

Not only blind; but dumb and deaf, the senses one after another were dulled by the clogging of the arteries of the brain, the immediate cause of her death. . . .Hers was almost five weeks of living death![58]

Although Mother M. Baptist saw the approach of death by repeated warnings for some years, even as late as July, 1898, she was able to perform her duties; but from July 4, she grew steadily worse until the day of her death, August 6, 1898. That morning Reverend Father Rooney, O.P., a patient in the hospital, came to her room and said the prayers for the dying at 6:00 a.m., giving her the last Absolution. He then went to the chapel to offer the Holy Sacrifice for her. About 6:20, she calmly breathed her last She was in the seventieth year of her life and the fiftieth year of dedicated service in the religious state.

Most of the facts of her life have already been stated, but no history of her community would be complete if it failed to pay honor to her memory, for it was she who laid the foundation of the Institute in San Francisco.

The San Francisco newspapers gave accounts of her condition day by day and at the announcement of her death the San Francisco *Call* stated:

. . .No death in recent years has been heard of with greater regret in this community than that of Mother Superior, Mary Baptist Russell, the sweet woman who watched over the destinies of various charitable institutions in this city during the past half century. The tidings of this calm leave-taking of life will fill with sorrow thousands who were fortunate enough to meet her and those who heard or read of her beautiful deeds of charity since her advent to this

State. A more lovable character than hers has rarely been found. Her constant aim in life has been to uplift the suffering and the wounded, and in this she was entirely successful. . . . [59]

So also did the *Chronicle,* the *Examiner* and of course, the *San Francisco Monitor* devote columns to enthusiastic appreciation of her life, dedicated to the most crucial needs of the growing city. Of special import is a letter written by Archbishop Riordan to her brother Reverend Matthew Russell, S.J. This letter was penned some time after her death. It serves as an Introduction to Father Russell's second work, *The Three Sisters of Lord Russell of Killowen.*

July 16, 1912

Dear Father Russell,

It gives me great pleasure to add my testimony about your saintly sister, who labored here so devotedly and so long. . . .

Mother Baptist was not here long before she realized that there was a great work to be done to save this floating population to the Church; and she lost no time in beginning it. She was gentle, calm, silent, but a strong woman who took in at a glance the necessities of the situation and laid plans accordingly. A hospital had to be built for the infirm, a house of protection and reformation for the erring ones of her own sex; a house of Providence for the unemployed, a home for the aged, both men and women; and above all, the most necessary of all, Catholic schools in which the children of our Catholic people, while learning the things that are useful for this life, would at the same time be solidly instructed in the principles of their religion which would sanctify their lives here on earth and bring them to their eternal home after this life is over.

At the present time, when churches and schools are numerous, it is not easy to understand the tremendous difficulties that confronted her, difficulties that would have deterred one less hopeful and less courageous than Mother Baptist Russell. She had a great work to do and with the courage of the saints she put her hands to do it without delay. She had God with her and with His assistance all obstacles could be surmounted. . . .

When she passed to her eternal reward she left as monuments of her great zeal a well-equipped hospital, a Magdalen Asylum, a large school for boys and girls in St. Peter's Parish, a school in St. Brendan Parish, a school in St. Anthony's Parish, Oakland, and a Retreat for the members of the community who needed rest, now and then, for their exhausting labors.

These material works would of themselves be sufficient evidence of the very great business qualifications which she possessed, and also of her tact and influence in bringing people to place at her disposal the means necessary for the construction and maintenance of all these institutions. The principal source of her ability to interest her friends in her works of charity was her deeply spiritual character. All who came in contact with her soon recognized that she was a woman of deep faith, great piety and of a great affection for the poor. She accomplished much because she was entirely disinterested; she asked nothing for herself, nothing for personal needs or comforts; always thinking of others, planning for others; she was in every fabric of her being a perfect religious. If I were to single out from her many virtues those most characteristic and prominent, I should say her obedience and her charity. The rule of her Community was the law of her life.

She inculcated by counsel and above all by example that victory over one's self comes only to the obedient.

. . .The union between her and her spiritual daughters

was perfect. She had obtained from God the gift of government, and obedience on the part of her subjects was an easy thing because it was prompted by a very deep affection. . . .

Her voice was low, sweet and deliberate. One always felt, when speaking with her, that she realized that words were the expression of thought and were to be used with deliberation.

She left her impress on her Community. It is today what she made it. . . . We all felt that a special blessing was left by her to her spiritual daughters. . . . [60]

From Saturday to Tuesday thousands visited the convent chapel where she lay in death, and many touched the remains with medals, crosses, etc. It was as though a saint had passed from their midst. On the day of the funeral, Archbishop Riordan celebrated a Solemn Requiem Mass in the presence of some fifty priests, her sorrowing Sisters and as many as the chapel could contain, about a tenth of those who sought admittance. Belatedly the Archbishop regretted he had not arranged to have the funeral from the cathedral.

The *San Francisco Chronicle* said,

No dead sovereign ever had a prouder burial than the Mother M. Baptist Russell whose life of self-denial and good works had crowned her in a city's memory.[61]

The farewell discourse was delivered by Reverend Hugh Gallagher, S.J., a nephew of the good priest who had brought her from Kinsale to her mission in San Francisco forty-four years before.

She was buried in St. Michael's Cemetery, at the Magdalen Asylum. With the consent of the city authorities, this beautiful cemetery had been laid out as the Sisters' burial plot and blessed May 8, 1867. On the twenty-second of July, 1899, a very beautiful Celtic cross was erected over her grave. It was carved by Mr. Zeglio, Sister M. Phillipa's father. The memorial bears this inscription:

In memory of Mother M. Baptist Russell, First
Superior of the Sisters of Mercy, San Francisco. Born,
April 18, 1829.   Entered Religion Nov. 24, 1848.
Professed Aug. 2, 1851. Died August 6, 1898

A fitting text from Proverbs 31:20, is inscribed on the base:

She opened her hand to the needy and has stretched
out her arms to the poor.

*The Spanish American War: Sisters Respond to Care for the
Soldiers*

On April 11, 1898, President McKinley sent his war message
to Congress, and eight days later Congress responded by
authorizing the President to employ force to establish Cuban
independence. The Teller Amendment was offered to assure the
world that the United States would claim no sovereignty or
control over Cuba save to secure and maintain peace. America
jumped into the Spanish-American War at popular demand, its
appetite for war whetted by yellow journalism then rife in the
country. The war lasted less than four months, Manila itself
capitulating the day after the armistice was signed on August
12, 1898. The American casualties were slight, but the high rate
of death from sickness, especially typhoid, was appalling.

On September 7, 1898, a request was made that Mother M.
Columba O'Kelly send some Sisters to nurse the soldiers arriving
at the Presidio Hospital. Reverend Mother, with the consent of
the Archbishop and the approval of the Sisters, responded by
sending four Sisters who had volunteered to go.

The Sisters chosen were Sister M. Pius Savage, Sister M.
Raymond Dunnigan, Sister M. Dolores Dunne and Sister M.
Clement Scully; they began their duties Sunday, September 15
1898.

On November 16, 1898, Mother wrote to Dr. Eddy, the
surgeon in charge of the hospital, to the effect that she would
expect her Sisters home from the Presidio on or about
December 6, as the sickness among the soldiers seemed to be
abating. On December 3 the Sisters received their release from
the Presidio Hospital. The soldiers were sorry to see the Sisters
leave but all save three patients were able to be up.

The following letter was received by Mother Columba on the
night of the Sisters' return:

Division Field Hospital
Presidio of San Francisco
December 3, 1898

Mother Superior

Dear Madam:

With the departure from our Hospital of Sisters M. Pius, M. Dolores, M. Clement and M. Louis of your Order and Hospital, permit me to thank you and them for the noble, unselfish and devoted work they have performed in caring for the sick and wounded men belonging to the Philippine Expedition.

I but express the opinion of the surgeons of the Hospital and the patients that were committed to the care of the Sisters, when I say that theirs were the model wards of our Hospital. Their unremitting labor for those who were stricken whilst in our Country's service is that true eloquence of loyalty to our land and Flag shown in heroic deeds and not in empty words. If the Country does not fully appreciate what a noble work you have done, it is because of that quiet, unasuming labor, not for show but of duty and love for humanity, which will not permit the heralding of its deeds before the public. Permit me to assure you that those who do know what has been done will not fail to credit you with the high value of your actions and the noble motives that induced them. Allow me again, on behalf of myself and staff and those under our charge, to express our great obligation and heartfelt thanks.

Very respectfully,
Your obedient servant,

R.G. Ebert
Surgeon, U.S. Army, Hospital[62]

The following week a similar letter was received from Dr. Ebert's commanding officer, Major W.S. Matthews:

Division Field Hospital
Presidio, San Francisco, California
December 8, 1898

Mother Superior
Sisters of Mercy
St. Mary's Hospital

Dear Madam:

I am very glad indeed to have had the pleasure of
reading Dr. Ebert's endorsement of the work of the
Sisters of Mercy and kindred Orders at this hospital,
and I most enthusiastically and cordially endorse all
that he has said.

On September 26, I had occasion to make an official
report to the Surgeon General, Washington, D.C., and
in that report the following report is found, which
will more clearly express my estimate of the services
of the Sisters than anything I can write.

> . . .we are blessed with the services of some Sisters
> of Mercy, who are receiving no compensation, for
> they will accept none, exhibiting a most commend-
> able, self-sacrificing and patriotic spirit. Their work
> is as good as could be desired, and in at least one or
> two cases the tide has been turned in favor of the
> patients receiving their tender and ever faithful
> care. . . .

Most sincerely yours,

W. S. H. Matthews
Major and Brigade Surgeon, U.S.V.
Commanding Hospital[6 3]

The Health Apostolate on Rincon Hill[6 4]

Many and varied are the cases where souls were healed as well
as bodies in the hospital on Rincon Hill. During May, 1899, a
man was brought to the hospital and registered from Seattle
where he held a good position. After a few days, his condition

being much improved, he remarked to the Sister attending him that he felt relieved to find someone to whom he could speak of his trouble. Sister asked him if he would like to see a priest. "Oh, no," he replied, "I have not been to the Sacraments for fifty years, and cannot come to make up my mind to do so now." Sister finally proposed that he allow her to bring in the priest to talk to him. He consented, and Father Butler, S.J., was asked to visit him. After remaining with him for some time, Father Butler left. On returning to his room, Sister found the man beaming with joy. God had touched his heart; he had commenced his confession and was to visit Father Butler at the college. For this he remained a week longer at the hospital. He received Holy Communion, probably his first, for he had left Ireland when a child of ten. He returned home a changed man. It seemed impossible to express his gratitude to God and to those who had been instrumental in bringing about his reconciliation. This is but one of many like incidents of the healing of souls on Rincon Hill.

During the month of July, 1900, Mrs. Giblin, an old friend of Mother Baptist Russell, called on Mother M. Columba O'Kelly to arrange for the endowment of four beds for the hospital. A few weeks later she called again, with her lawyer who brought the papers to complete the endowment; and at the same time she handed Mother a check for twelve thousand dollars. Mother M. Columba was given full liberty to select the occupants of the beds. Another endowed bed was made by the widow of Justinian Claire in Memory of her late husband.

It was in 1900 that the training school for nurses was established at St. Mary's. On October 4, Miss Kerwin, graduate of Mercy Hospital, Chicago, arrived to take charge of the School of Nursing which opened on October 14. By December 7, the first nine applicants to the school had completed their probation term and received from Mother Columba the nurse's cap. The first graduation from the school took place on November 21, 1902 at a very simple ceremony.

On September 28, 1901, Sister M. Joseph Crowley and Sister M. Vincent White entered the California College of Pharmacy, affiliated with the University of California in Berkeley.

During the month of May, 1903, President Theodore Roosevelt visited the Pacific Coast and in response to an invitation by President Benjamin Ide Wheeler of the University of California, the President attended the commencement exercises at Berkeley. Sister M. Joseph and Sister M. Vincent had intended to receive their diplomas in private but the Dean of the College of Pharmacy sent them a pressing request to be present with the rest, to do honor to the presidential party. With them, two Sisters of St. Francis who had taken the same course occupied front seats on the stage duringsthe exercises in which hundreds of students from the various colleges of the university received their diplomas.

In 1903 Sister M. Malachi White, R.N. was appointed to take charge of the school of nursing at St. Mary's.

Chapter 5

PLANS FOR A NEW ST. MARY'S HOSPITAL

South Park and Rincon Hill, both below Market, had once been the city's most desirable residential area mainly because of the mild climate and comparative freedom from wind and fog. Yet as the waterfront was developed, with its shipping interests, foundries as well as factories located near ready transportation, the district gave way to warehouses, distilleries, etc. Early in the spring of 1902, Mother M. Columba read the signs of the times, and she cast about for adequate space in a desirable location to build a new St. Mary's Hospital.

Because of the apparent need to act promptly, she wrote Archbishop Riordan, then in Chicago, concerning the purchase of property on Point Lobos Avenue. With little hesitation the Archbishop responded by telegram to Mother's letter and approved the purchase. Negotiations were commenced and on June 2, 1902, the property was secured.[1]

Mother Euphrasia Sullivan

On May 19, 1904, Mother M. Euphrasia Sullivan was chosen Mother Superior in an election presided over by the Most Reverend George Montgomery. During her administration, an entirely new era dawned for the Sisters of Mercy in San Francisco.

December 8, 1904, marked the fiftieth anniversary of the Mercy foundation on the Pacific Coast. For the convenience of many concerned, the festivities took place December 15.

Because the chapel on Rincon Hill could not accommodate the friends, relatives and benefactors of the community, a solemn pontifical Jubilee Mass was offered at St. Mary's Cathedral at 10:00 a.m. At the appointed hour the spacious cathedral was well filled when the augmented choir burst into joyful strains. At least fifty clergymen of the archdiocese proceeded to the sanctuary. Father A. P. Doyle, C.S.P., from Washington, D.C., was the orator of the day.

While the Sisters looked back on fifty years in San Francisco, they were almost jolted out of any complacency they might have had in order to meet the demands of the present.

After consultation with the doctors, the Point Lobos property was considered to be unsuitable for hospital purposes, being in the fog belt, and it was deciced to make a second investment near the park. Accordingly, a block of land near the park, bounded by Hayes, Grove, Stanyan and Schrader Streets, was secured at a cost of $125,000. This met with general satisfaction and, under the direction of Mother M. Euphrasia Sullivan, a concentrated effort was made in November, 1905, to procure ways and means for the construction of the new hospital.

St. Peter's Academy Alumnae held a meeting and expressed their wish to be among the first to assist the good cause. A series of events—socials, programs, and a garden party—were planned. Success crowned each undertaking and they realized one thousand dollars, a check for which was delivered to Mother Euphrasia in St. Peter's Hall, Sunday afternoon, November 26, 1905. On December 20, Dr. T. E. Bailey sent a check for another thousand dollars to St. Mary's building fund. The drive was on! How little did they dream that the fire in the spring of 1906 would wipe out the old St. Mary's on Rincon Hill and that they had already undertaken its replacement![2]

For some reason or other, December 21, 1905, brought the sad news that the board of directors of San Quentin had decided to refuse admittance to all religious women visiting the prison for the spiritual welfare of the prisoners. Notice of this decision was given to Father Walsh of San Rafael with the request that he inform the Sisters. They complied, and though permission had been granted by the Governor himself, more than forty years previous, they made no protest. More priests were available than when they had undertaken this work of Mercy, but they regretted that the opportunity of serving those

145

imprisoned was so abruptly cut short.[3]

Dr. Edward Topham has left us his impression of St. Mary's Hospital just before the fire.[4] His account is rather lengthy. In summary, he seems to cite facts that reflect the times, such as the limited use of tissue work and laboratory analysis, the single elevator with the large shaft activated by water power, the relatively recent introduction of x-ray, and the difficulty of getting doctors to submit to the use of rubber gloves in surgery (although within a year the practice was universal and considered essential).

In January, 1906, it became rather widely known that Reverend D. O. Crowley of the Youth's Directory, and Reverend John F. McGinty, pastor of Holy Cross, were about to depart for an extended European trip. Every arrangement for their proposed departure had been made when, within a week of it, it was learned that both Father Crowley and Father McGinty had determined to remain at home. Aware that the Sisters of Mercy were making a drive for funds to build the new St. Mary's Hospital, these generous priests decided to donate the funds for their contemplated trip to the endowment of beds for the poor at St. Mary's.[5]

The San Francisco Earthquake and Fire—April 18, 1906

About 5:13 on the morning of April 18, 1906, the sleeping city of San Francisco was rudely awakened by the most severe earthquake yet recorded on the Pacific Coast. The seismograph of the University of California reported the principal shock as two movements of maximum intensity that lasted less than two minutes. The first shock was followed by a number of tremors of varying intensity. Accounts of eyewitnesses indicate that destruction was considerable, but that it was not the earthquake that destroyed the city, although it was the basic cause of the greater destruction, for it snapped the city's water pipes. The buckled sidewalks and gaping fissures were but evidence of the dislocation of buried pipes, and although the water supply was adequate the network of the water system was rendered useless.

Dr. Edward Topham, resident physician of St. Mary's, Rincon Hill, describes his confused awakening on the morning of the eighteenth; but he states that the after the initial shock he saw no damage to the hospital:[6]

We had no electricity but it was daylight and our old faithful elevator still purred up and down for the simple reason it was run by water power and we were among the few who had a large tank full of water. The seriousness of the situation still did not impress me until I went to the roof. I was able from the elevation to count thirteen major fires in the downtown section encircling us from the Ferry Building and sweeping around toward the west. There was added consternation when I walked down to Second Street as far as Mission and saw firemen vainly trying to pump water from a sewer. Then it struck home! The hydrants were dry, there was no water! Trolley wires were lying entangled on the cobbled street. . . .

Dr. William C. Hopper, former resident physician, came in to advise the evacuation of the hospital. He offered to charter a vessel, to tie up at the Pacific Mail dock at South Beach, and to secure ambulances and wagons to convey the sick and infirm on board. Further, he would watch the progress of the flames and send a timely warning. Word came at about 1:30 p.m. that the ship was at the dock.

The story of the evacuation of the patients and the destruction of St. Mary's is vividly told by Father Yorke in an article in the *Leader*, April 28, 1906:

St. Mary's Hospital on Rincon Hill is a thing of the past. . . .When the earthquake had shaken San Francisco to pieces old St. Mary's proved the reliability of the builders. It was practically intact. But the rush of the flames from the southwest side, from the new flats on Rincon Place, carried off the Old Ladies' Home and soon gutted the main building.

The Sisters had decided to move the patients at 1:30 on Wednesday afternoon and the removal took until 5:00 p.m. Dr. Wm. C. Hopper interviewed Mr. Palmer of the Southern Pacific Steamship Company, and the Newark was sent up immediately, with the whole crew at the disposal of the Sisters, but the Modoc arrived at three in the afternoon, and being adapted for hospital purposes, the patients were transferred

147

there. The medical staff of St. Mary's was successful in obtaining vehicles of all kinds to transport the sick and the old, and last of all, the Sisters.

There were one hundred and fifty patients, of whom ninety were confined to bed, and one hundred old ladies of whom twenty were bedridden. The old men, in number about twenty, and the convalescents walked down to the Mail dock where all embarked.

Captain Wilson, officers and crew, showed the greatest kindness to the patients and Sisters, giving up their own accommodations for the comfort of the sick.

Many an eye turned to St. Mary's as they stood on deck. A sudden change in the wind had driven the smoke from the hill and the building stood out clear against the evening sky. . . .

Valuable papers of the house were saved by the foresight of the superior, who stuffed them all into two telescope baskets, and having forgotten about her own necessities, preserved for the community those valuable instruments which will be no inconsiderable factor in restoring its former prosperity and prestige.

The hospital burned slowly. A blue whirlwind of flame seemed to pass over the hill. The cross in St. Mary's glowed to the last like a beacon, and fixed forever on the eminence the title of Red Cross Hill.

By this time the Modoc was moored to the Broadway wharf. The St. Mary's Sisters left the ship and reached their own home, the Academy of Our Lady of Lourdes, in East Oakland, about 7:00 p.m.

The following Monday, April 23, Mother Euphrasia sent eight Sisters under the guidance of Mother Pius Savage to open the "tent hospital" on Hayes Street.[7]

The *Leader* was published during the crisis in a temporary

office, 371-373 Eleventh Street, Oakland, and a second temporary office was opened at 3000—24th St., San Francisco. One of the services supplied by the paper was a listing of damage to churches and schools and a schedule where one might hear Mass. Furthermore, the *Leader* published, free of charge, an "information wanted" column to enable the scattered people of San Francisco to contact relatives and friends. Among these notes was a column on hospital news which stated:

> The Sisters from St. Mary's Hospital, San Francisco, are now at Our Lady of Lourdes Academy, East Oakland. (The names followed.)

Another *Leader* article was entitled *Save the Girls*, and suggested a timely apostolate of the sisters of Mercy:

> The destruction of the big department stores in which thousands of young girls received employment has caused a form of distress which is very difficult to relieve, but must be relieved at once. In a great many cases these young girls are strangers to the city and have no friends. It is absolutely necessary that some provision should be made for homeless young girls until normal conditions are restored and the ordinary means of occupation reopened. The Oakland Catholic Central Relief Committee has opened a home for all girls where they can receive temporary shelter and food. This institution is in charge of the Sisters of Mercy, assisted by a corps of lay helpers. . . .

On April 19, 1906, the *Call*, the *Chronicle* and the *Examiner* published a joint effort, which is a journalistic commemorative:

EARTHQUAKE AND FIRE

San Francisco in Ruins

> Death and destruction have been the fate of San Francisco. Shaken by a tremblor at 5:13 o'clock yesterday morning, the shock lasting 48 seconds, and scourged by flames that raged diametrically in all directions, the city is a mass of smouldering ruins. . . .

After darkness thousands of the homeless were making their way with their blankets and scant provisions to Golden Gate Park and the Beach to find shelter. Those in homes in the hills just north of the Hayes Valley wrecked section piled their belongings in the streets; express wagons and automobiles were hauling the things away to the sparsely settled regions. Everybody in San Francisco is prepared to leave the city, for the belief is firm that San Francisco will be totally destroyed.

Downtown everything is in ruins. Not a business house stands. Theaters are crumbled into heaps. Factories and commission houses lie smouldering on their former sites. All of the newspaper plants have been rendered useless, the *Call* and the *Examiner* buildings excluding the Call's editorial rooms on Steveson Street being entirely destroyed.

It is estimated that the loss in San Francisco will reach from $150,000,000 to $200,000,000. These figures are in the rough and nothing can be told until partial accounting is taken.

On every side there was death and destruction. Hundreds were injured, either burned, crushed or struck by falling pieces from the buildings. One in ten died while on the operating tables at Mechanics Pavilion, improvised as a hospital for the comfort and care of 300 of the injured. The number of dead is not known but it is estimated that at least 500 met their death in the horror.

At nine o'clock, under the special message from President Roosevelt, the city was placed under martial law. Hundreds of troops patrolled the streets and drove the crowds back, while hundreds more were set to work assisting the fire and police departments. The strictest orders were issued and in true military spirit the soldiers obeyed.[8]

For three awful days and two nights, Wednesday through Friday, the fires raged until. . .

Five hundred and fourteen city blocks had been reduced to ruins—a region that included the entire business district and well over half of the better residential area. . . .The total number of houses burned was well over 28,000, one in five of which was of brick, steel or stone construction. The proportion of residences to business and commercial houses destroyed was about equal. The financial loss, including not only the enormous amount of property and goods destroyed, but incidental losses due to the destruction of businesses and the virtually complete cessation of commercial activity was fixed at not less than one billion dollars. In the nature of things the loss of life was never accurately known.[9]

The report of the Citizens Committee indicates that the fire was contained, roughly speaking, to the north at Filbert Street, to the south at Townsend, and to the southwest at Twentieth and Dolores. Because of the width of Van Ness Avenue, it was hoped to stem the flames, on the west, by dynamiting a number of houses on the east side of Van Ness. But the flames got through to Franklin, north of Sutter, and also took a good rectangle in Hayes Valley between Oak and Golden Gate.

Had there been no fire, few traces of the severe shock would have been visible a few months later. Broken chimneys, cracked plaster, loosened bricks, destruction of crockery, pictures, etc., were widespread. The majority of buildings, however, were structurally intact. The most severe damage occurred where foundations were insecure or construction faulty. The greatest destruction was evident in the filled-in area that had once been Yerba Buena Cove, between Montgomery and the waterfront, or south of Market, where creek beds and former swamps had been filled and built over. It is thought that most of the breaks in the water system occurred in filled-in ground where the movement occasioned by the severe shock dislocated the pipes.

The entire complex[10] of the Sisters of Mercy on Rincon Hill was swept away by the fire—the hospital, the home for the aged, the Mater Misericordiae and the novitiate, and all this even though the entire plant had withstood the earthquake. St. Peter's School and St. Catherine's Home escaped the flames, but both houses became heavily involved in relief work. St. Brendan's, on Fremont and Harrison, was totally destroyed and never rebuilt.

151

There was comparatively little disease or serious illness, and there was even less lawlessness, doubtless due to military vigilance. There was also little real suffering from hunger—food supplies were rushed in from nearby places, and relief trains were soon on their way from distant cities. Contributions for relief spoke well on the generosity of mankind. Within a week the relief chest reached almost $20,000,000. Congress contributed $1,000,000 in its first appropriation and added $1,500,000 later. The Canadian Dominion Parliament voted $100,000; the Dowager Empress of China sent $70,000; the Emperor of Japan, $100,000.[11]

Letters to the Sisters came from convents all over the United States, from Canada, and of course, from Ireland, expressing sympathy and concern as well as assurance of tangible help. Some who did not know anyone personally directed their contributions of food, clothing, money, etc., to Sisters of Mercy, confident that they would know where there was most need.

Many came to the Sisters' aid in supplying specific needs for the tent hospital on Hayes and Stanyan. The Sisters of the tent hospital were housed in a two-story building at 2201 Fulton Street. Mr. McHugh, a contractor, supplied them with two double-team gravel wagons and drivers; and with this help they were able to secure fifty tents, a field range, and necessary utensils from the Presidio Hospital. Medicines and food were supplied by the U.S. Government; several bales of cots and blankets were found at Third and Townsend. A John McCarthy, one of the male nurses who had served in the army, quickly set up camp. They could even boast of a pharmacy. Mother M. Pius Savage was the hospital superintendent while Dr. Edward Topham headed the staff of ten physicians.

Although conditions were hardly ideal, they carried on in some fifty tents for about two months. Because they intended to build on this same site as soon as possible they realized it was necessary to seek better accommodations, which could serve until the new hospital would be ready. This led to negotiations with Dr. Simon, who owned the Maudslay Sanitorium, on 2344 Sutter Street between Divisadero and Scott Streets. While the building needed renovation, it was well adapted to hospital purposes. It had been an old home, enlarged to three stories to accommodate some sixty patients in single rooms or twice that number with two beds. It had recently been used for mental patients. By June 17, 1906, it was ready for occupancy, and the eighteen patients still at Providence Hospital, Oakland, were moved in, a real step to reestablishment.

It was no great surprise when the first cases of typhoid were reported—all too frequently this is what happens when sanitation systems are disrupted. However, not only patients but even nurses and staff doctors contracted the fever.

The only hospital equipment saved from the Rincon Hill fire was that of the operating plant, but this in itself greatly facilitated the work of the physicians.

The following proclamation, issued by Governor George C. Pardee, on Thanksgiving Day, 1906, is evidence of the fine Christian spirit that prevailed in the state of California after the shattering experience of April 18.

Sacramento, No. 10
Executive Department, State of California

At the end of one of the most memorable years in their history—a year which witnessed one of the greatest disasters of modern times—the people of California have much for which to return thanks to the Giver of all blessings.

Although San Francisco and other cities were almost destroyed by fire and earthquake, the general prosperity of the State has remained unaffected. Even the cities which suffered from the stroke of April 18 are being rapidly restored, and, moreover, that misfortune was made one of the greatest demonstrations of brotherly kindness the world has ever seen. For the world-wide sympathy which was manifested toward us in our distress, gratitude is due to the people of other States and of foreign countries and most of all to Him Who causes the heart of man to feel for a brother in need.

By means of the help so generously extended, suffering was soon relieved and with the restoration of their industries, our people are now facing a future bright with hope. In recognition of these and other blessings, it is proper that the annual custom of

153

setting apart a day for thanksgiving and praise should be followed.

Now, therefore, by authority of the law invested in me, I, George C. Pardee, Governor, do hereby designate Thursday, the 29th day of November, 1906, as a day of general thanksgiving to Almighty God.

In Testimony Whereof, I have hereunto set my hand and caused the great seal of the State to be affixed at the Capitol in the city of Sacramento this tenth day of November, 1906.

George C. Pardee, Governor
C. F. Curry, Secretary of State [1] [2]

Rebuilding After the Fire[1] [3]

On June 7, 1906, Reverend P.C. Yorke had secured sufficient funds to erect a one-story temporary home for the aged, so that in six or seven weeks the old people, both men and women, were gathered from the various quarters supplied by the kindness of friends during the never-to-be-forgotten catastrophe and comfortably settled on Bray Avenue, Fruitvale.

When we read that school reopened July 30, we realize that in this eventful year the schools were very much affected. The reason they were so out-of-step was that all had been closed for Holy Week and Easter Week when the earthquake and fire had occurred, and they did not reopen until the new term. At St. Peter's the pastor considered it wise to open the academy and commercial departments three weeks after the great disaster. The classes were in session until June 28, when all studies were discontinued. After a month's vacation, the academy reopened with the rest of the schools, July 30, 1906. St. Peter's Academy and Our Lady of Lourdes carried heavy enrollments after the fire; St. Peter's because it was one of the few schools in San Francisco that had escaped the flames, and Lourdes Academy because many of the homeless victims of San Francisco's earthquake and fire had moved across the bay. Furthermore, Lourdes was a boarding school and could provide a home as well as an education for children during this trying period of readjustment.

The dauntless courage and unswerving determination of the people of San Francisco to rebuild their city and recoup their losses are evident in the contemporary press. Among the leaders who planned and built a new San Francisco, none deserves greater commendation than Mother M. Euphrasia whose work during these trying times was truly heroic. Even the Archbishop remarked: "She should be canonized for guiding the community so well and so efficiently during those days of trial."

Early in 1907, work was begun on the permanent building for Our Lady's Home, Oakland, California, and it was ready for dedication March 17, 1908. The L-shaped structure, facing 34th Avenue, was a spacious three-story frame building with rooms for eighty guests in addition to the accommodations for the Sisters. The main entrance was a beautiful approach to a carefully planned building, with large well-furnished reception rooms. The broad balconies with their eastern exposure, from which could be viewed the rolling hills, were a restful pleasure to elderly guests. Limitation of funds, however, made it necessary to use the temporary buildings as dining rooms, and the chapel, too, was not intended to be permanent.

In the summer of 1907, Mother M. Euphrasia was re-elected, and Mother M. Pius Savage was again chosen Mother Assistant; Sister M. Elizabeth Burscough, Bursar, and Sister M. Bernard O'Brien, Mistress of Novices. The novitiate, which had been located at St. Catherine's for the previous year, was transferred to St. Peter's Convent where Sister M. Bernard O'Brien was to act as Principal of St. Peter's Academy and Mistress of Novices. Plans had been drawn to erect a special building on the grounds of St. Peter's for the novitiate. On second thought, however, it was decided that the boys be sent to the Brothers and by rearrangement of rooms, it became unnecessary to build what would have been only a temporary expedient. In the building program of Our Lady's Home, in 1912, provision was made to accommodate the novitiate in a new wing and the novices were transferred to Fruitvale on August 16, 1912.

St. Mary's Hospital, Hayes and Stanyan—1911

Mother M. Euphrasia's second term as Mother Superior would have expired in 1910, in the midst of the heroic efforts to reestablish the works of the Institute, swept away by the fire of 1906. The community felt justified in petitioning Rome for an extension of her term of office. Accordingly they sought and obtained the necessary dispensation, and Mother M. Euphrasia was elected for a third term.

Meanwhile every effort had been made to complete the new St. Mary's Hospital on Hayes and Stanyan. The Sutter Street Hospital had served its purpose since June, 1906, but it certainly had its limitations. The magnificent steel and concrete building on Hayes finally was ready for occupancy on February 22, 1911. Chaste and beautiful in design, well-planned in accommodations and dimensions, it promised, when complete, to be one of the finest hospitals of the day. Nothing was spared in securing the comfort and recovery of the sick.

The gleaming white building, rated Class A, finished in white Medusa with a Spanish tiled roof, was certainly a monument to the quiet, noble woman, Mother M. Euphrasia, who conceived and supervised its construction. All associated with her in the trying period following the earthquake were grateful to God, Who spared her to see the fruits of her labor. At the time of the dedication by Archbishop Riordan, the main section and east wing were complete, with a capacity for about 150 patients.

It was a far cry from the hospital on Rincon Hill, built fifty years before. Every department and service incorporated the developments which marked the advance of time; and the experience of years was evident in setting up each. In addition to the most up-to-date heating and ventilating systems, the hospital was equipped with a signal system, its own ice plant, a sterilizing plant, and a power plant in the basement. The immense switchboard in itself was indicative of the vast extent of the plant. Here, too, in the basement was the electric master clock which regulated the time throughout the building. The sixth floor was devoted to the Sisters' apartments.

John McLaren, superintendent of San Francisco's Golden Gate Park, supervised the landscaping at St. Mary's. One attractive feature of the new hospital was its roof garden. Sheltered from the winds, beautiful with its array of flowers and fern, it commanded a breathtaking view in every direction.

The Annual Report of St. Mary's Hospital, published by the Sisters of Mercy in 1911, describes the several departments. By this time, the x-ray department was well staffed and equipped to handle "all kinds of radiologic work, both therapeutic and radiographic." The pathology department was described as "able to provide chemical, bacteriological and pathological analysis." The pharmacy department, staffed by Sister M. Vincent White and Sister M. Joseph Crowley, was given due space in the Annual Report of 1912. Mention was also made that the hospital had six endowed beds for the exclusive use of the sick poor and that during the year thirty-six persons had received 146 weeks of treatment gratuitously, and that reduced rates were given to fifty-three patients during 240 weeks.

In 1916, owing to the increased burden of the growing hospital, it was considered wise to appoint a superintendent for St. Mary's Hospital, thus relieving the Mother Superior for the work of the Institute. Accordingly, Sister M. Malachi White was chosen the first superintendent on June 1, 1916.

The War Era—1914-1918

With the assassination of the Archduke and Archduchess of Austria, July 28, 1914, Europe blew up. In a chain reaction, about thirty-three nations became embroiled in World War I. By April, 1917, the United States was caught in the maelstrom and, in one way or another, every American felt the hand of war.

The Preparedness Parade of 1917 in San Francisco was interrupted by a bomb explosion which killed eight and brought death to Dr. Painter, St. Mary's roentgenologist for some years. As Mother Euphrasia had heard him say that he would like to be baptized if he were going to die, she sent word to that effect to the emergency hospital and the sacrament was administered. She and a companion went to see the doctor but he had already expired.

About the time of World War I, a great movement was underway to standardize hospitals. The Superintendent's Report, St. Mary's Hospital, 1917-1918, speaks for itself:

> In January, 1917, St. Mary's Hospital became an Institutional Member of the Catholic Hospital Association. One of the pledges of the Association is a hearty cooperation with the American Medical Association and the American College of Surgeons to aid in the standardization of hospitals; therefore, in compliance we have made a complete change in our case histories and method of filing. Charts from the leading hospitals of the country were collected and what is most suited to our needs adopted from each.

157

Our present selected graphic and surgical charts were then designed with a view to having as much permanent data as possible on the fewest number of sheets.

The method adopted of filing is a modification of that used by the Massachusetts General Hospital, with the classification of diagnoses as used by the University of California. The system is being installed by Miss Genevieve Clark, former report clerk of Massachusetts General Hospital and University of California Hospital. Miss Mary Sheehan is in charge of records under the direction of Miss Clark.

Of course, the revamping of the record system was not the only way St. Mary's sought to follow the trends of the times or express cooperation in the then current movement to standardize hospitals and improve service.

The following letter to Mother M. Euphrasia, dated October 5, 1918, indicates another way in which the war affected St. Mary's.

Dear Reverend Mother,

The Surgeon General has just forwarded to me a communication of the Medical Reserve Corps of the United States Army and in all probability I will be called to active duty in a very short time; my term of service will be for the duration of the war and as that will necessarily cover an indefinite period of time, I feel it my duty to tender to you my resignation as a member of your Hospital Staff.

I regret very much the severance of ties which have for so long a period of time connected me with an Institution which has given me so much honor to serve and where I have received so much kindness and consideration, but it is as plain to me as it certainly is to you that there are obligations which have a higher claim to what little ability I may possess, and this fact makes it easier to say goodbye.

158

There are no words at my command that can possibly convey to you the gratitude there is in my heart for all that you have done for me and all the kindness which you have constantly showered on me that I can only hope that oft repeated "Thank you" will convey to you the feeling that goes with it. I shall be in San Francisco for about two weeks and will call personally to say "Goodbye."

Sincerely and gratefully,
T. E. Bailey[14]

Dr. Bailly had been connected with St. Mary's since his student days. Later, the doctor became a member of the staff and finally, chief surgeon. He was most skillful and always had a large patronage. His going would mean a great financial loss to the hospital, too, at a time when funds were badly needed.

About this time, the Spanish influenza epidemic swept San Francisco; in fact, it was world-wide. The Red Cross invited the Sisters to enter the service, with this condition—they were to don Red Cross uniforms including the cap! Needless to say the Sisters did not enlist. They did offer their services to Dr. William C. Hassler, Health Officer of San Francisco. He sent a gracious letter of thanks for the offer but stated that he believed the epidemic to be under control and the Sisters' services not needed.

The epidemic left lasting memories: wholesale making of masks and pneumonia jackets; numbers of Sisters, nurses, students, etc., so ill as to cause a problem of supplying someone to care for them; closed schools; Mass out-of-doors; and for some time, lists of deaths of appalling length in the daily papers—five times times the usual number. There were no fatalities, however, among the Sisters, but they were so hard-pressed that it was necessary to dispense them from the recitation of the Office.

Era of Expansion through Amalgamation—1917-1923[15]

By May, 1917, a union of the Sisters of Mercy, Rio Vista, with the San Francisco community had been effected. The amalgamation necessitated a number of trips and further taxed the already failing health of Mother M. Euphrasia Sullivan. It soon became evident that her active life was drawing to a close.

On May 18, 1919, she was stricken with paralysis. Although every possible medical assistance and loving care were lavished on the dear invalid, she gradually grew worse. By September 22, 1920, hypostatic pneumonia developed. On September 24, 1920, the Feast of Our Lady of Mercy, this valiant woman received the last sacraments, and surrounded by her sorrowing Sisters, she surrendered her soul to her Maker.

Her remains were laid in the chapel of the Novitiate until Saturday afternoon when they were removed to St. Mary's Hospital, whence the funeral took place Monday morning. Great were the numbers who came to take a last look at the kind face of a true Sister of Mercy who had spent herself to relieve the suffering of others.

Dr. Theodore Rethers, member of St. Mary's staff, was in Europe when he received word of Mother Euphrasia's death. He wrote the following:

> Hotel Rubens
> Buckingham Palace Rd., S.W.
> London
> October 21, 1920

Dear Reverend Mother,

I just received a letter from home today in which Mrs. Rethers told me of the death of Mother Euphrasia. It was quite a shock to me although I know she had been failing in health for some time past. When she passed from active participation in the affairs of your Order, I felt, as everyone did, that it was a great loss to your Institute in so many ways. I had always admired her great executive ability, her desire to do everything in her power to advance the interests of St. Mary's Hospital; she always seemed to be able to grasp every problem immediately, even in the minutest details, and her judgment was always excellent and unexcelled.

She was always open to advice and usually could improve upon any suggested ideas. I need not dwell upon the qualities of her disposition and temperament; ever modest, retiring, but firm, she made everyone feel the kindness of her heart. Her loss to any community could only be met with difficulty.

I wish to express to you and the Sisters of the Order my heartfelt sympathy.

I have thought of you all many times in my travels and had I, a very poor and neglectful correspondent, written half the times I had intended, I would have swamped the mail. . . .

Sincerely yours,
(signed) Theo. Rethers. [16]

When St. Mary's Hospital was built in 1911, it seemed to provide ample accommodations, but by 1917 the 150-bed hospital was already too small. The Superintendent's Report of that year clearly reflects the problem:

Since January 1, 1916, several changes have been made, thereby increasing the capacity by fifteen beds. The Typhoid Service Room was converted into a five-bed surgical ward. A dormitory on the second floor has become a five-bed Maternity Ward. The alcoves were closed in and transformed into private rooms. Our bed space was entirely too limited, and we were frequently obliged to refuse admittance to patients for want of accommodations. During the epidemic, a great number of extra beds were put up, and the sun court on the fifth floor converted into a ward as we refused no cases when there was any possibility of caring for them.

According to the annals, however, plans and specifications for an addition to the hospital were not prepared until 1923, and the new wing not completed before 1926.

St. Mary's Hospital, Modesto[17]

At the conclusion of Mother M. Euphrasia's term of office in 1919, Mother M. Bernard O'Brien was elected Reverend Mother. To her fell the lot of making decisions affecting the

161

spread of the community to embrace more than the Bay Region.

On April 20, 1920, came the first challenge. Rev. James W. Galvin, administrator of St. Stanislaus Church, Modesto, called at St. Mary's Hospital to ask the Sisters to establish a Catholic hospital in Stanislaus County. Mother M. Bernard was not at home, and Mother M. Gertrude, the Assistant, listened to his description of the future of the Church in this growing community. The matter, however, could not be settled then, and Father Galvin left. On his second visit, May 2, 1920, he interviewed Mother M. Bernard, who was deterred from taking on another hospital at a time when the community was in need of funds to enlarge St. Mary's and was already short of Sisters. She did agree, however, to visit Modesto to observe the possibilities, in hope that at some future time the project might become a reality.

Mother M. Bernard O'Brien, Mother Gertrude Reid, and Sister M. Agnes White visited Modesto on May 21, 1920, and were well pleased with all they saw. Negotiations were completed that day. At a council meeting held for this purpose, it was decided to send Sister M. Malachi White and three other Sisters to the new field of labor.

On May 31, 1920 they set out for Modesto in the company of Reverend Mother Bernard and Sister M. Pius Savage. The new mission was formally initiated under the title St. Mary's Hospital, Modesto, on June 1, 1920. The bungalow adjoining the hospital was converted into a convent and was furnished by the kind donations of friends. As soon as a chapel could be fitted up to reserve the Blessed Sacrament they had daily Mass.

The daily paper of Modesto carried the following news:

...The new St. Mary's Hospital, Modesto, will be conducted along the same lines of efficiency as is the renowned St. Mary's of San Francisco and will carry out the same high ideals which have ever characterized this oldest hospital of the Pacific, that is, the highest type of service to the patient, through the physician. The Sisters will endeavor to meet all the requirements now demanded by those great national societies, the American Medical Association and the American College of Surgeons, who are working so efficiently here in California, through our own League for the conservation of Public Health, for the standardization of hospitals.

The doors of the new St. Mary's will be open to all physicians of good standing and to patients regardless of race or creed.

Even before Mother Bernard undertook the venture in Modesto, events were taking place farther south which would eventually lead the San Francisco community to expand as far as southern California and Arizona. These trends foreshadowed a new chapter in the history of the Sisters of Mercy in the Far West.

Chapter 6

NORTH OF THE GOLDEN GATE

Yreka—1871-1876

What combination of circumstances led the Sisters of Mercy to Yreka, a small mining town in the vast wilderness of the extreme northern part of California, and in 1871?

The Siskiyou country was already familiar to early trappers of California and Oregon more than twenty years before the days of the Gold Rush. Trappers made regular expeditions from Oregon through the Sacramento Valley. And yet the Siskiyou area got off to a slow start for a mining area. It was primitive, and its transportation particularly so! For years the chief mode of travel was by horseback, over miserable and dangerous trails with such other hazards as the unfriendly Indian or the all too common highwayman, especially after the discovery of gold and the advent of the stagecoach. By 1856 the stage road reached Yreka by way of the Pit River; and the Pit River Indians had proven quite hostile to the white man's encroachment on their domain. By 1860 the new stage road was completed and one could board the stage for Yreka with a fair chance of arriving with scalp intact. A better stage route, however, seemed to invite California's masked gentry. Of the twenty eight stagecoach hold-ups credited to Black Bart, the Yreka stage figured in seven. Report has it that as late as 1880, when President Rutherford B. Hayes and General Wm. T. Sherman, of Civil War fame, passed through Yreka they were well received. But the crowd, for Yreka, was notably sparse because the men-folk were off in the mountains tracking stagecoach bandits.

Meanwhile the alert Archbishop Alemany of San Francisco studied the area of his jurisdiction, extending from the Bay of Monterey to the Oregon border. The discovery of gold, followed by the influx of Argonauts, had spiritual implications that the average historian might fail to observe; but the increase of people in the northern and central mining areas caught the attention of this saintly shepherd, and he took steps to send missionary priests to administer to the spiritual needs of these men.

Even as early as 1853, the Church had begun to function in Siskiyou County,[1] for it was in that year that Father James Croke, the traveling missioner from Oregon, came down as far as Yreka to hold services for the miners. But there was no resident priest until Father Hugh Gallagher returned to San Francisco in 1854 from his trip to Europe and brought back two young Irish priests who had been assigned to the California missions. In July, 1855, Father James Cassin and Father Tom Cody set out for the Siskiyou country. After a long trip by boat up the Sacramento and Feather Rivers from San Francisco, they were transferred at Marysville to the waiting stage for a bumpy drive of 125 miles. All this might well have disheartened the most zealous of missionaries. The faith, often neglected under the circumstances of frontier living, was strong here, and the priests were encouraged at the readiness of the people to avail themselves of the opportunities afforded. Almost immediately, Father Cassin erected a church at Yreka, and the records of baptism within three months of their arrival indicate the missioners went to work at once.

But it was a hard life, and missionaries came and went. In March, 1860, Father Hugh Gallagher was sent to Yreka where he remained until May, when arrangements were made to transfer Siskiyou County to the newly formed vicariate of Marysville.[2] In 1861 it was to pay his first visit to Yreka and to the missions in the area, as well as to administer Confirmation, that brought the zealous Bishop Eugene O'Connell to travel all 250 miles from Marysville up into the Siskiyou country.

When he found that Yreka was again without a resident priest in 1863, he began securing the services of temporary administrators and even went himself to help in the work of ministry. Finally, he secured Father Patrick Farrelly, an All Hallows man whom he only recently ordained in Marysville. From the start, this young priest showed exceptional missionary zeal, energy, vision, and promise.

It was he who, in 1866, built the second Yreka church, one entirely of brick, and next to it the rectory. Not not long after, he set about building a convent and school, and secured the promise of seven or eight Sisters from Canada. By 1869 his enthusiasm met its first jolt when he received word that the Mother General in France had revoked the permission she had given to ten Sisters to go to Yreka. Perhaps in the interim she had found out something of the nature of the mission and feared her Sisters would not be able to meet the challenge.

At any rate, Bishop O'Connell would not let matters rest there, and he applied to Mother M. Francis Warde, who was able to secure a group of Sisters from Mount St. Mary's, Manchester, New Hampshire.[3] The Manchester community was a dauntless group of Sisters of Mercy, hard-working and generous in answering, as far as they could, any demand made upon them, no matter where or how difficult the mission, and provided there were souls to be saved and a need for the works of the Institute. This was the spirit in which they answered the call of Bishop O'Connell in january, 1871, for some sisters for the foundation in Yreka.

Mother M. Camillus McGarr, who was appointed to head the little group of seven volunteers chosen for the California mission, immediately prepared to set out. The young superior,[4] baptized Elizabeth McGarr, was born in Auburn, New York, on June 8, 1844, the third of eight children of Daniel McGarr and Anastasia Lyons, both staunch Irish Catholics, people of integrity and great generosity to the poor. Surrounded by the wholesome influence of a truly Christian family, Elizabeth from her earliest years had nourished the desire to dedicate her life to God. On July 16, 1862, she entered the Convent of Mercy, Manchester, New Hampshire, which Mother M. Francis Xavier Warde had founded in 1858.

Here, too, Sister M. Camillus was professed on December 3, 1866. Doubtless she long cherished happy memories of her early days at Manchester, and of such associations as she had with Mother M. Francis Warde, one of the first seven Sisters professed by Mother Catherine McAuley at Baggot Street.

After her profession, Sister M. Camillus was assigned to teach in the parochial boys' school, as well as in the night school, which had been established to benefit the girls and women employed in the local factories. At the age of twenty-four, she was appointed local superior of a branch house in Portsmouth, New Hampshire and the burden of superior then placed up on her was lifted only by death.

Leaving Mount St. Mary's Convent of Mercy, Manchester, New Hampshire, in January, 1871,[5] the little group of Sisters traveled to New York, where they made a brief stop—long enough, however, to experience the kind hospitality of the New York Sisters of Mercy, which was supplemented by a certain Mr. Grace who put his carriage at their disposal and pressed into their hands, when leaving, a goodly sum of money with which they were to supply their needs in the new apostolate. As they crossed the country, they were to receive a network of religious hospitality and none more welcome than that received from their own Omaha Sisters, who had seen nobody from "home" since the Omaha foundation had set out from Manchester, New Hampshire, in 1864. It was at Omaha that the Sisters were met by their Yreka pastor, Reverend Patrick Farrelly.

The trip west coincided roughly with the completion of the first transcontinental railroad, for only two years before, the Union Pacific, building westward from Omaha, and the Central Pacific, building eastward from Sacramento had met on May 19, 1869 at Promontory Point, Utah. It was, therefore, understandable that the good pastor met the Sisters at Omaha, "out where the west begins"; and from there escorted them to Marysville, where they were introduced to Bishop O'Connell.

In a letter the Bishop expresses his appreciation to Mother M. Francis Warde for sending the Sisters to Yreka:

January 31, 1871

Dear Reverend Mother,

Yesterday afternoon our Sisters arrived in Marysville accompanied by their chaplain and pastor, Father Farrelly. Thank God! And after God, my best thanks to you, dear Mother. They all seemed to be in good health and spirits, and, as far as I can judge, correspond with the high recommendation which you gave of each of them. I thought to prevail on them, and so did the Sisters of this town, to rest for a few days; but, bent on reaching the end of their journey and in gladdening the hearts of the Yrekans before the Feast of the Purification, I was obliged to yield to their request and to let them go the same day! Not, however, till I had acceded to another request which they made, namely, to visit them in their new home and profess the Sister whom you wished me to profess in Marysville. So far, dear Reverend Mother, I hope you are satisfied. They gave me beautiful copies of the Mercy Rule and Constitutions, and the Ceremonial, which you so kindly sent me. Many thanks to you for this as well as for all the preceding favors received at your hands. You may depend on my requesting—nay, even if necessary, of insisting on their adhering strictly to the regulations of the Motherhouse which I look on as a model to be followed—a house which gave my destitute diocese such zealous, devoted Sisters. Again and again may God pour His choicest blessings upon you all that remain; may these, whom in your charity you sent to us, produce abundant fruit, and may their fruit remain. As soon as possible I shall say Mass for your intentions and I recommend myself to your prayers. You may depend on my hearty cooperation with your Sisters, as also on the cooperation of my clergy.

July 11, 1871

Excuse my delay, dear Reverend Mother, in answering your welcome and very kind letter. But as I hadn't visited the Sisters in Yreka at the time your favor reached Marysville, I postponed my reply till after my visit. Thank God, I found them well and happy, and quite content with their new mission and pastor. Up to my arrival they had met with no crosses but about a month after my departure, a most destructive fire broke out and destroyed fully one-third of the town, including the church and the pastor's house. Thank God, the convent escaped. It was only slightly damaged. Having met with such a heavy cross may we not hope that a bright crown awaits them?. . .

At the conflagration the citizens turned out en mass and by almost superhuman efforts succeeded in saving the convent. May they all obtain mercy from God in return for their exertions to save the Sisters of Mercy.

Your obliged and sincere servant in Christ,

Eugene O'Connell

The fire[6] referred to in the bishop's letter was a severe blow to Yreka. Official records show that more than a third of the town was reduced to ashes. People lost not only their homes but their means of livelihood. The parish was faced with the destruction of both church and rectory, and the recent building program had already placed them in a position of indebtedness not easily met in even the most favorable of circumstances. Father Farrelly, who had been the mainstay of the Catholic community, had labored so unceasingly to recoup the losses sustained by the fire as well as to pay off the debt already incurred by the convent and school, that his health broke. In June, 1873, he had to leave Yreka, where his vigorous administration during eight years of faithful service had endeared him to Siskiyou Catholics and non-Catholics alike.

Moreover, Yreka's boom times were on the wane. Mining had already begun to decline. Although the railroad had not yet reached into Siskiyou County, it was thought that the town would soon lose its commercial importance, with the passing of the stagecoach and the mule-team freighters. Even the highwaymen were going out of business or transferring their activities to more lucrative areas. True, some people of Yreka and the vicinity were turning to farming and were finding the soil and climate quite fruitful, especially in Scott Valley, but many families were so thoroughly discouraged by their declining fortune that they elected to move from the locality. This was soon reflected in the notable decline in school enrollment.

At this time, too, Indian troubles in eastern Siskiyou accentuated the isolated position of the Yreka mission. For some time, during 1872-1873, the Modocs outwitted the

Americans while the Indians sought an amicable and just settlement of their grievances. Led by Chief Kientepoos, popularly referred to as Captain Jack, they took refuge in the caverns and caves of the lava beds about sixty miles east of Yreka and quite successfully withstood the superior numbers of the U.S. regulars. Treachery met treachery and both the American commander, General E.R. Canby, and Captain Jack paid with their lives before peace was restored to Siskiyou.

It was therefore a combination of circumstances that would explain the withdrawal of the Sisters from Yreka. Undoubtedly, the fire of July 4, 1871, was the initial and perhaps major cause. In the face of a general decline of fortune in the area, it was evident that the Sisters could not shoulder the financial responsibilities that fell to them, and in 1876 they welcomed the invitation of Archbishop Alemany to send a group of Sisters to undertake a foundation in Rio Vista, where the needed support was more readily forthcoming.

Rio Vista, St. Gertrude's Academy—1876[7]

Rio Vista, about halfway between San Francisco and Sacramento, was once a part of the Rancho Los Ulpinos, the Bidwell grant of 17,725 acres along the western bank of the Sacramento River.

After a wharf was built, boats traveling between Sacramento and San Francisco touched daily at Rio Vista, making it a commercial center for the surrounding country. The name Rio Vista was adopted about 1860, although the town was not incorporated until January 6, 1894.

The original settlement flourished for about five years, until an event occurred that literally swept the town out of existence. The rains of the winter of 1861-1862 continued almost incessantly for an estimated "forty days and forty nights," until the river rose to unheard-of heights. By January 9, 1862, the entire town was flooded, and its populace barely escaped with their lives. All that remained of the old town were a few piles that had formed part of the wharf.

As in most places visited by a natural calamity, the former residents of the town began plans for building again, doubtless in a more elevated position, out of reach of the rising river. The new town grew rapidly and in a short time far excelled the old. A wharf was built by Joseph Bruning in the spring of 1862, and the riverboats ran regularly again.

Within a ten-year period, vast stretches of swamp and overflowed lands that lay below the Montezuma Hills and extended as far as Stockton were reclaimed, and Rio Vista developed as the heart of one of the most properous agricultural districts in the state. Highways and bridges facilitated travel and transportation, and canning industries were introduced, which furnished employment, especially during the summer months. The town took on a new look, and a new St. Joseph's replaced the temporary church that had been built after the flood.

In this period, Mr. Joseph Bruning proved himself one of the most civic-minded leaders of the era, a man of broad vision, kind heart and deep spirituality. Our Sister Annalist writes:

Mr. Joseph Bruning, the founder of St. Gertrude's Academy, is well deserving of honorable mention in the Annals of the Sisters of Mercy. He was born in Oldenburg, Germany, on July 18, 1812. As he was of a delicate constitution, on the advice of his physician he spent some time at sea. Afterwards he came to San Francisco where he conducted a hotel for several years. Here he married Miss Elizabeth Gertrude Blase, a woman of amiable disposition and solid virtue who in every respect proved a worthy partner for such an excellent man.

Soon he was forced to leave San Francisco and seek an outdoor life. He purchased a ranch on the Sacramento River where he settled and was able to be of great assistance to the first settlers of Rio Vista, after the flood of 1862. In later years many of the pioneers of the surrounding locality loved to recount the generosity of the Brunings during times of distress and how many a poor family was supplied with food and clothing as well as coal during a hard winter.[3]

Mr. Bruning was a man of remarkable faith and integrity. Deeply religious, his every effort seemed to be for the glory of God and the good of men. It was chiefly by his exertions that the first Catholic church was erected, as well as the first public school in Rio Vista. As a result of his benevolence and generosity, visiting priests were able to carry on their sacred duties amid the hardships of those early days. The priest was

170

always welcome to share their home during his stay, an invitation gladly accepted until the parish was able to afford a parochial residence.

Aware of the spiritual needs of the Catholics of the vicinity, it was also the great desire of the Brunings to establish a good Catholic school to meet the educational demands of the growing community. When Archbishop Alemany was consulted, he gave his hearty approval to the proposed undertaking. In 1876, the modest building was complete, and the Archbishop applied to St. Mary's Hospital, then the Motherhouse of the Sisters of Mercy, San Francisco, for Sisters to take charge of the new school. Mother M. Baptist Russell was forced to refuse his request because she was already involved in other foundations, and no Sisters could be spared. As a consequence, the Archbiship wrote to the Sisters of Mercy in Yreka, inviting them to come to Rio Vista and begin the good work awaiting them there. Mother M. Camillus McGarr and three Sisters agreed to accept the Rio Vista apostolate, and in May, 1876, set out from Yreka.[9]

God's blessing seemed to prosper the good work and from the beginning a day school for boys and girls was well attended. Within a short time it became evident that if provision were made for a girls' boarding school, the daughters of farmers in a much wider area would come to St. Gertrude's for their education, and such proved to be the case. The secondary school quickly developed to become fully equipped to offer a creditable high school education. The original building outgrew the demands made upon it, and, in 1882, the first addition went up. Ten years later a large wing was added, and some years after that the new chapel was erected.

In February, 1902, Mrs. Bruning died, and in September Mr. Bruning. Before the latter died, he deeded the property of the school and his home to the Sisters of Mercy. It was this home that was used for the first St. Joseph's School, a boarding school for boys aged seven to twelve. It was opened in 1903.[10]

About this same time, June 6, 1903, a small community of Sisters of Mercy in Ukiah was united with the Rio Vista community at the request of Archbishop Patrick Riordan of San Francisco, and the Ukiah Sisters took on the much needed undertaking of the St. Joseph's Boys' School.[11]

The Ukiah Community of Sisters of Mercy—1883-1903[12]

171

The foundress of the Ukiah convent was Mother Josephine Cummings, who had come with a group of seven Sisters from St. Catherine's Convent New York City, on April 14, 1871, to establish a foundation in Eureka, Humboldt County, California, then in the Grass Valley Diocese.

When Sister M. Josephine Cummings set out from the New York Motherhouse in 1871, she was but a novice who had had the courage to offer herself for a far off mission on the Pacific Coast. Eureka, which finally became the metropolis of the Humboldt region, had already assumed some importance as the port of entry to the Trinity mining district, expecially after a road was cut from eureka to the Trinity area. in mining days men were so busy raking in the gold that they were dependent upon commerce with San Francisco to supply most of their needs, and Eureka was the import town. After mining was superseded by lumbering, Eureka became the natural shipping center for the lumber interests. California's famous Redwood Highway runs through Humboldt County, and thousands of acres of redwood groves have been conserved as public parks. For any person from New York, the scenery must have been staggering indeed; but to a few timid women, in 1871, the wild remote country must have been lonely and awesome, too.

By 1877, when Sister M. Josephine was only twenty-five, she was chosen superior of the Eureka convent.[13] She was the daughter of John and Ann Cummings of Limerick, Ireland, who came to New York during the mid-nineteenth century, as did so many of their countrymen who sought to enjoy freedom of religion and freedom of opportunity in the new promised land. Here, in the same year that Mother M. Baptist Russell laid the foundation of the San Francisco community, Sister Josephine Cummings was born; and in her sixteenth year, she entered St. Catherine's Convent of Mercy, New York City. Little did she then dream that less than ten years later she would be the superior of the pioneer band in far off Eureka, California.

Beginnings are often difficult and disheartening, and the early years of the Eureka foundation were no exception. The Sisters soon found that they were surrounded by a very hostile community. The A.P.A.[14] movement was rampant in the area and persistently hampered their efforts. Under the guise of patriotism, this group carried out an intensive campaign of bigotry similar in expression to that fomented by the Know-Nothings in the 1850s. Such was her initial experience as superior, but there were also other even more difficult problems to face, and at the close of her term of office, Mother M. Josephine sought permission from her ecclesiastical superiors to return to the Motherhouse in New York. Right Reverend Bishop Patrick Manogue, who had always been a staunch friend, begged Mother Josephine to reconsider her decision. He suggested that she open a house in Mendocino County, where the Church had met with little success. "With your big heart and generous disposition," said the Bishop, "you can do much to help me in the cause of Christ in that district." And who could refuse this zealous prelate, who had given his life for the cause of Christ in the rugged mountains of California?

Having caught something of the Bishop's spirit, Mother Josephine set about to undertake the new venture. Through the kindness of Mr. John Reed, a prominent gentleman of the town, a suitable site was procured in Ukiah, the county seat of Mendocino. The building on the grounds had been a Methodist college. To this was added an entire front wing, and in the rear another addition was made. On June 21, 1883, Mother Josephine and three companions took possession of a new Mercy foundation under the title Sacred Heart Convent of Mercy, Ukiah.[15]

In September, 1883, the school opened with an enrollment of twenty-five boarders and nearly one hundred day pupils, Mother Josephine soon won the goodwill of even the most bigoted; and those who had most strongly opposed the coming of the Sisters soon became their best friends. To the work of the school was added the visitation of the sick and the afflicted, as well as the instruction of the children from the public school.

The foundation did increase in members. Within the first sixteen years, nine young women from the area joined their ranks and became Sisters of Mercy. In 1890, two mission schools were opened for the Indians of the nearby reservation, and much good was effected among those poor neglected children of God. Always a lover of music and a musician skilled in several instruments, Mother Josephine organized promising classes in both vocal and instrumental music.

For almost twenty years, the Ukiah Sisters labored effectively in the various works of Mercy in the Mendocino area, but because theirs was an independent community, they carried burdens which would not have been so heavy if shared by a larger affiliation. Archbishop Riordan recognized this and sought the agreement of both the Rio Vista and Ukiah communities to bring about a union, to take effect on the death of Mother Josephine. Finally worn out by her labors and an attendant illness, she passed peacefully to her reward on September 6, 1902, and was deeply mourned by her co-workers and the entire Ukiah community, whose love and esteem she had won by her tireless charity. On July 6 of the following year the little band of seven professed Sisters and one novice was welcomed at St. Gertrude's where the union was soon cemented by cordial and sisterly affection, the bond of a true convent of Mercy.

Nor were the charges of the Sisters of Mercy overlooked in the transfer. Arrangements were made for a continuation of their work among the Indians in Ukiah by the Dominican Sisters of Mission San Jose.

Rio Vista, St. Joseph's Boys' School—1903[16]

The Ukiah Sisters came to Rio Vista at a most opportune time, for the union coincided with the opening of the St. Joseph's Boys' School, Rio Vista. The almost unnoticed beginning of a boarding school for boys initiated a new era in the work of the Sisters of Mercy for the next fifty years. Circumstances had proven that little boys whose sisters were boarders at St. Gertrude's often were in need of a boarding school, too. The schools were so close that they seemed to afford a measure of holding together a family bereft of a parent due to illness, death or some other great tragedy. As the number increased, larger accommodations were built. The little boarders attended classes at St. Gertrude's.

St. Joseph's School for Junior Boys received the hearty approval of the Archbishop, and four Sisters took up residence in the new branch house, where a little chapel was fitted up. The house was dedicated on August 8, 1903.

Sausalito, Mount Carmel Academy—1910[17]

A few years later, at the invitation of Father John Valentini, pastor in Sausalito, Mother Camillus opened a school for the parish boys and girls. The school, which came to be called Mt. Carmel Academy, also promised to provide something of a resort, a place for change and rest during the summer vacation after the strenuous labors of the Sisters and because of the intense heat of the Sacramento Valley in the summer months.

The buildings needed some remodeling and adaptation for use as a convent and school. When completed, provision had been made for about six Sisters and twelve boarders, with classrooms for about eighty children.

On the first of August, 1910, the day school opened with an enrollment of 140 pupils, far more than had been anticipated. The growth of the school necessitated accomodation for eight Sisters, additional quarters for boarders, as well as needed classrooms. Despite the difficulty of transportation, pupils came from Mill Valley, Tiburon, Belvedere and even Fort Baker, brought by parents in the morning and picked up in the evening. This required supervised playground work as well as apparatus and equipment for games, etc. There was excellent support from the parents, the pastor and even the local public schools, for all felt that a healthy rivalry had improved the educational tone of the community.

For some time Dr. Charles Baschab was pastor , and the Sisters profited much from the visits of his highly gifted friends. The annalist remarks that there were three such visitors in one week; one of these was Dr. Zwerlein of Catholic University. When Dr. Baschab spoke in church, some thought he was talking over the heads of the children. Following such a comment one child said, "I could go along easily with Father; in fact, I knew what he was going to say next." This expertise was due to the fact that Father did not disdain to find time consistently to teach a religion class to the seventh and eighth grades. His was a well planned course and covered ten months, with ample evidence from the students that they understood the knowledge, love and service of God embraced in Jewish and Christian revelation.

For some time the health of Mother M. Camillus McGarr had been failing and despite all medical care it became evident that the Master would soon call her home. Her death occurred on September 20, 1911, and was keenly felt by her Sisters, the graduates of St. Gertrude's, and the people of Rio Vista.

Not very long after her death the Rio Vista community was amalgamated with that of the Sisters of Mercy of San Francisco, on May 19, 1917.

Chapter 7

THE SISTERS OF MERCY IN SOUTHERN CALIFORNIA

Difficult Beginnings

To a generation familiar with the phenomenal population increase and urban sprawl that has characterized southern California in recent years, it may be difficult to explain why the area seemed to be outside the sphere of growth and development that marked the northern part of the state in the last half of the nineteenth century. An analysis of the situation north of the Tehachapis during this same period will doubtless explain why the population of central and northern California mushroomed to more than half a million people as against a steady but much less observable increase in the south.

The northern gold rush, begun in 1849, and followed by the development of quartz mining and its attendant financial development as well as by the discovery of the Comstock Lode, paled to insignificance the feeble mining interests in the south. The search for gold in northern California opened up one county after another, and people poured in to share in the quest. Furthermore, mining not only lured miners and investors, but it promoted the expansion of agriculture and with it the introduction of new crops and new farming methods. It also stimulated industries to supply the needs of the many so far from eastern production; and it hastened the growth of towns and cities, as centers of commerce, banking and transportation.

The newcomers to the state in these decades were chiefly from the United States and northern Europe. They were aggressive and resourceful as they set to work to tame the wilderness, harness the forces of nature and initiate the development of what has become the most productive and most wealthy state in the Union.

However, the history of California did not begin here. We must recall that in 1969 San Diego celebrated its two hundredth anniversary, commemorating the establishment of the first white settlement in California. San Diegans have erected a bronze tablet on Presidio Hill which bears this inscription:

Here the First Citizen, Fray Junipero Serra,
Planted Civilization in California.

176

> Here he first Raised the Cross,
> Here he began the First Mission,
> Here, founded the First Town.
> —San Diego, July 16, 1769

We also read in the chronicles of the past that in the same year, 1769, a scouting party, led by Gaspar de Portola, visited the place which later was to give birth to the first Spanish pueblo, Our Lady of the Angels of Porciuncula, or Los Angeles, on September 4, 1781.

It was from Mission San Diego de Alcala that the Spanish padres began the El Camino Real, which served as a connecting link between the twenty-one missions, each a day's journey apart.

One of the most devastating acts in California's history was the secularization of the missions which followed, although not immediately, the Mexican Revolution against Spain (1810-1821). The very wealth and prosperity of the missions made them a target for the unscrupulous.

Presumably the legislation was an attempt to enfranchise the Indians and make them self-sustaining; but in actuality it led to the disintegration of the mission community; caused the natives, not yet able to live as white men, to revert to their primitive condition of squalor and poverty, and while it did bring an end to the flourishing missions, it threw open for grabs millions of acres formerly held by the missions and made possible the seven hundred private rancho grants of the Mexican government between 1834 and 1846.[1]

Life in southern California during the Mexican period was comfortable and lazy. Huge cattle ranchos supplied the commerce for meat consumption and for the hide and tallow trades. It was the latter that drew Boston skippers to southern California, bringing for exchange the East Coast products so much needed in an area almost devoid of industry. The huge ranchos were grants to men whom the Californians like to call the Silver Dons.

The first Bishop of California, Garcia Diego y Morena, appointed in 1841, was unable to check the steady decay that confronted his diocese as a result of the confiscation of the mission lands and the development of sprawling ranchos.

Following the Treaty of Guadalupe Hidalgo (1848), which gave the United States all the territory below the forty-second parallel, excluding Lower California, it was necessary for the Church not only to replace Bishop Moreno but also to reconstruct the diocese. The Most Reverend Joseph Sadoc Alemany, therefore, was named to the new see of Monterey by Pope Pius IX, on May 31, 1850.[2]

At the time of his arrival, the diocese of Monterey was one of the largest of ecclesiastical jurisdictions in the United States. The problem was partially settled by April 17, 1853,[3] when Rome separated Lower California from Upper California, and more completely by the erection, three months later, of the metropolitan see of San Francisco, with Alemany as Archbishop.[4] The territorial bounds of the new archdiocese of San Francisco became the forty-second parallel on the north; the Pacific Ocean on the west; the Colorado River on the east; and on the south, the limits of the city of San Jose. The diocese of Monterey embraced all of the rest of California south of San Jose to the Mexican border and extended from the Pacific to the Colorado River. Bishop Thaddeus Amat, C.M., became Bishop Alemany's successor to the see of Monterey, March 12, 1854.

To return to the story of southern California during the Mexican era, it was characterized by the extensive ranchos of the Silver Dons whose immense holdings have often become a cause for criticism. The day of the Silver Dons were numbered, however, by the tragic weather that befell California in the sixties. The winter of 1861-62 was one of the wettest in California history. For all of a month the rain fell in torrents; there were floods throughout the state and havoc was widespread. Thousands of livestock perished and a fourth of the state's taxable wealth was destroyed.

In southern California, the damage caused by the rains was insignificant compared with the Great Drought that followed the flood (1863-1864).[5] For two years, grasslands reverted to desert and livestock died by the thousands. Like the ten plagues that beset the early Egyptians, a devastating swarm of locusts contributed to the distress; and finally, there came a virulent plague of smallpox. Then followed a collapse of property values. By 1865 the total evaluation of real and personal property in Los Angeles, the Queen of the Cow Country, had fallen to little more than half a million dollars. It was this natural calamity that wiped out the era of the Dons and started the subdivision of most of the Spanish or Mexican grants. A new economic order emerged.

The post-Civil War period marks the beginning of the agricultural era in southern California. The influx of farmers in quest of land drove what was left of the cattle industry to the hill country.

Wheat farming, the grape industry, and most important to southern California, the citrus industry in the seventies, were the beginnings of an agricultural revolution that would give California her worldwide reputation in agriculture. Nevertheless, the California farmers, especially in the southern part of the state, met with almost insurmountable obstacles. To acquire the land itself they often had to outwit the land sharks, monopolists and gamblers who had acquired tremendous holdings, sometimes through illegal means. The Silver Dons had relinquished their holdings, but land titles were in a sad state of uncertainty and confusion, and in many cases there was also need of prolonged and expensive litigation to obtain necessary water rights.

The railroads were tremendous landowners, having received immense land grants from the federal and western state governments. This land was often the most desirable in the West because of easy access to transportation.

It is certainly clear that San Francisco and Los Angeles received more support from the railroads to become great metropolitan centers than did San Diego. Towns could be doomed or made by the wand of the railroad magnate. Booms and busts followed each other with the promotion of each new major line.

In the 1880s, the Santa Fe touched off the rate war[6] when the Southern Pacific refused to consider a prorata agreement. For a short time one could travel from the Mississippi to southern California for as little as one dollar, and freight rates underwent a like cut. Streams of people poured into southern California, some with land options attached to their railroad tickets. Property values skyrocketed and people made fortunes on paper.

By the late spring of 1888, it had all ended. The bottom fell out of the boom. Departing trains now had a heavier business. Some towns became deserted villages. But even after the departure, Los Angeles came out of the boom with a population of better than 50,000 and the county more than 100,000. San Diego, which had also shared in the boom, had acquired a

179

population of 35,000, which according to the 1890 census, dropped to 16,159 and the county to 34,987. Even then it was more than three times larger than it had been before the boom.

Gradually Los Angeles and San Diego recovered some of their confidence and developers were once again comparing California to sunny Italy. By 1894, there were 3,000,000 fruit trees in San Diego County, 2,000,000 more than at the end of the boom. The orange and lemon industry seemed promising.

San Diego had by the turn of the century reached some level of contentment. There were comfortable homes, neat orchards and some promising civic leaders. It remained, however, for the opportunities offered by the twentieth century for San Diego to realize her potential. She was still at the end of the line; her port had not yet caught the eye of Washington. She was still too dependent on railroads to be able to capitalize on her own resources.

Meanwhile, Los Angeles became the hub of southern California commerce. The growth of Los Angeles and the prosperity of the surrounding communities—Riverside, San Bernardino, and Redlands—diverted much of the trade with the interior that San Diego had once enjoyed.

It was in the wake of the boom in the 1880s that both Mother M. Bonaventure Fox and Mother Michael Cummings arrived in southern California to undertake the work of the Sisters of Mercy. Not only was the area filled with people holding inflated land certificates, often fleeced of their life's earnings, but the region was so devoid of industry as yet, that it was difficult to assure the jobless a means of support. Many of the industries that have taken care of the present day expanding population in Los Angeles had not yet even been conceived. A wave of calamities—floods, bank failures, and the impact of the nationwide depression of the early nineties,—had robbed southern California of much of her confidence. In such an economic climate, it was hard to initiate projects which required money especially if one were forced to depend upon gifts and loans.

In 1888 the Most Reverend Francis Mora, Bishop of the Monterey-Los Angeles diocese, made application to the Mother-house of the Sisters of Mercy in Big Rapids, Michigan, for a few Sisters to take over a school in Salinas, California. Mother Bonaventure Fox and one companion, a postulant, Miss Julia Coe, later Sister M. Philomena Coe, offered themselves for the mission.[7]

To those east of the Mississippi, Salinas in 1888 was probably an obscure place. It is about nine miles from Monterey Bay in the Salinas River Valley. It was even then served by the Southern Pacific. By 1888, it had already replaced Monterey as the county seat, and Monterey had been the capital of California from 1775 to 1849. The Salinas Valley is one of the richest agricultural regions in the United States, producing, especially, vegetables. The Californian of today would be familiar with the place because of the annual rodeo or because it is but a few miles from Fort Ord.

Mother M. Bonaventure, who was to initiate the works of Mercy for the Los Angeles diocese, was well fitted for the task that lay ahead. She was the youngest daughter of John and Bedelia Fox, comfortable Irish parents whose yet more precious heritage was the faith of their fathers. Elizabeth Fox was born in Kilconnell, Galway, in 1840, and from her infancy she was reared in such an atmosphere of Christian piety that it was not difficult for her to hear the Master's call. Two of her sisters became Sisters of Mercy in Galway convents, Mother M. Magdalen at Gort and Sister M. Bernard at Tuam. Her brother, Reverend Bonaventure Fox, O.F.M., offered himself to the Santa Barbara province and became a zealous California missionary. Sister M. Bonaventure also had a marked inclination toward the missions, which drew her ever westward. Although some years lapsed before she was able to follow her strong attraction, in her late twenties she made her way to America and entered the Sisters of Mercy in Greenbush, New York, on February 4, 1868, where she was professed on September 11, 1870. She loved children, and her generous heart readily went out to meet the needs of the poor. For some years she was happily engaged in the works of the Institute in New York.[8]

From Greenbush, New York, Sister M. Bonaventure went to Michigan. She had been fired by the account of the pioneer country she received from Mother M. Alphonsius Thielmann, Superior in Michigan.

In 1880, Sister M. Bonaventure volunteered to assist on a comparatively new hospital project at Big Rapids, established by the Sisters of Mercy of Grand Rapids, Michigan, in 1878. Here she labored for several years in the care of the sick and the suffering, giving herself generously as the need presented itself.

In November, 1887, Sister M. Bonaventure Fox joined Mother M. Teresa Dolan and sister M. Dolores Drew from Big

Rapids, and went to Fort Scott, Kansas, to establish the works of Mercy in the diocese of Wichita. Because of ill health, Mother M. Bonaventure returned to Big Rapids in the spring of 1888. It was in 1888 that an application was made to the Motherhouse of the Sisters of Mercy in Big Rapids, for Sisters to take charge of the school in Salinas, California. Sister M. Bonaventure Fox offered herself for the California mission. Meanwhile Sister M. Michael Cummings of the Denver Sisters of Mercy had also given a ready response to the plea sent to Bishop Matz[9] of Denver by Bishop Mora[10] of the Monterey-Los Angeles diocese, for co-workers to assist Mother Bonaventure in Salinas.

Chapter 8

THE LOS ANGELES FOUNDATION—1890[1]
Mother M. Bonaventure Fox

Enroute to the new field of her labors, Mother M. Bonaventure Fox stopped at St. Mary's Hospital, San Francisco, where she was warmly received by Mother M. Baptist Russell. The latter had much to share with a Sister of Mercy about to begin an apostolate in an area as yet untilled. Mother M. Baptist had the experience of thirty-five years, replete with the trials and successes, the joys and sorrows attendant on working in the Lord's vineyard thousands of miles from home. Both women had a thirst for souls and a readiness to meet whatever challenge presented itself.

One fruit of the friendship between Mother M. Baptist and Mother Bonaventure that grew during the next ten years was the development of the works of Mercy in southern California. Mother Russell had been asked to extend the labors of the Sisters here, but neither Archbishop Alemany nor Archbishop Riordan, his successor, felt that any of her religious family could yet be spared, so great were the demands in the northern diocese.

Sacred Heart School, Salinas, California—1889

It was at St. Mary's that Mother M. Bonaventure arranged to meet the pastor of Sacred Heart parish, Salinas, California, and agreed to take over the school from which the Sisters of Loretto had lately withdrawn. Before proceeding to Salinas, however, she made a long anticipated trip to Santa Barbara to visit one very dear to her, her missionary brother, Father Bonaventure, O.F.M., who was in residence at the old Mission.

By September, 1889, Mother Bonaventure and her companion from Big Rapids, Michigan, Sister M. Philomena Coe,[2] assisted also by a lay teacher, opened the school in Salinas. Within a few months they were joined by Mother M. Michael Cummings and Sister M. Alphonsus Fitzpatrick, who had been asked by the Most Reverend Nicholas C. Matz, Bishop of Denver, to go to the assistance of Mother Bonaventure.

By the end of the term in Salinas and after a fair trial of a year, it was evident to all the Sisters who had undertaken the mission that the area was not ready to support a school. This merely endorsed what the Sisters of Loretto had decided when they left Sacred Heart School a few years before.

Mother M. Bonaventure was not disheartened, but journeyed to Los Angeles with Sister M. Philomena to present the facts to the Bishop. Because the latter was out of town when she arrived, she was warmly received by his Vicar General, Reverend Joachim Adam. Ready to undertake any mission the Bishop might advise, she nevertheless suggested opening a home for working girls in the growing city. Father Adam lent a kindly ear and promised to present her project to the Bishop.

Saint Martha's Home for Working Girls, Los Angeles—1890[3]

Not long after her return to Salinas, she received a telegram from Bishop Francis Mora, encouraging her to return to Los Angeles. Mother M. Bonaventure lost no time in answering the invitation, and on April 7, 1890, she and her companion arrived in Los Angeles, which incident marks the foundation of the Los Angeles community. By this time she had but fifty cents in her pocket.

The Bishop heartily agreed with Mother M. Bonaventure's suggestion that a House of Mercy be opened for young women of good character working in offices or stores, and also those in domestic service who might need a safe home while seeking employment. Thus it was that the first house of the Institute established in the Los Angeles diocese was St. Martha's Home for Working Girls. In 1890 Los Angeles was not the sprawling city that it is today; but the recent boom had brought in many people who were friendless. Now that the excitement had passed with the arrival of the bust which followed the boom, such an institution met a real need.

Meanwhile, Mother M. Michael and her companion had resolved to return to Denver or St. Louis where they were promised a warm welcome. At this point Mother M. Baptist Russell suggested to them that they undertake a mission in San Diego, where Bishop Mora had begged the San Francisco foundress to send some of her Sisters. Mother M. Baptist Russell advised Mother M. Michael not to leave California until she had sought direction from Bishop Mora. The zealous Bishop was only too happy to receive Mother M. Michael and her companion on May 29, 1890. He persuaded them to go to San Diego to open a hospital. The following Sunday he himself went to San Diego and before leaving gave an autographed endorsement to certify their status. How the mustard seed took root and flourished will be described in detail in the story of the Sisters of Mercy in San Diego.

There is need now to return to the Los Angeles foundation. For a short while Mother M. Bonaventure and Sister M. Philomena occupied a tiny cottage on Los Angeles Street close to the cathedral. At this time the new episcopal residence on East Second Street was in the course of construction. As soon as it was ready, the Bishop turned over his former place, on Main near Second Streets, to the Sisters at a nominal rental. Mother M. Bonaventure was glad to accept his offer, and before long the convent and home for working girls were ready for occupancy. Here also a novitiate was fitted up to provide for four candidates for religious life, who had already made application (1890).

St. Martha's Home for Working Girls was not, however, a very lucrative project, for these young women had little or nothing to pay their way. Nevertheless, God seems to have blessed the undertaking by proofs that He would not be outdone in generosity. The four aspirants to religious life in 1890 truly provided the hundredfold; they brought not only great fervor to the work in hand but also considerable financial help. Doubtlesss a large part of the success of the struggling community and certainly great joy and encouragement to the brave Sisters who had undertaken the task should be credited to these pioneer postulants.

Mother M. Bonaventure lost no time in seeking the necessary permission to visit the local institutions. Soon the little band radiated the work of Mercy from Main and Second, visiting the sick and poor in their homes and in the county hospital and bringing consolation to those in prison. In the exercise of the works of Mercy, the coming of the Sisters was acclaimed by priests and people as an answer to a long felt need. During these early years of the foundation, Reverend Joachim Adam proved a prudent counselor, an invaluable friend, and a saintly spiritual director.

In 1891, another work was undertaken—the care of aged women.[4] The cost varied according to circumstances. A life home could be secured for a thousand dollars; many, however, found a home with the Sisters for very much less. At this time there was no such thing as Social Security, and it was to take some fifty years to condition the public to assume the responsibility for the less fortunate members of society in an industrialized nation.

It soon became evident to the Sisters that their present place could no longer accommodate those who applied for admission. Therefore in 1892 a piece of property was purchased on East Third Street near Main. This property had a spacious house giving ample accommodation for the increased number of boarders and life members. Not long after, the Sisters added a large brick building, which provided a chapel, community room, novitiate, dormitories, etc. And yet, at the end of three years, this Mercy compound had to be abandoned for still larger quarters.

Mercy Hospital, San Bernardino—1891[5]

Meanwhile Father Stockman of San Bernardino prevailed upon Mother M. Bonaventure to undertake the erection there of a small hospital, chiefly for miners, and the good priest donated a thousand dollars to the project. A fair sized frame building was erected, with accommodations for thirty or more patients. By 1897, however, the silver mines were closed. This, together with the railroad strikes, created conditions detrimental to maintaining a hospital, and it was decided to discontinue their San Bernardino venture after five years. The building was sold and moved to another location and a year or two later, the land on which it had stood was also sold.

The Sisters were not quitting in any sense of the word; they were merely transferring their efforts to a place where they could effect the most good. About this time another need of the diocese presented itself to Mother M. Bonaventure rather graphically. The Sisters of Charity had provided for orphan girls, but at this time there were no Sisters caring for the little boys of Los Angeles. One evening a burly but good natured policeman presented himself at the door of the convent. He was holding the hand of a little Mexican boy of about three years and in his arms was this little fellow's baby brother, perhaps a year and a half old. Invited into the convent parlor, the officer told a pathetic story of neglect and abuse that touched the motherly heart of Mother Bonaventure. She took the boys in that night but requested that the officer report the case to Bishop Mora. The latter was only too happy to give her full permission to undertake the care of orphans, both boys and girls. The year 1895, therefore, initiate a new work of Mercy in Los Angeles—the opening of the Home of the Guardian Angels, for orphans, half-orphans and abandoned children. As the number increased, the Sisters sought and received state aid, but the cost of maintaining the little ones, even with the aid of such funds, overtaxed the resources of the Sisters. Again the Giver of all good gifts rewarded their trust in Divine Providence. As the work of Mercy became known to the people, donations and help of various sorts enabled Mother Bonaventure and her Sisters to meet the obligations incurred and to continue the care of the little ones for about twenty-three years. For some years the Sisters were able to accommodate these children by renting a house suitable for the purpose.

The year 1895, which marked the opening of the Home of the Guardian Angels, was also the occasion for the Silver Jubilee of Mother Bonaventure, September 11, 1895.[6] Among the gifts she received was a check for one hundred dollars from Bishop Mora who noted that "this Sister could make it go a long way. Witness what she had done in Los Angeles on a 'shoe string.' "

During this year, too, the Sisters decided to leave East Third Street, for the works of the Institute had expanded to such a degree in three years that they had outgrown all the possibilities of the Third Street property. They were able to purchase a desirable site, 150 by 115 feet, on Boyd Street, only a few blocks from St. Vibiana's Cathedral.

At the new location, a very substantial frame building of

three stories was erected. It was a happy day for the community when, on January 23, 1896, Bishop George Montgomery, who had succeeded Bishop Mora, blessed the new Mercy Mother-house[7] at 326 Boyd Street. When he used the occasion to give encouragement to the Sisters, he did not lose the opportunity to speak to the many friends of the Sisters and of the Church, who were present for the occasion, requesting help in the works of Mercy. The Sisters had given themselves, but without substantial help from the laity they were limited in what they could accomplish for the poor, the sick and the afflicted.

On the new property, a separate building was also erected for aged men who desired to spend their declining years in the peace of such a home. They were able to secure life membership on the same conditions as the women.

The Home of the Guardian Angels which was opened in 1895 was not a part of the new Mercy complex on Boyd Street. For some years the Sisters had rented a house suitable for the purpose. This work too, grew until the great number of abandoned or neglected little ones forced Mother Bonaventure to seek a new location. After some search, she found a large house in St. Vincent's parish at 333 South Figueroa Street, to which she transferred the orphans until the opening of the place on West Washington in 1906.[8]

Not long after the Los Angeles community had moved to its new convent, the Sisters had the great pleasure of entertaining Mother M. Baptist Russell and her companion, Sister M. Columba O'Kelly, of St. Mary's Hospital, San Francisco. Mother's health was beginning to fail, and it was hoped that this little change of climate would do her good. After all, did not the posters and advertisements that drew so many to Southern California say that the climate was a "sure cure" for almost everything?

Mother M. Bonaventure was delighted to see Mother M. Baptist again after almost a decade, and how much more did she now have to share of her experiences and early struggles on the Los Angeles foundation! Mother M. Baptist had gone to Ireland in 1879, and she sparked the recreation hour by recounting incidents of the trip. As most of the Sisters were daughters of Erin they were absorbed by her tales. Of great interest to them as well were the stories she told of early San Francisco and the pioneering efforts of her Sisters in the city that was then taking shape.

Before returning to San Francisco, Mother Baptist also visited

Mother Michael in San Diego, taking Mother Bonaventure with her. From there the two Sisters traveled to Santa Barbara, where Father Bonaventure, O.F.M., had died the previous year, and to Rancho Camulos in Ventura County, a place remembered as the setting for *Ramona*, Helen Hunt Jackson's popular novel which dramatized the plight of the California Indian.

In the spring of the next year, 1898, Mother M. Bonaventure began to show signs of failing health, and for several weeks she was a patient at St. Vincent's Hospital. Although not much improved, she returned home, and because she assumed her various duties for a few months, her anxious community became somewhat encouraged. To their great sorrow, however, she again became so seriously ill that on March 25, 1899, she received the sacraments of the dying. Two weeks later, on April 6, surrounded by her grieved community, she passed to her heavenly Spouse who had promised a fitting reward for even a cup of water given to the needy in His Name.

At the request of the Most Reverend Bishop George Montgomery, her remains were brought to St. Vibiana's Cathedral, where on the eighth of April at nine a.m. a Solemn Requiem Mass was celebrated for the repose of her soul. Very Reverend Joachim Adam delivered the eulogy in which he dwelt on her great zeal for souls, expressed especially in the various works of Mercy she had initiated and developed in the diocese of Monterey-Los Angeles.

Mother M. Bonaventure left behind her a community of twenty-one professed Sisters to carry on the works she had commenced.[9] It was a rather phenomenal growth in membership in the first nine years.

On April 20, Sister M. Joachim McBrinn succeeded Mother M. Bonaventure, and, save for the interim terms of Sister M. Bernard Daley (1905) and Sister M. Philomena Coe (1914), she gave excellent leadership to the Los Angeles community for more than two decades.

About the same time as Mother M. Joachim was elected superior (1902) the Very Reverend Joachim Adam, V.G., of the Monterey-Los Angeles diocese resigned his office because of ill health and returned to Spain, his native land. He had been a strong support to Mother M. Bonaventure and a staunch friend of the Sisters of Mercy. He recovered, however, and in 1907 he yearned to see California again, but he was stricken with paralysis and died at Mercy Hospital, London, on July 30, 1907.[10]

The turn of the century marked not only a new era in the history of the Sisters of Mercy but a real turning point in the history of Los Angeles. In a scant fifty years Los Angeles had grown from a little pueblo of 1,600 people in 1850, to what was at that time a major city of 103,000, ninety percent of whom had arrived since 1880, lured by visions of economic opportunity.

When Mother M. Joachim assumed office, California seemed to be awakening upon a new era of confidence, and Los Angeles had begun to feel the results of the trend toward urbanization. A steady, though perhaps not spectacular, influx of people to southern California had been caused by the development of a broader economic base and the introduction of new industries. One phase of the new economy was the development of the oil industry. For some time the drag in the California petroleum industry stemmed from the fact that it seemed to have but limited use. To the California oil men must go much credit for finding multiple uses for oil products and due recognition for their share in the technological advances in methods of locating fields, drilling and refining.

What is known as the Los Angeles—Salt Lake Field was opened in 1893, largely the result of the ingenuity and leadership of E.L. Doheny,[11] who was to become the chief figure in Los Angeles oil. To him must also be given the credit for persuading the Santa Fe Railroad to experiment with crude oil as a fuel for its locomotives. Not only was the experiment a success, but it provided a cleaner, more convenient, and cheaper fuel. Within six years, several thousand wells were crammed into a small strip of western Los Angeles. For a while the market became glutted with oil but the conversion from coal to oil in railway transportation and industrial furnaces, to say nothing of the timely arrival of the automobile, strengthened the industry and started Los Angeles on the road to industrialization.

Thanks to her climate, southern California also became the center of two relatively new industries—the production of motion pictures and the airplane industry. Both were due to become "blotting paper industries" and affect the entire world.[12]

But if Los Angeles were to achieve her industrial potential, her leaders saw that two needs must be met: an adequate water supply for a growing city and a good port to acquire her share of the West Coast export-import trade.

The acquisition of San Pedro harbor[13] and the thirty-mile stretch to the sea, a unique "shoestring" annexed in 1906, brought the harbor into the city and legalized the spending of municipal funds for port improvement. In 1909 the consolidation of San Pedro and Wilmington with Los Angeles gave Los Angeles an extended shoreline and a wider window on the Pacific; and yet, Los Angeles could never have become the largest city in California had she not made provision for an adequate water supply. In 1913, the Los Angeles Aqueduct[14] was the first step taken, bringing water from the Owens River to Los Angeles. The project was made possible by the voters' authorization of a twenty-five million dollar bond issue for the development of municipally owned hydro-electric power, thereby assuring an adequate water supply for the growing city of Los Angeles for years to come.

California was a changing state in the first two decades of the twentieth century and nowhere was this more evident than in the growth in population south of the Tehachapis. In 1900 southern California had a population of less than 350,000 as compared with that of northern California's 1,150,000; by 1920 southern California had reached 1,431, 000 and northern California could claim slightly less than 2,000,000. And yet, in the same year (1920) the city of Los Angeles itself had passed San Francisco in population.

This factor alone, which was given further impetus by a corresponding growth in industry, explains why California played so prominent a part in urging the construction of the Boulder Dam to bring water from the Colorado River.[15]

In tracing the story of the growth of Los Angeles in the first quarter of the twentieth century, we are probably better prepared to understand some of the changes and developments in the Los Angeles community of the Sisters of Mercy which enabled them to meet the changing times.

What had been a very commodious home for working girls and could make ample provision for the aged when the Sisters purchased the property on Boyd Street in 1895, was utterly inadequate ten years later. Such, too, was the case with regard to the home for the orphans, who were transferred to a large house on South Figueroa Street. The new Bishop, Most Reverend Thomas Conaty, recognized the need for larger quarters and recommended that the Sisters look for a suitable site. This suggestion was acted upon promptly, and in 1904 the

Bishop approved the tract that Mother M. Joachim had selected—ten acres on the western rim of the city, on the southwest corner of West Washington and Concord Streets. Here they constructed the very substantial three-and-a-half-story brick building which became known as the Convent of Our Lady of Mercy. Facing West Washington and well set back from the street, with broad lawns and good structural lines, it was an imposing building as well as a very serviceable one. The main building or central block was the convent proper. The west wing, called St. Patrick's Home, had accommodations for one-hundred elderly people; the east wing, the Home of the Guardian Angels, provided ample room for two hundred children. By June 30, 1906, the Sisters were able to take possession of the new Mercy compound.[16]

The move from Boyd Street made it necessary to find a suitable place for the working girls. For a few years they rented a house on the corner of Hope and Pico Streets, until more satisfactory arrangements could be made. In 1908 they were able to lease a large brick building at 1626 South Figueroa Street. In a few months, the community took possession of a well planned convent with accommodations for at least forty boarders. St. Martha's Home for working girls on Figueroa Street exerted a salutary influence on this type of young woman for about ten years, when other needs of the diocese caused the Most Reverend Bishop John J. Cantwell, who had succeeded Bishop Conaty, to advise the discontinuance of the home. It was indeed a source of regret to the Sisters to abandon this, their first work in the diocese. The Sisters were, however, mindful of the need for schools and hospitals in the rapidly growing city and recognized the Will of God in the counsel of their good Bishop. In 1918 St. Martha's Home was closed after a service of providing a refined home for working girls for twenty-eight years.[17]

Sacred Heart Elementary School, Redlands—1908-1938

In 1908 Rt. Rev. Monsignor T.J. Fitzgerald of Redlands asked Mother M. Joachim for Sisters to take charge of the Sacred Heart Elementary School in his parish. Redlands lies at the foot of the San Bernardino Mountains, about sixty-five miles east of Los Angeles. It was one of the towns that grew with the citrus industry and is in the midst of the largest navel orange growing district in the world.

Our Lady of Mercy—1918[18]

Within a few years, Monsignor Fitzgerald opened another school in Redlands for many of the poor Mexican children in the area; he named it Our Lady of Mercy, doubtless, in deference to the Sisters as well as to Our Lady. For more than thirty years the Sisters of Mercy maintained the only Catholic schools in this thriving district.

With the increase in population in southern California, the creation and staffing of schools became one of the most crying needs of the diocese. To meet repeated requests for Mercy schools, two Sisters were sent to Ireland, in 1908 to recruit subjects. They returned with a sturdy group of young women, eight of whom persevered and creditably answered a timely need either in hospitals or schools.

Mercy Hospital, Bakersfield—1910[19]

It was in 1910 that the Sisters of Mercy of Los Angeles undertook hospital work in Bakersfield at the request of Bishop Conaty.

Bakersfield, the seat of Kern County, lies about one hundred miles northwest of Los Angeles, In 1900 it had a population of less than 5,000; but by 1920 it had reached 18,638, and it has continued to grow. This rapid rate of population increase was due to the agricultural development of Kern County and to its oil fields. More than a hundred oil companies have offices in the city, and Elk Hills Naval Reserve is about twenty-three miles west. Until recently, communication and transportation have steadily improved. Both the Santa Fe and the Southern Pacific have served this city. In the more recent past, Bakersfield has come to depend much upon United Air Lines,[20] as well as on bus and truck lines.

In 1910, however, it was what might today be called a small town. From the materials available, here is a brief history of St. Clair's Hospital, Sixteenth and H Streets, before the coming of the Los Angeles Sisters.

Mother M. Vincent Mahoney, a member of the Sisters of Mercy of Macon, Georgia, had gone to Colorado, presumably for her health, as records indicate that she was asthmatic.

Perhaps she envisioned relief from asthma and a life of further service in the highly advertised health-haven of sunny California. At any rate, she induced Sister M. Alexis of the Denver Sisters of Mercy to join her in a hospital enterprise in Bakersfield. In 1905 she was able to secure the St. Clair residence on Sixteenth between G and H Streets, and to open it as a fourteen bed hospital in 1908. In an effort to secure much needed help for the hospital, she sought recruits at the Convent of Mercy, Los Angeles, but without success. In San Diego, however, at the Convent of Mercy which had already established St. Joseph's Sanatorium, she received a response from Sister Mary Augustine Quinn and Sister M. Teresa O'Donnell. These are the two which the Kern County Medical Society Bulletin, May, 1961, states "came to Bakersfield enriched by a large nursing and managerial hospital experience in Chicago." Both were Sisters of Mercy of the San Diego Community and both received the chapter votes and the approval of Bishop Conaty to transfer to the Sisters of Mercy, Bakersfield, on December 10, 1908. Miss Marguerite Castro, a Kern County nurse who had been trained at Fabiola School of Nursing, in Oakland, also initially assisted them in setting up the hospital.

For a while it was operated quite successfully, but difficulties arose, followed by disagreements among the administrators. The Catholics of Bakersfield reported the matter to Bishop Conaty because Bakersfield at that time belonged to the Monterey-Los Angeles diocese.[21] It was then that Bishop Conaty asked Mother M. Joachim McBrinn of the Los Angeles Sisters of Mercy to take over the project.

From letters and fragmentary articles it seems that Mother M. Vincent had already departed for Salt Lake City to secure relief, since Bakersfield had not proved to be the health-haven she had expected. A photostatic copy of a financial statement of the hospital made by Mr. W. A. Howell for Bishop Conaty indicates that his report covers the period "from the date Reverend Mother M. Alexis assumed the management of St. Clair's, November 8, 1909, to date" (Feb. 17, 1910). Sister M. Joachim of the Los Angeles Sisters, who took over the hospital in Bakersfield at the request of the Bishop, writes:

We arrived in Bakersfield on February 9, 1910, and took charge of the hospital which had been opened in 1908 by Sister M. Vincent. . . . We remained in what was known as the St. Clair Hospital until 1913 when we built our new hospital and named it Mercy Hospital.[22]

Sister M. Augustine Quinn and Sister M. Teresa O'Donnell were the last two of the original group to leave St. Clair's when the Los Angeles Sisters assumed the management of the hospital in 1910. Sister M. Alexis is reported to have gone to the Sisters of Mercy, San Diego, for awhile and then returned to her own community in Denver. Sister M. Vincent seems to have participated in the Salt Lake City foundation (1910) and even to have entered into the projected transfer of a Utah foundation to Pocatello, Idaho, in 1916. Her plans, however, were apparently intercepted by death on September 9, 1916. She was buried in the Sisters' plot in the Catholic cemetery in Salt Lake City.

The Los Angeles Sisters had been reluctant to step into a difficult situation, but they looked upon their Bishop's request as a valid test of obedience; therefore, cost what it might, they accepted it as such. Doubtless, Bishop Conaty felt it was wise to put the management of St. Clair Hospital in the hands of Sisters of Mercy, both for the subsequent image of the Church and for that of the Institute of the Sisters of Mercy; but it was with heavy hearts and considerable apprehension that Mother M. Joachim, accompanied by Sister M. Philomena Coe, Sister M. Pius Brosnan, Sister M. Berchmans Labelle, and Sister M. Agnes Hallisey, boarded the train for Bakersfield.

On their arrival they were graciously welcomed by Reverend F. Freund, pastor of St. Francis parish, Mr. W.A. Howell, and a number of the parishioners. Whatever homesickness or loneliness they may have felt was quickly dispelled when they entered the chapel of their new home and found themselves in the Presence of their Changeless Friend. On February 9, 1910, the Los Angeles community took over St. Clair Hospital. There was no misapprehension about the difficulty of the situation, and the initial transfer was particularly trying, especially when two of the former members of the hospital staff began a rival hospital, the San Joaquin, in the same town.

Almost at once it was found necessary that two more Sisters be added to the group, Sister M. Gertrude McQuillan and Sister Margaret Mary Holihan.[23] During these trying times good friends who gave every encouragement to the new administra-

194

tion were not lacking. Mother M. Joachim's personal support was an additional source of strength to the Sisters who were initiating the project. She remained with them about six weeks, by which time the last of the former staff had withdrawn.

St. Francis School, Bakersfield—1910[24]

Meanwhile Father F. Freund had been pressing the question of undertaking a much needed elementary school in his parish, and preparations were made during the summer of 1910 to meet his request. The school could not be ready for some time, and so the Sisters adapted themselves to four makeshift classrooms set up in the basement of the church. St. Francis School opened on September 12, 1910. Sister M. Benedict Rooney was appointed as principal, and her assistants were Sister M. Raphael Fraga and Sister M. Ursula Hart. The Sisters resided at the hospital pending the construction of a school and convent. Even though the principal shared the teaching burden, it soon became evident that they were shorthanded and in 1911 Sister M. Joseph Keane was added to the school force.

Gradually support came in for the school, and a simple but comfortable building arose next to the church, with every necessary facility to carry on the good work. Not long after, a very suitable convent was provided near the church and school.

Neither schools nor hospitals can flourish, however, without needed hands, and southern California was not yet a seed-bed of vocations. In 1912 a second visit to Ireland in quest of subjects was planned for early June. For the two lucky travelers it meant a visit home, likely the only one in a lifetime, but the stay was relatively short. Much of the time was absorbed in gaining generous, promising candidates. On both trips, in 1908 and 1912, the Sisters were cordially received at the convents visited, and everywhere a true spirit of Irish hospitality and courtesy was shown them. The bishops and priests were kind and understanding, in spite of the fact that many were opposed to the young women of the flock leaving Ireland. Nevertheless, the mission met with quite good success, and they returned with a band of prospective postulants, ten of whom persevered.[25]

By 1912 the Sisters were convinced that St. Clair Hospital was totally inadequate for the wants of a growing community, and they presented to the Bishop their aspirations to build an up-to-date Mercy Hospital in the near future. He heartily endorsed this laudable ambition and suggested the purchase of a proper site. It was about this time (1912) that Reverend John Holden became pastor of St. Francis parish, To him Mr. William de Gana, one of the parishioners, expressed a desire to donate a substantial sum of money to a truly worthwhile cause. Father Holden recommended that he give it to the Sisters who were straining themselves to give Bakersfield a representative Catholic hospital and were just then entertaining plans to start the building of an up-to-date structure. This is the way prayers are answered, for on November 1, 1912, Mr. de Gana gave Mother M. Joachim a check for $45,000 with but one stipulation, that the gift would not be publicized during his lifetime.[26] In compliance with the Bishop's wishes they had already sought a suitable location and had reached an agreement to secure part of Tevis estate, situated on Truxtun Avenue and valued at $9,000. It was deemed advisable to move the St. Clair Hospital, the cottage which served as a convent, and other buildings to the new site. The cost of this moving and of putting the buildings in good condition came to $7,000. The site of the St. Clair Hospital was sold for $20,000, a tidy sum for projected developments. Father Holden, who contributed five-hundred dollars from his limited resources, was also generous with his time and advice, as well as with his ability to encourage interested benefactors.

In November, 1912, the Bishop, accompanied by Rt. Rev. Monsignor J.M. McCarthy, Reverend H. Weber, C.S.S.R., and Reverend John Laubacher, came to the Bakersfield Hospital where they met the builder, Mr. F.J. Amweg of San Francisco. The plans were approved and the contract signed. The expenditure was to be $41,000. That evening a banquet was served at the Southern Hotel, an invitation having been extended to the physicians and surgeons of Bakersfield to meet Bishop Conaty and hear his words of encouragement regarding the new hospital. About thirty physicians attended the banquet, one of the most successful gatherings of doctors as yet held in Bakersfield. There was a general good feeling especially when it was learned that the work on the new building was to begin at once.

The cornerstone was laid on February 9, 1913, by Bishop Conaty. The large number who attended the ceremony gave evidence of the enthusiastic support of the Bakersfield people.

By November 9, 1913, the new three-story concrete structure with accommodations for fifty patients was ready.[27]

Before the year was out the Sisters were already making plans to make this new hospital function in the best possible manner by establishing a three-year training school for nurses. In implementing this plan, they were fortunate to secure the services of Miss Julia Donnelly of Mercy Hospital, Chicago, as Superintendent of the Training School.[28]

Cognizant that a well-trained nursing staff is absolutely essential to the operation of a good hospital year after year, Sisters also entered the training program, so that by 1921, Mercy Hospital had acquired eleven trained nursing Sisters.[29]

The former hospital, St. Clair, now called the "Annex," served as the nurses' home until about 1922 when the new nurses' home was completed. The Annex was then converted into the convent and the convent cottage sold.

St. Thomas Tubercular Sanatorium, Mentone—1911-1917[30]

Meanwhile Rev. Monsignor T.J. Fitzgerald and Dr. Gayle Moseley called on the Los Angeles Sisters to interest them in a tubercular sanatorium at Mentone, a town three miles east of Redlands. Here a large hotel located on a seven-acre tract had to be remodeled for the purpose, and a cottage sufficiently large to serve as a convent was provided. The property and buildings, including several modern tents, valued at $25,000, was offered to the community for $8,000, just a little more than the cost of the improvements. After due consideration, the offer was accepted on October 3, 1911. Five Sisters, led by Sister M. Philomena Coe, were sent to prepare the place. About six weeks later, St. Thomas Aquinas Sanatorium was opened, and almost immediately filled to capacity. For several years the Sisters of the Los Angeles community gave themselves to this nursing apostolate in Mentone. In this wholesome environment they offered hope and encouragement to those who could profit by their care and they also gave consolation to others whom they prepared for death, victims of this dread disease in those days when medical science had not yet discovered adequate measures for tuberculosis control or effective drugs to stay the disease. The majority of patients could not meet even the moderate rates charged, and those who had some means found that the long period of enforced rest ate up their funds. And yet, as the community had no funds upon which to draw to support them, they found they had no choice but to close St. Thomas Aquinas Sanatorium on June 1, 1917. The buildings and the land were finally sold.

The Bakersfield hospital, called Mercy Hospital since the move to the new site in 1913, grew in reputation and facilities with the growth of Bakersfield.

On September 18, 1915, Bishop Conaty died at Coronado, and was succeeded in 1917 by the Most Rev. John J. Cantwell.

The new Bishop thought seriously of the needs of the diocese and weighed them against some of the works of Mercy currently provided. It was a question of relevance and priority of demands. By this time the diocese had six orphanages, three for boys and three for girls, but there was a great need for boarding schools for small boys. Consequently, the Bishop recommended that the Home of the Guardian Angels be closed; the orphan boys were to be sent to Watsonville and the girls placed with the Sisters of Charity or the Italian Sisters, who also had an orphanage in Los Angeles.

St. John's Military Academy—1919[3][1]

After due preparation, St. John's Military Academy, as it was henceforth to be called, opened at 4060 West Washington, in September, 1919. Boys from age six to fourteen years were accepted as resident students, but day scholars were not excluded. St. John's was to be a select school, designed to provide a well-balanced academic program in an environment that would afford the comforts of home, the companionship of boys, the motherly care of religious women, a military discipline that would contribute to manliness, self-control, courage, resourcefulness, and character development, molded according to Christian ideals. Here was nothing of the goose-step or militaristic jingoism so decried by modern society; but the military training was authentic, by officers who had served in the regular army. While they handled the athletics and put the boys through drills according to *Butt's Manual* they were themselves men of high ideals who conditioned the boys to become both manly and thoroughly representative Christians.

The reputation of St. John's Military Academy was early established and continued through the years. Due to its educational advantages, well-rounded program, and attractive environment for growing boys, it drew not only from the Los Angeles area but from the whole Southwest, as well as from Latin America. That the academy was both necessary and successful during the period of its existence is well attested.

Watsonville Orphanage Interim Assignment—1919-1921[32]

In 1919 Bishop Cantwell asked Mother M. Joachim again to come to his aid when the Franciscans, who had been conducting the boys' orphanage in Watsonville for forty-five years, resigned their charge. It was a call for an interim service; some of the Sisters would carry on until he could secure priests to take over the work. Rev. Vincent Shepherd was in charge. Five Sisters, three from Los Angeles and two from San Diego, were assigned to the mission. They took care of the housekeeping and general supervision of the domestic departments and in addition did catechetical work. By 1921 the good Bishop had succeeded in securing Salesian Fathers to accept the charge. The Sisters had enjoyed their work with the boys and at the same time had the satisfaction of knowing they had enabled Bishop Cantwell in a time of need to sustain the good work.

St. Aloysius Elementary School—1921[33]

This same year, 1921, Reverend Francis Becker of Florence, on the outskirts of Los Angeles, had announced to his people the opening of a new school in September. He had engaged a community of Sisters from the East and all arrangements had been made. Then, at the eleventh hour, the Mother Superior notified him that she would have to cancel the project. Father Becker hopefully turned to Mother Joachim who reluctantly had to disappoint him as all plans for the coming year had been completed and the assignments made. Undismayed, Father Becker took his problem to the Bishop, who was supposed to work miracles. This he seemed to do and Mother Joachim helped him; for, after a bit of juggling of schedules and post changes, she had Sisters ready to open St. Aloysius School on September 13, 1921. Sister M. Aloysius McNamara was chosen as the first principal. As there was as yet no convent, the Sisters who were assigned traveled about twelve miles every day from St. John's Military Academy. It would have been a real tragedy to disappoint the pastor and the parish, for about 160 children were already enrolled for the first to the eighth grade. The people of St. Aloysius parish, from the very beginning, were very cooperative and appreciative of the work of the Sisters. Nor were the efforts of the Sisters confined to the school. In addition to their classwork they brought the word of God to public school children within the parish and in the outlying neighborhoods.

By mid-September, 1918, the union of the Sisters of Mercy of southern California was effected, with Mother M. Joachim[34] the new Mother Superior and the convent at 4060 West Washington as the Motherhouse.

Mother M. Joachim McBrinn surely played the part of second foundress of the Los Angeles community. She served her Sisters through the history of the foundation, succeeding Mother Bonaventure Fox in 1899; and she was repeatedly chosen Mother Superior for as long as was in keeping with canon law. To her also fell the delicate role of acting in the best interests of her Sisters and in accord with the wishes of Bishop Cantwell during the difficult period of the amalgamation.

Chapter 9

THE SAN DIEGO FOUNDATION—1890[1]
Mother M. Michael Cummings

While Mother M. Bonaventure Fox was laying the foundation of the Institute of the Sisters of Mercy in Los Angeles, Mother M. Michael Cummings was at work in San Diego building another Mercy community. The latter had taken Mother M. Baptist Russell's advice and had sought direction from Bishop Mora before leaving Los Angeles. In his signed endorsement of the foundation in San Diego, he wrote:

San Diego
June 5, 1899

We confirm the appointment of Sister M. Michael as Mother Superior of the Community of Sisters of Mercy in this city and give permission to said community to build a hospital with their own means in or near said city.[2]

We might be inclined to smile when we read "build a hospital with their own means." They had no means; and the words seem almost ironic. And yet their simple Bishop had no such intent; his note was to serve as an official authorization for whatever they might do.

One of the first questions that might be raised concerning the establishment of the Sisters of Mercy in San Diego is, "Why a hospital?" or, as it was at first called, St. Joseph's Dispensary. Most of Mother M. Michael's religious life had been devoted to the nursing apostolate.[3] She had scarcely pronounced her vows and promised to serve God in the poor, the sick and the ignorant, than she was assigned by Mother de Pazzi Bentley to tend the sick in St. John's Hospital, St. Louis, where she labored for nine years. Subsequently, at the call of Bishop Joseph Machebeuef of Denver, Colorado, she offered to go to Durango to assist Mother M. Baptist Meyers. After five years there, Sister M. Michael was sent to another hospital at Ouray, Colorado.

And yet, despite years of Mother M. Michael's hospital experience, probably no foundation was initiated under less auspicious circumstances than that of San Diego. She and her companion, Sister M. Alphonsus Fitzpatrick, arrived in San Diego almost penniless and friendless. The city was facing a serious recession following the collapse of the land boom of 1888. The population had dropped from 40,000 to 16,159. Business was at a standstill, evidenced by the numerous shops and firms that had cancelled their leases. Hotels were empty. To secure loans, even in favorable times, friends are necessary, and the San Diego community was hostile to the Sisters. Despite all this, Mother M. Michael felt she was acting under the inspiration of the Spirit in following the wishes of the good Bishop. Surely God would provide. This indomitable trust was probably the special charisma of Mother M. Michael.

Bishop Mora and Father Antonio Ubach, pastor of San Diego, scoured the environs to select a proper site. They had little difficulty in making their choice—a site on the mesa in the northern part of the city, sufficiently removed from the business center, with easy access.

No one would question their judgment on the selection of a site, but what of the funds necessary to secure it? Mother Michael was more realistic, and for the time agreed to rent the two rooms on the second floor of the Grand Central Block;

201

corner of Sixth and H Streets, in the business section of the city. Here the Sisters opened St. Joseph's Dispensary on July 9, 1890.

The seemingly insurmountable difficulties and the opposition to the Sisters would have broken a less staunch spirit. In fact they did prove too great for Mother M. Michael's companion, Sister M. Alphonsus Fitzpatrick, who withdrew and with the Bishop's approval joined the Sisters of Mercy in Los Angeles, July 23, 1891. Burdens carried alone are doubly heavy, and despite her invincible trust, these were trying days for Mother M. Michael. True, she soon had two prospective Sisters to aid her in her work, but while they certainly helped her, they were also a part of her heavy burden because to her fell the responsibility of their formation. Meanwhile Mother de Pazzi Bentley, who had been her superior when she had left the Midwest, wrote to her urging her to come "home."

St. Charles Convent of Mercy
Clayton, Missouri
Feast of the Transfiguration, 1890

My very dear Child,

Your welcomed letter of the 29th ult. received 4th inst. Why did you not write to me at once or come to me when Bishop Matz left you free and advised you to go to California on the ground that you were needed there and could do more good? I had hoped that as soon as you should be free you would write to me that you were coming back to your first convent home. Did you not know that I wrote to Bishop Matz to beg him to leave you to return to us, but he would not. How could he suggest California when he knew we wanted you back? We are about to open a hospital on Lucas Place at 23rd Street. . .and you could help us a great deal. . .Be assured of prayers and unchanged affection for you. I constantly think of you before the Tabernacle.

As ever with love from the Sisters,
Your loving Mother in J.C.,

SISTER M. de PAZZI [4]

The ties that bound her to Mother de Pazzi and to the convent of her early religious life now accentuated the sufferings of this dedicated woman. The sincerity of Mother de Pazzi's letter, with its bid for peace and security, were weighed against the obligations of the moment. She had given her word to Bishop Mora; she had assumed the responsibility of a loan to lease the property on Sixth and H Streets; and she could not disappoint the two postulants who had offered themselves for the work.

With unbounded confidence in God, she shouldered her burdens: forming the two aspirants, managing the dispensary and reaching out to secure support for the permanent hospital of her dreams. She was tried as gold by fire and yet despite the crosses that were hers she was ever mindful of the sustaining Hand of God. One of her greatest consolations was a postulant, Miss Anna Smith, later Sister M. Josephine, who came to her November 1, 1890. She was the first Sister of Mercy professed in San Diego. Father Ubach received her vows on the feast of Our Lady of Mount Carmel, 1893. This priest always looked upon himself as the link between the Spanish padres and the new order. In 1866 he was appointed pastor of Old Town, the original San Diego.

The aggressive Yankee found Old San Diego an unsuitable seaport town, and a new San Diego, located on San Diego Bay, superseded it. The coming of the railroad in 1884 and the land boom of 1888 did stimulate the city's growth but the development of San Diego dates largely from the increased federal interest in the city as a port and naval base.

At first Father Ubach was enthusiastic about the Sisters' work and even so expressed himself; but he seems to have become rather alienated when Mother Michael took steps to have the hospital incorporated in 1893, even though the move had been approved by Bishop Mora. Perhaps this is another case of the peculiar interpretation of the position of religious institutes as held by this frontier pastor whose jurisdiction was so extensive that he seemed to exercise the authority of a bishop; or, at least he considered himself the arbiter of the affairs of the religious, for he sought to thwart the move toward incorporation. The Sisters knew that they were not only acting according to good business procedure, but that they were also so counseled by their Bishop. Therefore, they were not dissuaded. On March 16, 1893, St. Joseph's Hospital and

Sanatorium was incorporated under the laws of California.[5] Father Ubach found this hard to take, and although the Sisters sought to improve relations, he could not understand that anything short of his way could be right. He ended his days at the hospital and with kindly feelings toward the Sisters, but it saddened them that a misunderstanding could have clouded his declining years.

Sister M. Josephine Smith proved to be a strong support for Mother M. Michael during twenty years of poverty, prejudice and frequent crises. To her ability, zeal and energy, the San Diego Institute of the Sisters of Mercy owes much of its subsequent prosperity. She was a thoroughly good religious, a genial companion, a clear-headed businesswoman and one truly devoted to the nursing apostolate. With such support, Mother M. Michael courageously forged ahead.

A year had not passed since she had opened St. Joseph's Dispensary in 1890, before she secured a site for a new hospital, the very property recommended by both Bishop Mora and Father Ubach—ten acres of the mesa on the northern edge of the city. Here on an eminence near where the road begins to descend into the historic Mission Valley she erected the center building or first unit of St. Joseph's Hospital and Sanatorium, which was finished and blessed before the end of 1891. It was an imposing three-story structure with 252 pleasing architectural proportions. The entrance faced University Avenue and could be reached by the electric car line from any part of the city.

This same year (1891) Mother Michael began another work of Mercy dear to the hearts of her Sisters—the care of the aged. At first a few rooms in the hospital were set aside for them, but as their numbers increased it was necessary in 1892 to erect a separate building for the aged on the hospital grounds. To meet growing demadns, the building had to be enlarged twice, to become a sixty-five-room home able to serve one-hundred guests.[6]

In 1898, a west wing was added to the main hospital building, and this nearly doubled the capacity of St. Joseph's. San Diego was beginning to be appreciated by those who sought a change of climate. Here asthmatics, rheumatics, and consumptives were numerous, but there was scacely an illness for which man did not seek relief, under doctor's orders or on his own initiative. The mild temperature and abundant sunshine seemed to help many. Needless to say, St. Joseph's Hospital and Sanatorium also profited by the demand for place. It was constructed so as to receive the sunlight in all the rooms most of the day. The rooms were kept spotlessly clean, and everything possible was done to contribute to the comfort of the patient. Careful nursing, nourishing food, and good medical service in such a promising environment soon made St. Joseph's a much-sought health center.

No sooner had the west wing been added than it became evident that a new chapel had to be erected. The tiny chapel that had served the Sisters was now inadequate for the increased number of Sisters and their patients. Mother M. Michael put her heart and soul into building a chapel worthy of the Spouse she had long before come to depend upon. When asked if she had funds to build, she readily responded in the negative; nevertheless, she just as promptly retorted: "The Lord will provide." He did. By this time she had made friends among non-Catholics as well as Catholics. Contributions came in, and Mother Michael went ahead with her plans for the chapel. It was truly beautiful, with a capacity for about three-hundred. In order to facilitate access to the chapel, it was connected by an arcade with the west wing.

On November 14, 1898, the hospital chapel was dedicated by Bishop George Montgomery. The day was advisedly chosen to coincide with the celebration of the Silver Jubilee of Mother M. Michael, and to add even further joy to the occasion, Mother M. de Pazzi Bentley and Mother M. Liguori Galbraith came from St. Louis, Missouri.[7]

While Mother Michael was truly grateful for her blessings, she did not pause long to look back, because there was yet much to do. She was especially solicitous for her own religious family, which was growing with the demands made upon the community. The turn of the century saw an upsurge in population, an awakening of the national economy, and a remarkable trend toward urbanization. Before enlarging the hospital any further, she determined to construct a real convent. The foundation was begun March 17, 1900. It was near the hospital but in a more retired area of the grounds. Although she consulted competent builders, the plans were basically her own for this was to be the Motherhouse of the San Diego Sisters. It was a large, roomy two-story structure with a basement and an attic sufficiently high so as to be readily converted into a third story. It faced a beautiful lawn on the east, and to the west, north, and south were well kept gardens. On the west, too, was a deep terraced canyon with row upon row of fruit trees and vines. Arbors and benches, conveniently placed, invited rest and quiet contemplation. For the Sister involved in the active apostolate, moments of prayerful quiet are a must, although the uninitiated are generally more impressed by their activity. One patient who observed the endless round of duties said of the Sisters:

> Animated by true charity they labor indefatigably for the sick, the aged and the poor, and their admirable devotedness has brought renewed health and usefulness to many. . . .The same care is given by the Sisters to all their charges. They minister to them, prepare their meals and look after their wants. You may see them in the kitchen or laundry, in the dispensary or operating room, the kindest and most intelligent attendants, ever busy but with a smile and a pleasant word always on their lips. You would never suspect that long watches, labors without end, ever fatigued them. . . .Their day's work begins long before daylight; they kneel in prayer and meditation long before their patients waken to receive their care. Every hour of the day finds them at their post, vigilant and attentive, and only after every inmate of their hospital has been provided for to make the sufferer's night as painless as possible, do they seek rest. . . .[8]

It was a priest patient who penned these lines and he followed up the description of a busy day by this query and response:

> What is the secret of this immense, this ineffable charity?. . .The Sisters are religious, schooled in the interior life, ever recollected and devoted to prayer and meditation. This is the well-spring, at once of their indefatigable charity and their wonderful a-chievements.

The convent of St. Joseph's Hospital-Sanatorium provided also for the novitiate and training school for the community.

Here the novice was initiated into religious life and here she was prepared to assume the vows of religion. Here her love of God was nourished and strengthened, as it would be the lodestone during her entire religious life of dedicated service to her fellowmen for the sake of Him, Who said, "Whatsoever you do to the least of your brothers, that you do unto Me."

The School of Nursing was established in 1903. Nursing education was still in its infancy, but Mother Michael was quick to see its prime importance as a major move toward providing competent professional service for the hospital. She obtained the services of Miss Kate Sullivan, graduate of Mercy Hospital, Pittsburgh, to superintend the nursing school. At the first graduation, May 31, 1906, distinguished by the presence of both Bishop Thomas Conaty and Mayor Sehon of San Diego, ten Sisters of Mercy received their diplomas in nursing education.

Scarcely had the nursing school gotten underway when Mother M. Michael sponsored the construction of the large east wing of St. Joseph's Hospital, which made provisions for classrooms, surgery and x-ray. To some, such expansion seemed folly, but within three years this now 220-bed hospital was fully occupied.

When the completed hospital was dedicated in 1904, Bishop Conaty noted that St. Joseph's had come into some prominence, for city officials and businessmen were now ready to lend their presence to the occasion, proud to be a part of a progressive trend in their city. Again the Bishop noted how much had been accomplished with so little, and in only fourteen years. On the same day a profession ceremony of six novices took place, very encouraging evidence of the growing religious community in San Diego.

Just when prospects appeared to be encouraging, the San Diego Sisters suffered a veritable calamity. Mother M. Josephine, who had been Mother M. Michael's mainstay for almost twenty years, was stricken with a fatal illness on November 24, 1909. After a little more than a year of pitiful suffering she died peacefully on March 24, 1911. Her death was keenly felt by the entire community. Reverend J. J. Conlan delivered her eulogy and a few lines from his fitting tribute should be recalled to preserve the memory of this great-souled religious.

> The loss of Mother Josephine will be felt by her Sisters beyond the usual tribute of feeling. . . .She

was the courage and strength of the whole family, and a light for their feet when all was dark. This perhaps would not mean much in the ordinary religious community but in the case of San Diego, only a soul of heroic qualities could have maintained its poise and serenity as did Mother Josephine through the weary struggle of twenty-one years with poverty and the opposition of prejudice. . . .During the frequent dark and apparently hopeless crisis of the early days at St. Joseph's her bright spirit rose to deal with each problem. A truer or stauncher soul never lived. . . .The two-fold story of her life is easily understood when we remember that her religious and social qualities were hidden in the cloister where she was the most genial of companions, the most thoughtful of friends, and the most affectionate Sister of every member of the community while, on the other hand, the world of businessmen knew her only as the clear-headed, resolute woman of affairs, the masterful agent of the community's interests. [9]

St. Thomas Hospital, El Centro—1910-1917

That Mother M. Michael and her Sisters had won the recognition and esteem of even a wider circle than San Diego can be seen in the requests received from neighboring towns to establish branch hospitals. In response to such a request, a hospital was opened in El Centro in 1910. This was the first venture of the Sisters of Mercy into Imperial Valley. By 1905 the valley had a population of 14,000, and 120,000 acres were then under cultivation, thanks to the George Chaffey scheme to bring water from the Colorado and to the transforming power of irrigation.[10] It was the people of the valley who urged Reverend H. Eummelin to present their pleas to Mother Michael and her Sisters. There was a small hospital in El Centro, operated by the local physicians, but they too were eager to have the Sisters take over. Bishop Conaty approved the proposal for a Catholic hospital and helped Mother M. Michael purchase the thirty-bed institution.[11]

When Mother Michael brought the new superior, Sister M. Gabriel Gardiner, and her assistants for the opening of the hospital, March 20, 1910, they were warmly received by the citizens of El Centro who presented them with a deed to ten acres of land just north of the town. The hospital now became known as St. Thomas Hospital in recognition of the Bishop's effort to bring a Catholic hospital to the valley. For seven years it accomplished much good; but in 1917, when the United States entered World War I, it became increasingly difficult to staff the hospital and provide adequate help during the hot season. Hospitals were not as yet air-conditioned. For this reason, and with considerable regret, the Sisters were obliged to close St. Thomas Hospital.

St. John's Hospital, Oxnard—1912[1][2]

Meanwhile Reverend John Laubaucher, pastor of Santa Clara's Church, Oxnard, sought to elicit the interest of Mother Michael to build a small hospital in the very promising but as yet small town of Oxnard, which had been incorporated in 1903. It lies midway between Los Angeles and Santa Barbara, about four miles from the ocean. Today, it is a prosperous trading center for an extensive agricultural district, has a large beet-sugar factory, as well as other growing industries, and serves as the business center for Port Hueneme. From the very beginning the citizens of the community showed great willingness to assist Mother M. Michael and to accept financial as well as personal responsibility for the hospital project. Almost immediately, Mr. John Borchard offered a ten-acre site as well as $20,000, the latter to endow two hospital beds for the poor in perpetuity.

The Oxnard hospital was called St. John's to honor Father John Laubacher, pioneer pastor of Oxnard. Again, Mother Michael chose Sister M. Gabriel Gardiner as Superior and, according to custom, she shared the difficult period of getting the little hospital underway. According to the Oxnard convent annals, the raising of money for the new hospital was a real community enterprise:

> The collecting committee consisted of Mr. Charles Donlon, Mr. A. Levy, and Mr. Dean Lehman with two Sisters of Mercy. That one touch of nature makes the whole world kin was evidence again when the bankers of Oxnard united in the common cause of soliciting funds for the hospital. . . .Mr. Donlon made his

209

appeals to the people of Irish lineage, while Mr. Levy and Mr. Lehman, proficient in German, addressed their petitions to the Germans.

The population at that time [1912] was about 3000 and only about 500 citizens were financially able to assist in the work. Undertaking to build a hospital in so small a community must necessarily be uphill effort, and that so much was accomplished in so short a time proves that the good people of Oxnard were not only impressed by the oratory of the solicitors, but that they responded nobly to the call for generosity. The sum of twenty-one thousand dollars was donated in the first drive.

The Sisters of St. Joseph of Carondelet were already established in Oxnard as teachers of the Santa Clara School. As in so many instances of Mercy history, the most cordial relations developed between the school Sisters of St. Joseph and the hospital Sisters of the prospective Mercy institution. Never can the Sisters of Mercy forget all that they did for them during their pioneer days. Especially kind was Mother Hortulana, whose knowledge of German and influence with their kind benefactor, John Borchard, served them so well. After a hard day in the classroom, she would take the Sisters of Mercy for a "buggy ride" to Mr. Borchard's ranch. What seemed a rather casual trip was really deliberately planned to seek his counsel or to induce him to help them solve some financial problem. It was she who gave assistance in securing from him a $50,000 loan at a four percent rate. Subsequently he even cancelled $20,000 of this debt and, in addition, made a grant of land valued at $10,000. The Sisters of Oxnard acknowledge him as their principal benefactor and pray that God has richly rewarded his great generosity.

The first little hospital was a very temporary frame building which was blessed by Bishop Conaty, May 19, 1912. It was a matter of service while waiting to acquire sufficient funds for a St. John's that would do credit to the community. And yet even this little hospital secured some renown. It was at this time that twilight sleep was a pioneering method of painless childbirth. One of its principal and early exponents was the late Dr. William Livingston, of Oxnard. He was a native of Port

Hueneme and had traveled to Baden, Germany, to study the method under its originator, Professor Gauss. Two years after St. John's itself was born, Dr. Livingston introduced twilight sleep there. The method, involving carefully supervised injections of certain drugs, aroused both interest and controversy back in 1914. Even some of Dr. Livingston's own colleagues opposed him. But the doctor's success put little St. John's on the map.[13]

On April 25, 1915, a handsome new structure on the same spacious property, Fourth and E Streets, was ready for dedication. Although only a forty-five-bed institution at the time, St. John's was not long in winning recognition from the American College of Surgeons in 1927 and the full approval of the American Medical Association, in 1929.

While Mother Michael and her Sisters were pioneering in hospital work in southern California and had to strain every fiber of their beings to meet the changing standards of the times, they never became so absorbed in institutionalism that they forgot the poor and unfortunate for whose benefit they had really offered their lives. In fact, they found that it was largely through their success in hospital work that they were better equipped to be of service to the unfortunate members of society whose needs called out for Mercy. The care of the aged and the poor has certainly been an inseparable interest of their early hospitals, when social welfare was left to the compassionate few and the United States Government had not yet assumed the reponsibility for such services. No adage is more true than "the poor you have always with you." Only occasionally does the convent annalist comment on baskets of food for the poor, clothing drives, and the services extended through the hospital clinics. And yet, all year round, the needs of the poor were met in answer to cries for help in every form.

From time to time some disaster, epidemic or crisis furnished the occasion for a special service by the Sisters of Mercy of San Diego and because of its inherent human interest reached the press. One such instance was the tragedy which occurred July 21, 1905, when the U.S.S. *Bennington* blew up in San Diego harbor. The official count listed sixty dead and forty-seven injured. The *San Diego Union* of that date announced:

The wounded men from the *Bennington* have been taken to St. Joseph's Sanatorium where every effort is being made to save their lives.

About the same time, an editorial in an out-of-town paper read in part:

> Not the last nor the least of the efforts put forth on the sad occasion were those shown by the Sisters of Mercy. St. Joseph's Sanatorium, San Diego did its full duty to the gallant jackies of the *Bennington.*

A year later when the awful earthquake and fire struck San Francisco, the Sisters of San Diego reached out to offer their care to three hundred victims of the terrible tragedy. It was in reference to this that Mr. Sehon, Mayor of San Diego, made the observation in an after-dinner speech that in time of calamity the Sisters are foremost in coming to the relief of the afflicted.

About 1916 it became evident to Mother Michael and the hospital staff that San Diego needed a large and more modern hospital. The *San Diego Union* gave this report of the opening drive:

> More than $20,000 in pledges were announced last night at the Mercy Hospital Banquet given in the Cristobal Cafe at the Exposition, with 475 of San Diego's most prominent citizens supporting the new edifice to be named for the devoted order of the Sisters of Mercy and to supplant the present St. Joseph's Hospital.

Although their assessment of need cannot be disputed, the timing was doubtless inopportune. The world was teetering on the brink of a global war and Europe was already embroiled. What happened in Europe also affected the American economy and political fortunes. People did not want to commit themselves, even though they did not yet know that the following year would find them caught in World War I and sending their boys to fight in the trenches of western Europe. When the hospital undertook the fund-raising campaign to construct a new hospital, the facts were not yet all in. After a whirlwind twelve-day drive, only enough money had been raised to build an annex to the east wing, so the plan was re-assessed. Certain needs were imperative, and to meet these it would be necessary to construct another building connected with the eastern wing. For this Mother Michael was authorized to take the $21,000 obtained from the recent citizens' campaign. The *San Diego Union* noted:

> By reason of the War and unfavorable building conditions, St. Joseph's Hospital has not been able to construct the proposed new hospital, but due to urgent demands has devoted resources to the building of an additional wing for surgery and x-ray. The surgery is one of the largest and most complete in Southern California and several operations may be carried on at the same time.

Another important factor concerning St. Joseph's Hospital was brought out at the time of this drive. Dr. Paul Wegeforth, who was not a Catholic, compiled statistics from the records which he thought served to explain the non-sectarian attitude of the Sisters of Mercy in dispensing charity during the years preceding. This, in itself, seemed to him a talking point in seeking support.

Mt. Carmel Ranch, Del Mar

For the Sisters who were long associated with the San Diego community, the "ranch" had a nostalgic interest. Here they spent happy days of rest and relaxation which strengthened community ties, refreshed drooping spirits and reinvigorated those whose long hours on hospital floors had quite depleted. This property came to the Sisters before the turn of the century from the McGonagle family, which had extensive holdings but were what is sometimes called "land-poor." They were unable to pay the $4,000 mortgage due on a tract of land in Carmel Valley. The family had planned to offer the property to a religious institution, and when pressured for the mortgage they offered it to Mother Michael in return for sufficient funds to clear the mortgage. With Bishop George Montgomery's approval, the Sisters acquired the ranch under these terms. Here a vacation house was constructed which was soon named Carmel, and for many years it provided a haven of much needed peace and refreshment.

During World War I Mother M. Michael used the ranch to

213

take care of twenty-two neglected children. Somehow the community managed to shoulder this additional burden. Through their own efforts and with charitable contributions that did come in, it was possible to adequately meet their needs, and great was the satisfaction of serving Christ in the orphan, half-orphan, or abandoned children who are so dear to the Heart of Christ.

St. Joseph's Hospital had begun with a staff of two Sisters in 1890; by 1904, when the east wing was added, it had grown to twenty-eight. By the time the first nursing class graduated, in 1906, there were thirty-three Sisters. By 1910, after twenty years of service in San Diego, Mother Michael's community numbered forty. Yet despite this steady growth, Mother Michael was concerned about the future of her community, since vocations in southern California were scarce. As a kind Mother who realized that she was approaching her allotted span, she began to reflect on how best to provide for her wonderful family and safeguard the interests of her Institute. Doubtless she prayed as well as pondered.

The amalgamation of the San Diego community with the Sisters of Mercy in Los Angeles in 1918 seemed to be the answer to Mother Michael's prayer. Her own appointment at that time as Mistress of Novices is especially deserving of comment, for despite her rare administrative ability, her religious family pay first tribute to her for her consummate skill in the formation of young religious. Doubtless much of her success was due to the impact of her own example of fidelity to rule, reverence for authority, candor, simplicity, and generosity. She knew how to convey to each what psychologists so strongly emphasize today: the conviction that the Sister is needed, is wanted, and is loved. Those who knew her best loved her most. By the time she died, in 1922, she knew she had achieved her goal of stability for her community.

The post-Vatican II period tends to decry long terms for superiors and usually interprets such as an abuse. It is a rare rule, however, that admits no exceptions. The long administration of Mother Michael could not be called an abuse of power. San Diego documents show clearly that it was the San Diego community that sought Mother Michael's re-election. Four times they asked the Holy See to grant a dispensation to make Mother Michael eligible for re-election and each of these documents are in the Burlingame archives. Only one has been selected to give evidence of the guarantee to all Sisters of their freedom of choice. All the letters are in the same vein.

Most Holy Father,

The Sisters of Mercy, living in San Diego, in the diocese of Monterey-Los Angeles, prostrate at the feet of your Holiness request the faculty by which Sister M. Michael Cummings may again be elected superioress in the coming chapter. This Sister has for many years, to the delight of all the Sisters, governed the community, and those who present the petition cherish the hope that, on account of the particular gifts with which she is endowed, she will be of much benefit to the community.

By virtue of special faculties granted by Our Holy Father, the Sacred congregation of Religious, due attention being given to the things which have been explained, kindly grants to the Ordinary of the Diocese of Monterey-Los Angeles, in accordance with his best judgment and according to the dictates of his conscience, the power of confirming the aforesaid Superioress in her office for another term according as defined by the Constitutions; provided, however, that she be elected by secret ballot and have a majority of the votes, and provided, moreover, that she first render an account of her former administration.

> Given at Rome on the 23rd day of December, 1916
>
> D. Cardinal Falconio, Ep. Valit Praef.
SEAL   Veni La Puma Subsec. [14]

After the union of the Sisters of Mercy of the Diocese of Monterey-Los Angeles-Tucson with the Sisters of Mercy of San Francisco in 1922, Mother M. Bernard O'Brien was appointed Mother General of the United Sisters of Mercy of California, Arizona, pending the meeting of the first general chapter, scheduled to be held at St. Mary's Hospital, San Francisco, July

10, 1923. In the summer of 1922, a letter from Archbishop Edward J. Hanna asked that all local superiors, while awaiting the approval of the new constitution and the decision of the Sacred Congregation of Religious concerning the new mode of procedure in the work of the Sisters of Mercy, continue in office. Therefore, on July 2, 1922, Mother M. Michael was appointed local superior in San Diego.

Meanwhile, an important event in San Diego took place on November 14, 1921—the Golden Jubilee of Mother M. Michael. Anyone who is familiar with religious knows the extensive preparations involved in making a golden jubilee an auspicious occasion. In the case of Mother Michael, we also have the foundress of the San Diego community, and her life in San Diego is closely interwoven with the history of the Institute. Mother Joachim McBrinn, who thoroughly appreciated the regard in which Mother Michael was held by her Sisters, sent Los Angeles Sisters to replace the San Diego Sisters so that all of them would be able to attend the festivities on this occasion.

Rt. Rev. Msgr. Harnett, V.G., was celebrant of the Solemn High Mass in the hospital chapel, and Bishop John J. Cantwell assisted from the throne in *cappa magna*. It was he who preached the jubilee sermon, a glowing tribute to the jubilarian. He was at no loss for words, which rang with conviction, but space will permit only an excerpt from his address.

> Until Mother Michael arrived in San Diego, this city was without a hospital; through her untiring and whole-hearted efforts, St. Joseph's Hospital was built. The jubilee of a nun is not altogether a personal affair; it brings before us in a concrete way the ideas of self-sacrifice, of self-denial, of humility, justice, and patience....The recording angel alone can tell the blessed work that has been done in this house. He alone can tell how many souls have been rescued from the pit of darkness, how many times a heart has turned to God when before his dying eyes the figure of Jesus Crucified was lifted up....We hope that God will permit Mother M. Michael to abide a long time with her community, to be a guide and an example for the younger members. . . .

But God's ways are not our ways, nor even in line with the

216

hopes of the good Bishop, for in less than a year Mother M. Michael was dead. Her death came rather unexpectedly from angina pectoris, on October 6, 1922, and was a distinct shock to her friends. With her community she had been planning the erection of a modern fireproof hospital and no one seemed quite so well equipped to undertake the project. To say that her Sisters were crushed would be an understatement, and yet she had prepared them to face even this.

The Most Reverend John J. Cantwell celebrated a Pontifical Requiem on Monday morning at 9:30, on October 9, 1922; he also gave the funeral sermon. There was no longer any evidence of civic hostility toward the San Diego Sisters of Mercy. Men and women of every class and creed gathered to mourn her loss and to give public testimony to the honor in which Mother Michael had come to be held.

Before closing this chapter of the history of the Sisters of Mercy, it is fitting that we make an effort to put into focus the true picture of Mother M. Michael. Just who was she? What are the factors in her life that contributed to her undaunted character?[15] She was born July 8, 1853, on a farm in the Midwest, near Madisonville, Illinois, and at baptism received the name Rose Anna. She was the youngest of seven children. Her parents, County Galway people, undoubtedly had come to this country to take advantage of the availability of lands that came with westward expansion.

Like most children in the rural areas of the Midwest at this period, Rose Anna spent her early years in the local one-room school, where one teacher often taught eight grades. While the situation was not ideal, both teachers and pupils often obtained unbelievably good results.

Steps had already been taken to improve American education by the addition of more and better schools, adequately trained instructors, longer school hours, and greater uniformity of instruction. Better schools meant better textbooks. Noah Webster's monumental work had already gone far to unify and standardize the American language. Great, too, was the influence of William H. McGuffey (1800-1873), whose series of grade school readers, first published in 1830, became immensely popular for more than a half century. They contained gems of literature that not only elevated cultural standards but drove home lasting lessons of morality, idealism and national patriotism. Probably no other American did so much to shape the

217

character of the American people in the nineteenth century.

Public elementary education spread from state to state after 1830, but it was not until the last quarter of the century or later that it became compulsory. Public secondary education did not become compulsory until after World War I. Even then it was not universal as it was up to each state to determine how much education was to be compulsory.

It should not surprise us to learn that Rose Anna's education was somewhat limited. Her parents are to be commended on taking advantage of educational opportunities that were not compulsory especially when, on the farm, every hand makes the work lighter. Indeed, much of her education came with life on the farm. Father Henry Brinkmeyer gives some snatches to support this contention.

> During the high water in spring, she would cross the creek every day on stilts to gather the cows in order that her brothers might not get their feet wet, waste time changing their shoes, and thus be retarded in finishing their chores.

and again,

> Rose was a born nurse, for she was able to save so many of the little animals around the farm who were injured or sick. . . .She would dig a hole in the warm ground, put the sick chick into it and cover it up, until the little thing would crawl out and run to its mother.

She attended the local school until she was eleven, when her deeply religious parents decided that it was time that she be properly prepared for the reception of the sacraments. For the next two years she attended the parochial school in Madisonville, and walked five miles each way daily until she received her first Holy Communion, on May 5, 1866.

The scanning of this simple life is likely to create some pity and some amusement for the sophisticated adolescent of today: such hard work, so much time wasted and such monotonous chores. And yet, within this very pattern was forged a love of the out-of-doors, a strong sense of responsibility, a compassion

218

for the less fortunate, a love for good books, and an appreciation of the Faith of her fathers; nor does this exhaust the formation of character traits that distinguished her as a model religious, an understanding formation director or superior, and an able administrator.

A strongly knit family, such as she enjoyed, was a vital part of her education. She listened to no TV, and probably saw no daily paper, but she was nonetheless a part of the world about her—and a stirring world it was during her formative years.

Only a year after she was born, the "Little Giant," Stephen A. Douglas, had begun to loom large, both in her state and in national history, as the Senator from Illinois who introduced the Kansas-Nebraska Bill. She was only seven when Lincoln's election precipitated the secession of the first seven Southern states and started a chain of events that led to one of the bloodiest wars in our history—the Civil War.

She did not need to hear an explanation of the influence of the frontier, the prairies, the story of the receding Indians, and the building of the transcontinental railroad. Her life was a part of this period of history—the time when America developed her strongest national traits.

In her tender years, she became aware of a call to religious life. Margaret, an older sister, had entered the Sisters of Mercy in St. Louis, but had died nine months after profession. At the age of seventeen, Rose Anna was permitted to enter the convent of the Sisters of Mercy in St. Louis. Here she was formed to the religious life by Mother de Pazzi Bentley, who had been chosen by Mother Agnes O'Connor as Superior of the group that set out from St. Catherine's, New York, in 1856, to bring the Sisters of Mercy to St. Louis.

During her years of formation in St. Louis, Mother M. Michael Cummings must have often thanked God that she was schooled in the principles and practices of religious life by Mother M. de Pazzi. The latter had been formed as a religious by Mother Agnes O'Connor, foundress of the New York convent, the first foundation in the United States from Baggot Street.

On November 14, 1871, Rose Anna Cummings was clothed in the habit of the Sisters of Mercy, Archbishop Peter Richard Kenrick of St. Louis presiding. It must be noted that it was this occasion that was commemorated in her Golden Jubilee on November 14, 1921. On October 6, 1922, God called her to

Himself, but she still lives in the memory of those who were
fortunate to have been formed to religious life under her able
guidance.

Chapter 10

THE SOUTHWEST—NEW MEXICO AND ARIZONA

An Introduction

The Southwest was slow in gaining acceptance into the
family of the United States. In fact, in the coast to coast
expansion, New Mexico and Arizona were the very last states to
be admitted to the Union. In the scramble for admittance in the
last half of the nineteenth century, all the other states, save the
Indian Territory (Oklahoma), were readily welcomed into the
fold. The best supported reasons for the rejection of the
Southwest states of New Mexico and Arizona were cultural,
political, and economic. Howard R. Lamar puts it this way:

> Here was a real confrontation of different races and
> different cultures, all in varying stages of develop-
> ment which for its range and complexity was unique
> in the story of the westward movement.[1]

Following the Anglo-American invasion, the Southwest contained not only groups of peaceful farming Indians, tribes of
fierce nomads, often even wild Indians, but also a large
Spanish-Mexican population as well as the American frontiers-
men with all their Yankee characteristics. Perhaps this is a key
to some understanding of the absence of the typical frontier:
the presence of intrigue that colors the political evolution of the
Southwest, the cultural antipathies that express themselves in
strong ties and stronger hostilities, the struggle between church
and state, the school question, and the delaying tactics in the
admission to statehood.

That the Church was truly aware of her responsibility to
meet the needs of the times is evinced in the meeting of the
American bishops in May, 1849, at the seventh Provincial
Council of Baltimore, where they submitted names to Pope Pius
IX in quest of a permanent Bishop for California.[2] It was at this

same meeting of American bishops that the Pope was petitioned to establish the New Mexico Territory as a vicariate apostolic, separate from the see of Durango, Mexico. They nominated Father Jean Baptist Lamy, a young French missioner in Kentucky. The following year, Santa Fe was erected into a diocese, and Bishop Lamy was consecrated in Cincinnati on November 24, 1850.[3] As his companion in Santa Fe he had brought with him Father Joseph Machebeuf, a long-time friend.[4]

Bishop Lamy went to work immediately with tremendous zeal and energy to bring about the long delayed reforms, riding into remote areas to learn the needs of his people and spreading the Kingdom of God. He was a true frontiersman with remarkable endurance despite his apparent delicate health. In six months, he rode all of 3,000 miles to visit his scattered flock. His jurisdiction embraced New Mexico, Arizona and eastern Colorado. By a decree of July 29, 1853, Pius IX raised the vicariate of New Mexico to the rank of an episcopal see, attached to the city of Santa Fe.[5] To meet the challenge in this vast diocese, on August 15, 1868, he was finally given the able assistance of the Most Reverend Joseph P. Machebeuf D.D.,[6] who was appointed Vicar Apostolic of Colorado and Utah, and the Most Reverend Jean Baptist Salpointe who was, in the same year, appointed Vicar Apostolic of Arizona.[7]

No one realized more than the zealous Bishop how necessary schools were to the effective spread of the Word of God and the strength of faith among his people. Indian mission schools were revived; education was promoted by free schools and academies where none had existed before; and even the first hospital in New Mexico was established, in 1866. The first Sisters who came to his aid were the Sisters of Loretto.[8]

Chapter 11

NEW MEXICO—1880
Mother M. Josephine Brennan[1]

La Mesilla—1880-1895—Academy of the Sacred Heart and St. Joseph's School for Boys opened in February, 1881

The Sisters of Mercy came to New Mexico late in 1880,

invited by the Vicar Apostolic, Rt. Rev. Jean Baptiste Salpointe, who introduced them to Rev. Agustin Morin,[2] pastor of Mesilla.

Mother Josephine Brennan, the first Superior in New Mexico, had come from the Convent of Mercy, Moate, Ireland, in response to a plea of Sister M. Ignatius Gaynor for recruits for East St. Louis, Illinois. On this mission to the United States was a former pupil of Sister M. Josephine, Miss Bridget Kearney, who had been teaching at Moate. After the trio arrived in east St. Louis, they were confronted by a difficulty that arose when a niece of Rev. P.J. O'Halloran, pastor of the parish in East St. Louis, was not admitted to profession. Sister M. Ignatius refused to yield and the girl withdrew. When time failed to heal the wound, Mother Josephine was only too happy to respond to the plea of Bishop Salpointe for Sisters to teach in New Mexico, and arrangements were made for her to go to Mesilla.[3] Six Sisters volunteered for the New Mexican mission: Mother Josephine Brennan, the Sisters M. Augustine Bambrick, M. Margaret Hessian, M. Bernard Connor, M. Teresa Connor, and the novice, Sister M. Antonia Kearney.

Mother Josephine waited only long enough for the reception of Miss Kearney, who received the name Sister M. Antonia. The records are not complete but it is conjectured that she was received in Cynthiana, Kentucky,[4] where the Sisters spent almost two years before proceeding to Mesilla, New Mexico. Mother M. Josephine, Sister M. Teresa Connor, and Sister M. Antonia Kearney set out first, arriving on Christmas Eve, 1880. The other three Sisters, M. Bernard Connor, M. Augustine Bambrick, and M. Margaret Hessian had reached Mesilla by mid-February, 1881.

New Mexico was still a rough untamed territory. Only two years before, Major General Lew Wallace,[5] the newly appointed territorial governor, had come from Indiana to take over the civil government at Santa Fe. He was even then better known as a writer of historical novels, but it was as an experienced Civil War veteran that he was sent to put down a cattle war in Lincoln County and to handle the current territorial gunman, Billy the Kid. Both Lew Wallace and his wife found Santa Fe an ideal place for writing; for it was here that he completed *Ben Hur, a Tale of Christ*, and Susan Wallace, her sketches of Mexican and Indian life for the *Atlantic Monthly*.[6] The governor had another talent, less publicized than his writings.

The picturesque character of the locality caught his eye and he illustrated his wife's magazine articles.

The trip of Mother M. Josephine Brennan and her companions, from St. Louis to La Mesilla, was a frontier experience. The first stage of the journey was the easiest, a few days by train to Kansas City. From there to New Mexico they had to take what was called the "burro" train, so-called because one never knew when it would stop or go. The railroad was the first and at this time the only one into this part of the Southwest.[7]

The Mesilla passengers then boarded a stagecoach to Rincon, stopping for meals, to change horses or exchange passengers. At Rincon they changed coaches again for the final stretch along the bed of the uncompleted railroad. Here they met Mr. Charles Reynolds, dubbed "Jose," who had been sent to Rincon to accompany them on the last lap of the journey.

Quite late at night, when the coach arrived at Mesilla,[8] Mrs. Reynolds and Mrs. Griggs were there to welcome the Sisters and accompany them to their convent. Mr. Reynolds acted as porter and interpreter, for the women could not speak a word of English. The Sisters were soon to learn that the surnames did not distinguish the Yankees from the Spanish or the Mexicans and, as yet, they knew very little Spanish.

But what could not be expressed in words was conveyed clearly by gestures and deeds. It was Christmas Eve, and a blazing fire and hot refreshments bespoke a warm welcome to the tired, shivering travelers. As the Sisters knelt on the earthen floor of their new home to thank God for His loving providence, the church bell rang out the call to Midnight Mass. Father Agustin Morin gave the Sisters a warm reception and led them into the little church, where they felt truly at home. After Mass, a shy congregation gathered about them to get a glimpse of the *Hermanas* whom they felt had been dropped from heaven.

Mesilla means tableland in Spanish. La Mesilla, in the Rio Grande Valley, was not unlike an oasis in the Sahara Desert, but this one was in the American desert. The little town was surrounded by small ranches or farms. The agriculture of this fertile area was hardly typical of the Southwest. All kinds of fruits and vegetables were grown but, due to the isolation of their position, the farmers had little market for their crops. It was a river town about 250 miles east of Tucson, and had prospered at the crossroads of the overland route from San

Antonio to Tucson and the trail from Missouri to Chihuahua, Mexico.

The people of La Mssilla were for the most part of the old Spanish-Mexican type, as might well be expected in a town only thirty-five miles from the Mexican border. And it was long a part of the Southern Republic. They looked upon the coming of the Sisters as a blessing from heaven and vied with each other in ministering to the wants of the *Hermanos del Cielas*, as they spoke of them.

The convent and Motherhouse of the Sisters of Mercy was a long, one-story adobe structure with four rooms on each side of a hall; at the front of the house there were three windows, and four windows on each side of the building. The windows were large but they were fitted with iron bars instead of glass, perhaps to keep the Apaches out, while beautiful Spanish curtains draped the windows within. The house was, until the coming of the Sisters, the residence of one of the old Spanish aristocrats and was considered to be the best in the area.

The ladies of the town had prepared it for the Sisters. The mud floors had been nicely sanded. The sleeping apartments were unique—in each bedroom was a homemade wooden cot provided with a native mattress and simple bedding, all very fresh and clean. On the floor, by each cot, was stretched a dried goat skin to serve as a rug. The toilet table and wardrobe for each Sister consisted of a wooden orange crate standing on end, the top to be used as a washstand, the compartments as a wardrobe. Everything was very simple and primitive, and the good ladies who had prepared the rooms were happy because the Sisters were so pleased with their new home, *El Convento*.

Behind the convent was a garden of about half an acre, with shade and fruit trees and a fine assortment of vegetables enough to supply the table. From the first, this little garden was a favorite spot for all the Sisters. The fertility of this place was due to the waters of the Rio Grande, carried into the garden by one of the many irrigation canals. During the flood season, the canal overflowed and inundated the countryside. Although much damage was done, it was generally offset by the good harvest that followed.

The schools, which opened in February, 1881, were at either side of the convent but separate from it; the girls on one side, the boys on the other. They were partly parochial and partly private until 1891 when they were placed under government control. As long as they remained in Mesilla, the Sisters continued to teach in the government schools. This, for the Sisters, was most satisfactory, though all had to take the examinations to hold the schools, and attend annual institutes, as directed by the New Mexican territorial laws.

In 1881 the Reverend Antonio Fourchegu, parish priest of Los Alamos, later the Vicar General of the archdiocese of Santa Fe, visited Mesilla. When he observed the benefits of the religious training by the Sisters, he sought Sisters for his own schools. Los Alamos was, even then, a flourishing little town about three hundred miles north of Mesilla in a much higher and colder climate than the Gila Valley. Because he pictured hundreds of children calling to the Sisters to come to them, and because he was so kindly and fatherly, the Superior would have liked to accede to his wish immediately. But it was scarcely possible then, due to lack of Sisters and the special claim Father Morin had on those at hand. Though a holy and zealous priest, the latter was a rather hard person "to get along with." He wanted to know the ins-and-outs of everything; not only those that pertained to the schools, but to even the most minute details of community life. He wished to be consulted about everything. Mother Josephine especially experienced his displeasure for she did not think it her duty to inform him of the private concerns of the Sisters. This caused a breach, which soon afterwards brought a change to the little community. On July 2, 1881, the profession of Sister M. Antonia Kearney took place, with Father Morin officiating. It was the first of its kind in La Mesilla and the first in the new community; for this reason, it took place in the parish church with a large congregation in attendance.

About that time, Father Fourchegu again appealed to the Sisters. He also solicited the aid of Father Morin who was quite pleased at the deference shown him. This was in the interests of the Sisters, too, as Father Morin could be instrumental in making things pleasant or otherwise for them. Father Fourchegu's strategy worked. Encouraged by Archbishop Lamy of Santa Fe, the Sisters gladly accepted Father Fourchegu's invitation and began plans.

But it was evident that if the Sisters hoped to meet the demands of the New Mexico vineyard of the Lord, they must do something to secure recruits. For this reason, Mother M. Josephine Brennan and Sister M. Augustine Bambrick went to

Ireland in the summer of 1881. They returned with five well-educated young women who had offered themselves for the New Mexico mission.

On reaching Mesilla they began their postulantship at once. To fit themselves for their expected duties, they also went to work immediately studying Spanish. The call was not long in coming, for they were to furnish much of the help in the project at Los Alamos.

On December 12, 1881, the anniversary of the foundation of the Congregation of Sisters of Mercy in Ireland, the Sisters were overwhelmed by the celebration in New Mexico, not because the new community took root this day, but because of the Feast of Our Lady of Guadalupe, the patron saint of Mexico. It was a gala day in every Mexican settlement, where houses and shops were festooned in the Mexican national colors: red, green and white; and where often, too, there hung the familiar picture of Our Lady of Guadalupe as depicted on Juan Diego's cloak. There was much music and rejoicing but less commercialism than usually accompanies a Yankee holiday. Yet these were trying times for the young religious, some of whom had been in the United States only a few months. That they were young and healthy counted a good deal at such times.

Los Alamos—1882-1893

On January 10, 1882, Mother M. Josephine, Sister M. Bernard Connor, and two postulants, Miss Bridget Bambrick and Miss Marie McTernan, left Mesilla for Los Alamos to open the new school prepared by Father Fourchegu. The opening day of school in Los Alamos was an interesting day for the Sisters. All sorts and sizes presented themselves for admission. Some were very small, four or five years old; some were like children entering any American school; and then there was the broad span of children of all ages, to twenty-one and over. All were very simply waiting for classification, as if they could be classified. It was no unusual thing to see a Sister with a class of thirty consisting of tots of five or six, beside a bewhiskered man of over twenty, the latter just as intent on learning to read. All, tiny or grown, showed great respect for the Sisters and were very obedient and studious.

The children of Los Alamos were a very good type of Mexican and the people did all in their power to make it pleasant for the Sisters, ever trying to help them with the language, their greatest difficulty. They were naturally polite and therefore easy to deal with. Their gestures were so true that if one failed to understand their words, she was sure to understand the intended meaning. The love of the children for the Sisters and their absolute dependence on them as a means of learning something inspired the Sisters to devote themselves to their charges.

About two months later, on March 18, 1883, Sister M. Alacoque Bambrick and Sister M. Peter McTernan were the first and only Sisters to receive the habit of Sisters of Mercy in Los Alamos. Because Father Agustin Morin refused to relinquish the Sisters in Mesilla, it was decided to hold the reception for two of their group after their arrival in Los Alamos. This explains the life records of Sister M. Alacoque Bambrick and Sister M. Peter McTernan: Entrance, Mesilla, September 19, 1881; Reception, Los Alamos, March 18, 1882, and Profession, Los Alamos, May 5, 1884.

Soon after the Los Alamos foundation, Mother M. Josephine Brennan's health began to give her Sisters some concern and, to give her assistance, Sister M. Bernard returned from Los Alamos. Her place was filled by her natural sister, Sister M. Teresa Connor.

Father Fourchegu proved a valuable friend and strong support in the difficult problems that face pioneers. The winters proved cold; sometimes for three months they were blanketed with snow. He was proud of his school and convent, the usual adobe, finished in Spanish style, comfortable, and neatly furnished. It was long enough to provide school rooms and quarters for boarders. The entire building was surrounded by porches, which sometimes served as classrooms when there was an overflow. The equipment was simple but sufficient; for the good pastor did all he could to supply their every need. The people were generous and, according to their custom, ranchers and merchants set aside a portion of their stores to supply for the Sisters.

The chief difficulty was the water supply, or rather the lack of it. All water used in the convent and for the use of the children had to be carried from the river, which was about one hundred yards from the house. This entailed real hardship for the Sisters, especially during the winter. It was quite a task to draw water and haul wood. The most formidable undertaking on this mission was the sinking of a well. The laborers, although willing to work, were quite ignorant men and the implements were of the crudest kind. It was not until Father Fourchegu went to work him with the men that they understood how to go about the business. The Sisters then had water in abundance and were spared the job of hauling it.

The people themselves could not do enough, often supplying provisions, although money was scarce. One Mexican woman was very kind to the Sisters, bringing them chickens every week. She chose, however, a strange time to deliver her gifts. Usually after the Sisters had gone to bed, she would come up on the porch and cry out, *"Politas Hermanas!"* (Chickens, Sisters). The Sisters did not at first know what she was saying but knew that her coming meant a chicken dinner. After some time, the Sister mentioned the gifts received at such an unusual hour. Father Fourchegu smiled and said, "Do you know why she comes at this time? She has to rob the chicken coops to get the chicken dinners for you. I think the lady is not responsible for her act. She is very good-hearted and probably thinks she is doing a great deal for the Church in thus feeding you." The Sisters decided they could forego the chicken dinners.

While the Sisters were at Los Alamos, schoolwork was exhibited each year and a playlet or drama at Christmas became traditional. The Mexicans were very graceful, and they delighted in the things for which they seem to be naturally gifted. Doubtless, this entailed much preparatory work and additional sacrifice, but with all this, these days were the occasions of great joy for the Sisters, too, as the Sisters of Charity and the Sisters of Loretto always came from a great distance to attend the Los Alamos festivities. Priests also came from the surrounding missions, as such programs were almost the only recreation they allowed themselves.

When the school year closed, the Sisters of Los Alamos returned to Mesilla for a joyful reunion. Since they had departed, Sister M. Paul O'Grady[9] and Sister M. Julia Derwin had received the habit and two postulants, Sister Elizabeth Cox and Sister Nora Egan, had arrived.

Between the time of her arrival at Los Alamos and the Sisters' return to Mesilla for the summer, Sister M. Teresa Connor had suffered a severe fall. While standing on a chair to arrange some drapes, she had fallen backward and struck her head. Although she seemed to have lost consciousness for some minutes, she was able to get up. Soon she was about her duties and since she made no further complaint, the Sisters thought no more of the incident.

During 1882 relations in Mesilla between Father Morin and Mother Josephine had become quite strained. Although Mother M. Josephine's term of office, six years, still had almost four years to run, a change was pending. Just who initiated the change is not certain. One account states that Mother M. Josephine asked Bishop Salpointe for permission to be released from office due to recurring illness and increasing difficulty with Father Morin. Bishop Salpointe, who knew that the Mesilla pastor was not likely to make things easy for one whose views differed from his, agreed to the request, and appointed Sister M. Bernard Connor as Superior. Another account states that Father Morin thought it best to have, for superior, a Sister who was not educated and might prove more inclined to do as he wished. He had learned that one of the Sisters who came with Mother M. Josephine had been a lay Sister in her former convent home and that Mother M. Josephine had made her a choir Sister so as to have Sisters of only one status in so small a community. Mother M. Josephine, however, despite her culture and refinement, was very humble and as simple as a child. She was, nevertheless, firm in maintaining the rights of the Sisters against encroachment by the pastor on the privacy of the community's affairs. At any rate, Sister M. Bernard Connor became the Superior, and Sister M. Paul O'Grady, still a novice, was delegated to the office of secretary to the Mother Superior to carry on business matters. Much of the burden of office fell on Sister M. Paul and this paved the way for her own appointment as Mother Superior later on.

Mother M. Bernard was a good and saintly woman, and very thoughtful and kind to all the Sisters. She simply had not had the benefit of an education. In this trying circumstance, Mother M. Josephine showed herself a true religious and very gracefully slipped into her place in the ranks, a difficult thing to do for one so young and energetic and who had served as the leader of the community in its pioneer days. It was in her new position in the ranks that she revealed so vividly how well imbued she was with the true character of a Sister of Mercy, a self-effacing, generous and truly dedicated Sister.

On New Year's Day, 1883, when things began to look very hopeful, a smallpox epidemic broke out to frighten the Sisters and decimate the school. The Mexicans did not seem to be afraid of smallpox, and they visited each other and spread the contagion. Although victims increased daily, schoolwork continued. The parish priest would not allow the schools to close. One of the victims asked for one of the Sisters, and Mother Bernard, not wishing to expose any of the other Sisters more than they were already in school, went herself to see the girl who, though very ill, eventually recovered. Soon Mother Bernard became ill and was isolated; smallpox was suspected. Mother M. Josephine at once offered to take care of Reverend Mother and thus spare the other Sisters as much as possible. Notwithstanding all the care and attention she received, Reverend Mother succumbed to the disease and died a victim of charity on April 16, 1883.

Mother M. Josephine, who had taken care of her during the two weeks of her illness, finally felt the effects of her prolonged vigils and untiring work. Never very robust, she suffered a complete breakdown and in May, 1883, she left for Mercy Hospital Durango, Colorado, where she had been very kindly invited by the Sisters. Under their skillful care, she seemed to grow much stronger, regaining some of her old spirit and looking forward to a complete recovery. But she was not to return to New Mexico. She was suddenly stricken by a heart attack and the Lord called her to Himself on January 16, 1884, in the thirty-sixth year of her life, twenty-one of which she had spent in religion. She was buried with the Sister of Mercy in Durango, Colorado.[10]

Like many founders of a religious community, Mother M. Josephine lived in the shadow of the Cross. She had met with one disappointment after another, and encountered considerable misunderstanding. She was a gifted woman, whose ability was recognized even before she left Ireland, for as a very young religious she was already Mistress of Novices in Moate. She was well-educated and endowed with musical gifts which she generously used for God's glory and the development of the talents of those she served. Her early death, doubtless induced by her selfless devotion in the care of Mother M. Bernard, makes us wonder what she might have accomplished had she been spared for further service. But the very brevity of her work in Mesilla is evidence that she had planted a seed strong enough to take root and produce a very permanent institution.

Shortly after the death of Mother M. Bernard, her sister,

Sister M. Teresa Connor, was appointed Superior by Bishop Salpointe, again at the request of Father Morin. This, according to one account, was in opposition to the wishes of the Sisters, who wanted Mother Josephine. Sister M. Teresa, unlike her sister, was fairly well educated, but she was reputed to be a rather rigid type of person. She served the remainder of the late Mother M. Bernard's term as well as three years of her own appointment by the Bishop.[11]

During Mother M. Teresa's term of office, the schools at Silver City (1883) and Belen (1884) were opened, as well as the invitation accepted to staff a school for the Jesuits in El Paso, Texas (1886). In the spring of 1887, however, she began to show signs of failing mental health. An appeal was sent to the Bishop. In June, Bishop Peter Bourgade called for an election, but as no one received a majority vote, he appointed Sister M. Paul O'Grady to the office of Superior. This office she was to hold by election every three years thereafter until 1914, and again from 1920 until the amalgamation in 1921. The long years of Mother M. Paul in the office of Superior of the New Mexican-Arizona community will explain the common reference to her as the second foundress of the community. Certainly no other Sister has left such an imprint as she on the history of her Sisters.[12]

Meanwhile the Sisters at Los Alamos lost their beloved pastor, Father A. Fourchegu,[13] who was appointed Vicar General of the Santa Fe diocese. While the Sisters were very happy to see the pastor so honored, they regretted it would take him from their parish.

Silver City—1883-1916—Our Lady of Lourdes Academy and Parochial School (1883-1916); St. Joseph's Sanatorium (1887-1915)

As the Sisters of Mercy had given assurance to Reverend Father Bourgade that they would come to Silver City as soon as they were able to undertake the work, he began to make plans for a convent and school. In February, 1883, he secured a piece of property referred to as Block #132 and turned the deed over to the Sisters of Mercy. It was a fine site, a lot consisting of a city block northwest of the Catholic Church and about a block away.

Silver City was so-called in reference to the mines operated there before the Mexican War. At that time the yield was great, so that mine owners thought the supply unlimited. This was rather soon disproved. After the silver fever abated it was found that the same area was a great producer of copper. This caused a boom in the early 'seventies, which lasted to the 'nineties, during which time millions of dollars worth of the red metal was taken from the mines in and around Silver City. Silver was also found again, but not in anything like the quantities earlier discovered. In the early 'nineties, depression occurred when the price of copper fell and the mines closed for a time. The coming of the railroads gave new life to Silver City, as it did to Raton, Deming, and other nearby towns.

Silver City is situated at an altitude of about 6,000 feet; it nestles among the mountains by which it is surrounded. The number of clear, sunny days in a year is put at 266; the winters are short but make up in severity for their brevity. This place with its pure, high and dry air is very healthy and became a great health resort for those afflicted with tuberculosis. In 1883, however, it was not yet a health center or a resort town. Children were plentiful, and the need for schools was great. It was for this reason that Father Bourgade was intent on building good schools and a comfortable convent for the Sisters.

The Silver City school project made the news on August 10, 1883, in the Silver City *Enterprise:*

> The foundation of the convent and schools of the Sisters of Mercy is almost complete. Brick-laying will begin in two weeks. The building, four stories, will be completed in October. It will be one of the finest buildings in the territory and will reflect credit on the Sisters who have undertaken the enterprise. It has been said that every single miner, regardless of creed, in southwestern New Mexico and Arizona has contributed one day's wage toward the cost. . . .[14]

In September, 1883, Mother M. Teresa and Sister M. Antonia Kearney, Superior of the Silver City convent, Sister M. Alphonsus Cox, and Sister M. Francis Egan left Mesilla for the mission in Silver City.[15]

Because all could not be in readiness for the opening of school in the fall of 1883, Father Bourgade had rented two cottages, one for the convent and one for the school. The cottage school was soon filled to capacity and another Sister was sent to help, so great was the number of children. Across the street, on the opposite terraced hill, the new schools were going up and many a longing glance was directed toward them. The annals of 1884 state that the building program in Silver City was completed in June of that year.

The Academy of Our Lady of Lourdes was the pride and joy of the pastor, by whom it was classified as a "select day and boarding school for girls." A three-story brick building with a stone foundation, it also served as the Motherhouse and novitiate of the Sisters of Mercy.

Belen, New Mexico—1884-1890

About the same time that Father Bourgade asked for Sisters for Silver City, an appeal was made to them by Reverend Francisco Gatignol for the Sisters to come to Belen; both places were in New Mexico but about three hundred miles apart. The Santa Fe Railroad and the re-opening of the coal mines were bringing workmen to the town. The children at Belen were numerous, and at the time there were no public schools.

Some years earlier the Sisters of Loretto had been forced to leave Belen when the mines closed down, and the convent and school were sadly in need of renovation. The parents promised to do their part if the Sisters would come. Mother M. Teresa Connor could not refuse the earnest invitation of the eager parents and their bashful children. A promise was given to send some Sisters. Meanwhile, the people of Belen cleaned and painted the school before the Sisters would arrive in August, 1884. Little or nothing, however, was done to the convent. This did not deter the pioneers. The young Sisters went to work and soon made it quite liveable.

When the four Sisters opened the Belen school in 1884, they found it almost impossible to handle all the children who came. They would do the best they could. The pupils were of mixed nationality and so receptive that it was a pleasure to teach them.

The little mission was sufficiently prosperous to provide the moderate needs of the Sisters. Had the schools, which were left entirely to the Sisters, been the only matter at hand, Belen would have been a very happy place, but in all matters spiritual, much was to be desired. The pastor had many missions to attend, some of these a hundred miles apart. In his anxiety to encompass them all his health began to fail. He was seldom at Belen so that at times there was no Mass on Sunday, and on weekdays very seldom, nor was there regularity about the sacraments. The community suffered from a lack of spiritual direction. The Sisters were spiritually starved, and most of them were very young. The pastor always promised improvement when he got an assistant, but the assistant never came. Father was growing stranger every day, always alone, going from one mission to another in all kinds of weather. He was soon relieved of his pastorate due to ill health and mental strain, caused no doubt by overwork. He returned to France, his native land, and lived but a very short time.

Mother M. Paul O'Grady, who was Reverend Mother at the time, seeing no prospect for change, felt it her duty to withdraw her Sisters in 1890. All the Sisters who had taught at Belen loved the place and the children who had been very quick to respond to all things good.

There was certainly much good effected during their stay in Belen, and some of the students even followed the Sisters to El Paso, Texas, where they were enrolled as boarders.

In April, 1884, Bishop Salpointe, who as Vicar Apostolic of Arizona and several parishes in southern New Mexico, had invited the Sisters to make the foundation at Mesilla in 1880, was promoted to a new position Coadjutor to Archbishop J.B. Lamy of the see of Santa Fe.[16] He remained, however, as administrator of the vicariate of Arizona until the appointment of his successor. On the resignation of Archbishop J.B. Lamy, July 18, 1885, Archbishop J.B. Salpointe succeeded to the see of Santa Fe.[17] Meanwhile, Father Bourgade, the pastor in Silver City, became the Vicar Apostolic of Arizona.[18] Needless to say the Sisters of Mercy regretted losing their pastor at Silver City, but were happy to see his worth recognized by his new promotion.

In August, 1885, the railroad officials were generous in furnishing passes so that the Sisters from Mesilla and Los Alamos could go to Silver City for retreat. In Mesilla the people were puzzled at the departure of the Sisters, but were satisfied when they learned that it was to be a temporary absence, for retreat and vacation only. During the summer absence, the people had the convent repaired and painted. Each year thereafter, those good people planned some surprise for the Sisters on their return.

El Paso, Texas—1886-1892[19]

In the spring of 1886, the Jesuits in El Paso, Texas, appealed to Mother M. Teresa for schools in El Paso, Texas. By September, the Sisters were established there, four being sent at first and later more as needed.

The Fathers provided a two-story brick building to serve as both convent and school, and large enough even to accommodate boarders. The children from Juarez, across the Rio Grande, in Mexico, were anxious to have a school near enough to attend during the week and to go home for the weekends; consequently, the accommodations for the boarders were insufficient from the beginning. The schools were good for El Paso, which at the time was but a small town of a few thousand. Of these more than half were Mexican or half-Mexican. Needless to say, the Jesuits expected good results from their schools, and they seem to have gotten it; for they so expressed themselves when the Sisters had to withdraw. As elsewhere, the beginnings were hard but the results rewarding. Many years later, the matrons of El Paso claimed the Sisters of Mercy as their former teachers. It being a pass city from Texas to Mexico and on the Southern Pacific line from New Orleans to California, the Sisters had many visitors. Among those in these early days was Cardinal Gibbons who, with a Chinese bishop and his secretary, honored them with their presence at dinner.

The diocesan boundary changes of this time were the cause of the Sisters leaving El Paso. In 1892 that part of the vicariate of Arizona was annexed to the diocese of Dallas. The Jesuits did not like the idea of withdrawing the Sisters but the Bishop was in favor of it; and so nothing else could be done as the community was not large enough in numbers for two dioceses. In 1892, after examinations and the close of school, the Sisters departed and the Sisters of Loretto from Las Cruces took over the schools for the fall semester.

Silver City (continued)[20]

The growth of the apostolate in New Mexico and Arizona put quite a strain on the young community. Demands for teaching Sisters were frequent, and the Southwest was not, at that time, a very fertile source of vocations. Again and again, with the permission of the Bishop, the Sisters journeyed to Ireland for recruits. In 1881, when five aspirants were secured; in 1886, when the Sisters returned with eight candidates; and again, in 1890, when eleven prospective postulants offered themselves for the missions in the Southwest. This was an era when a response to a vocation to foreign missions meant good-bye forever to home and country. Yet, there were few who turned back once "they had set their hand to the plow," and dropouts were negligible. This same fruitful method of securing very much-needed vocations was continued well into the twentieth century.

Our Lady of Lourdes Academy, the well-patronized boarding school of Silver City, and the parochial grade school, were popular and thriving. Silver City was constantly calling for more Sisters for their schools, and additions were made from time to time to relieve congestion.

By 1904, Silver City was experiencing another boom. The mines were working again, bringing workmen and their families to town. This was good for the schools, too, although the boom might not be of long duration. When the schools were closed in Phoenix in 1904, the Sisters went to Silver City and to Prescott. It was this year that Sister M. Peter McTernan and Sister M. Berchmans McCormick were sent to Ireland in quest of much-needed aspirants.

The eight young ladies who arrived from Ireland this year faced one of the worst floods in the history of New Mexico. In this section of the Southwest, after a heavy fall of snow or much rain, floods are likely to follow the melt, causing much destruction on the lowlands. When the Sisters, with their charges from Ireland, got to the border of New Mexico, they found one of these floods in progress. The train went on for a time, but it, too, had to submit to nature's demands. In Albuquerque, New Mexico, the passengers were taken off, the car being unable to proceed farther until the waters had abated. Here the Sisters had to remain for two weeks and even when the trains began to move again, they had to detour around the state, going into Arizona and on to Phoenix, because the road bed to Silver City had been washed away in several places. It took some months to rebuild the road, and they remained in Phoenix for over a month. The young ladies enjoyed the situation and had one more adventure before reaching the novitiate. Silver City, which had experienced a secondary flood, had not yet recovered, and traveling was somewhat difficult. On reaching the station they heard the driver call out, "Catholic bus." It was something new but seemed to promise safety and they piled on. They finally found themselves in the channel of the flood where after much swaying and grasping at each other, they were at length overturned. A bit shaken up, they made the rest of the way to the convent on foot.

In the fall of 1909, school attendance in Silver City was very large, and the prospects of a good school year seemed evident. When things were going along well, however, a serious diphtheria epidemic posed an alarming threat to the students. At first, only sporadic cases appeared in October, but toward Christmas it got into the schools. While every precaution was taken to keep it from children of the other schools, it made its way to these as well.

On December 30, a girl of fifteen awoke about 3:00 a.m. and complained to the Sister in the dormitory that she could not breathe. Sister gave her the remedies she thought would give relief; the girl was made quite at ease and went off to sleep. The doctor, who was called in the morning, examined the girl and said she had a very malignant type of diphtheria. Consulting physicians considered her condition grave. She had been taking instructions in the Catholic faith and she said if she was going to die she wanted baptism at once. She was baptized and seemed to grow better. Her relatives were notified and her aunts, who lived rather near, were summoned. She bade her aunts goodbye, thanked Sister for some little service and peacefully died.

The convent and schools were at once quarantined. Frantic letters came from parents who wanted to take their children home at once. This the health officers would not allow. The city physician came every day to examine throats and watch for additional cases. The convent was kept in quarantine for six weeks, the priest, the doctor and the sheriff being the only ones admitted. The sheriff, Mr. Gill, was very kind and did a great deal more than his duty required. He saw to the mail, wrote to some of the parents to allay their fears, brought provisions, and met every need. In the years after, he remained the friend he showed himself to be during these trying hours.

School for the boarders was held in the open during the quarantine, and Silver City was blessed with beautiful weather through the period. The children were sorry when the quarantine was lifted. The epidemic spoiled the school for that year, but all were grateful that only one of the students had died. It was thought that the death might affect school enrollment in the fall, but such was not the case. Enrollment was better than expected and with the opening of school there was the added joy that Reverend Edward Gerard had come as chaplain to the convent. All the children, Catholic and Protestant, loved him as a grandfather. Many a barrel of apples from Father Gerard found its way into the boarders' storeroom.

Silver City is nicely situated in a valley between surrounding hills covered with pine and other evergreens. One of the happiest memories in the schools was the trip to the hills for a Christmas tree, not a very long or dangerous event; however, always an occasion of great pleasure to the girls, almost as much as the old British custom of bringing home the Yule log.

It was at Silver City in 1909 that Mother M. Paul celebrated her Silver Jubilee. Her life in the Institute coincided with the history of the little community. She was professed in La Mesilla the very same year that Mother M. Josephine Brennan died (1884). It was she who was made secretary to Mother M. Bernard Connor, the second Mother Superior, in 1882. In 1887, when no election was made of any Sister, the Bishop appointed Sister M. Paul O'Grady to the office and she held it for twenty-seven consecutive years thereafter. After the Jubilee celebration of 1909, Mother M. Paul O'Grady and Sister M. Peter McTernan went to California for three months. She was already looking westward and envisioned her community affiliated with that of San Francisco, but it would be twelve years until the fulfillment of her dream.

St. Joseph's Sanatorium, Silver City—1887-1915[2][1]

In 1887 Mother M. Paul was asked by the pastor and citizens of Silver City to open a small hospital for the use of the mining men who had to be taken to El Paso for treatment when an accident occurred. It was a hard journey of ten hours duration for a poor sufferer. A small hospital was accordingly opened and three Sisters sent to ready it for service. Many a poor broken body was cared for and often, too, a very neglected soul reached. With loving gratitude could the Sisters recall countless consoling experiences in this little hospital where they served the Lord in the ministration of the sick.

After a few years a new hospital was built by the Sisters in the hills to meet the growing needs of the community. The new

St. Joseph's received a grant from the Territory of New Mexico for the care of their indigent sick; this was a help because the Sisters were called upon to care for many patients who, although without means, could hardly be refused.

The location, in the mountains and among the pines, threatened to make it a tubercular sanatorium. The physicians of the town did not wish it to so develop, but by 1905 St. Joseph's in Silver City was changed to St. Joseph's Sanatorium and closed to all other cases except for a ward in the cottage that was maintained for some old-timers. It was much in need of more accommodations for patients, but labor and materials were very high. New additions were made in 1906, and the new parts occupied almost as soon as completed. The medical director had patients coming from almost every state in the Union. Fort Bayard, the government sanatorium near Silver City, gave impetus to many to come to this section who believed that because the government had located its sanatorium here, it must be the best climate for sufferers from the disease. Silver City even came to be called "the City of Silver with the climate Golden."

The reputation of St. Joseph's was not confined to the United States; its reputation for good even bridged the Atlantic. The son of Lord J. Kennedy, of the High Court of England, had come to Silver City suffering from the so-called white plague. After a stay of over two years, he began to grow steadily weaker, and with this, kinder and gentler. His whole aim was to die well. The *Imitation of Christ* gave him great consolation, and he kept it with him begging the Sister to whom it belonged to let him use it. He asked every Sister who came to visit him to say some prayer with him. His favorite was "Into Thy Hands, O Lord, I commend my spirit." Because he wished to have the home folks know that he knew how to die all this information was given to them after his death. The dear old mother sent for the *Imitation* and for a list of his favorite prayers, as she wanted them to be her consolation. On a stone in the family burial plot, the aspiration, "Into Thy Hands I commend my Spirit," was engraved.

It was with great regret that the Sisters had to leave Silver City when it was caught in extensive diocesan changes. When Mesilla had to be closed after almost thirty-three years of service, in 1913, the Sisters felt Silver City was likely to follow. It was almost certain that the Bishop of Tucson's diocese would include only the state of Arizona, extensive enough. The sanatorium was transferred to the Sisters of St. Joseph in 1915 They were to take over the schools, too. It would have been a herculean task for even three times their number; therefore, it was not surprising that they asked the Sisters of Mercy to keep the schools for another year until they could establish their hold on the sanatorium. The Sisters of Mercy withdrew from the sanatorium in Silver City in 1915 and from the schools in 1916. For two years the Sisters of St. Joseph stayed on, but because they were not able to buy nor pay rental for the property, it was sold to the Hospital Corporation of Silver City for their work. Despite all reluctance to give up an apostolate of thirty-six years duration, the work of the Sisters of Mercy in New Mexico, which began in December of 1880, was terminated in November, 1916, with the closing of the schools in Silver City. The annalist notes, "One step nearer the Golden Gate." The Motherhouse was transferred to Phoenix, temporarily at least.

Emplazada, New Mexico—1888-1898

Emplazada, a small town five miles from Los Alamos, became a cathechetical center for the Sisters about 1888. Every Sunday morning a Mexican boy drove two Sisters by horse and buggy from Los Alamos to the little church to teach cathechism. Here boys and girls from the nearby ranches and the children of those employed on the railroad gathered to learn the divine truths. Doctrine was impressed by the teaching of beautiful hymns, often in their native Spanish tongue. In this way the Sisters reached their hearts as well as their heads, for the children loved their faith and wanted to know more about it.

From this beginning the Board of Education turned over the management of the one-room public school to the Sisters, who had taken and passed the examinations. Thereafter, each weekday two Sisters would set out with their lunch boxes from Los Alamos for Emplazada.

Many boys and girls did their share of the work on the family ranch. In winter the weather was very severe. Both of these factors made attendance very irregular. Sometimes the Sisters had twenty students, at other times, fifty. Nevertheless, it was encouraging to teach the children of Emplazada, all of whom were receptive, and some of whom were very intelligent. When attendance was good the school looked like a frontier trading post: burros, ponies, carts of every description were tied to every available post or tree. After ten years the Sisters gave up the catechetical school, with genuine regret, when the community withdrew from the Archdiocese of Santa Fe.

Los Alamos (continued)[22]

For some time, the prosperity of Los Alamos seemed to be declining, and the business that before was theirs now appeared to be transferred to Sapello, five miles farther on. This town was attended from Los Alamos parish and once a month the pastor used to drive there for Mass. This meant that on this day the privilege of Holy Mass was taken from Los Alamos and given to the people of Sapello. After a while the ranchers began moving into the Sapello area so that this place became the parish center, instead of Los Alamos, where the crops had failed for three consecutive years. The people had become so discouraged that many had moved on. It was rather easy for the Mexican to pick up stakes at any time because his household goods were usually very scant.

Today it seems strange to us that the Sisters moved from Los Alamos because the town seemed to be dying. Little did anyone dream that with the dawn of the atomic age it would become the site of an atomic energy laboratory.[23]

Sapello—1893-1897

In 1893 Father Juan Picard, who had succeeded Father Fourchegu at Los Alamos as pastor, told the Sisters of the impending change and asked the Sisters to move to Sapello, where they would have many of their old pupils; otherwise they would have Mass only once a month and be in all respects like Sapello had been during the time Los Alamos was the principal town of the parish. The Sisters moved to Sapello, and many of their former pupils did come to the Sapello school. Sometimes Father Fourchegu, now Vicar General at Santa Fe, called to see his children and regretted their having to leave Los Alamos. After five years of real hardship in Sapello, Mother M. Paul withdrew her Sisters. This branch house from Mesilla at Los Alamos, later Sapello, lasted fifteen years, closing in 1897.[24]

The beginning of the nineties brought real changes in the Southwest. Probably this was due in large measure to the development of the railroads between 1890 and 1900. This prompted many moves that brought more civilization to the wild, rugged country. Commerce was stimulated and new industries developed, all of which tended to bring the area closer to the American way of life. The public school system was initiated between 1891 and 1912, when statehood was granted. The progress of the public schools was slow, and we note that the local authorities engaged the Sisters as teachers. In Mesilla, the Board of Education built a modern brick building close to the church to replace the old adobe structure but hired the Sisters to continue the schools in Mesilla.

With the advent of statehood for New Mexico and Arizona, expenditures for the public schools were increased. Then, too, the governing authority of the public school system was the State Board of Education, which tended to systematize and standardize education under its control. In many places all or almost all of the children were Catholics, as were many of the local Board of Directors. Even the few non-Catholics were happy to have the Sisters as teachers. As time passed, state control became more evident. If religion was taught, it had to be after school hours, and the Sisters were required to take periodic examinations to attest their qualifications to teach. They gladly did so, and their excellent records gave further distinction to the teaching Sisters. As the public schools were gradually edging out the Catholic schools, Mother Mary Paul decided to withdraw her Sisters, and this was one reason she did not find it hard to take her Sisters from Mesilla when the new diocese of El Paso absorbed Mesilla in 1914.

Silver City was an ideal location for the Motherhouse because the railroad made it accessible to all the branch houses, and further, it was located in a more American community than Mesilla. The schools were thriving and even necessitated additions to take care of the congestion but Mother M. Paul could read the signs of the times. Silver City would likely be absorbed by the El Paso diocese, too.

In 1890 Mother M. Paul was confronted with another change; the former pastor of Mesilla, Reverend Agustin Morin, was made pastor of St. Vincent de Paul, Silver City. The Sisters, who had regretted the loss of Father Bourgade, were not much elated over the appointment of Father Morin. Like a series of chain reactions, one change seemed to set another in motion.

Mother M. Paul was very anxious to get a house in Arizona, and this late change in pastors seems to have made her more anxious. Even before leaving for Ireland, she had sent three Sisters to Florence, Arizona, where the Sisters of St. Joseph had a convent and parochial school which they were leaving. There Sisters had recently received a grant from the government to take care of the Indian children. This necessitated their giving up the school in Florence, since otherwise they had not sufficient Sisters to care for the Indians. The Sisters of Mercy returned from Arizona with very enthusiastic reports of the convent, the school, and the wonderful climate.

And yet it was almost twenty-five years before the Sisters of Mercy transferred their Motherhouse and novitiate to Arizona and then it was due to diocesan charges.[26] The Sisters had to make a choice and they threw in their lot with the Most Rev. Henry R. Granjon, Bishop of Tucson when the diocese of El Paso was erected in 1914.

Chapter 12

ARIZONA[1]
Mother M. Paul O'Grady

Florence—1890-1892

The year 1890 marks the beginning of the work of the Sisters of Mercy in Arizona. It was agreed that they would take over the schools in Florence, where the Sisters of St. Joseph were required to give them up . Little preparation was necessary because the convent was well furnished and the schools in good condition, ready to begin school as soon as the Sisters got there.

To get to Florence, the Sisters had to take a train at Deming, New Mexico, to Casa Grande, Arizona, and then go by stage, a distance of twenty-eight miles, to Florence. The climate, as they came into Arizona, was much milder than that of New Mexico, and that of Florence, very warm and tropical. It is said that the town was so-called by one of the pioneer townsmen who came from Italy and named it after his home city. To one coming from arid plains it was an oasis and a pretty one at that.

The Sisters' first acquaintance with Arizona was quite pleasant, perhaps too pleasant to last. The pastor, Father Wurlazel, seemed very strange, absentminded; and, once the schools were taken over, he was seldom to be seen even when the Sisters wished to speak to him on business matters. The western missions often worked havoc with the young priests who responded enthusiastically to a call to missionary life. They were soon much alone, with too much work, no care, and no regular meals, all of which combined to undermine their health and interfere with the fruits of their labors. The diocese was so large and the missions so many that recourse to their Bishop was almost an impossibility. The children of the school were quite heterogeneous: Irish, French, Italian, and Mexican, and they seemed to have the best qualities of each nationality. It was a pity that they could not have the benefit of a Catholic education when they were so eager for it. The Sisters stayed at the school for two years, but when conditions did not improve, they had to give up the school. The pastor, who had gone to France during the Sisters' stay, had really returned to his native land to die. Here, indeed, was a flock without a shepherd. Some of the children went to boarding schools, and some went to Phoenix when the Sisters left Florence.

Yuma—1892-1894

When the school at Florence was about to close, Father Gheldof, who was pastor at Yuma, Arizona, wrote Mother M. Paul to ask if the Sisters leaving Florence would take over a school in Yuma. The Sisters of St. Joseph who had been conducting the school had to withdraw to fill up the numbers required for their Indian school near Yuma. Mother M. Paul had intended to send the Sisters to help in the schools in Silver City and Mesilla, where they were in need of more Sisters, but she disliked refusing the appeal of a priest when she could possibly grant it. The Sisters, therefore, went from Florence to Yuma.

As they had done at Florence, the Sisters of St. Joseph left all the household effects for their successors, and all the Sisters had to do was to step into the schools and begin work. The schools in Yuma were very good. As at Florence, the Italian merchants, who were quite comfortable, were very good to the Sisters. The climate was warm and humid. The schools were

244

supposed to be parochial, but the Sisters were expected to collect school fees, as best theycould. No bills were to be sent to the homes of the children, and th parish paid nothing at all the Sisters. This was a queer way to do business. For a month or so things went all right, for the children brought their school and music fees; however, little by little, these dropped off. When the matter was brought to the attention of the pastor, he said, "Get what you can, but do not send a bill and I will not speak of it in Church. The Sisters can live on very little and with what some of the families give, it ought to keep you." Of course this state of affairs could not go on. The Sisters spoke to the parents of the children, and the result was an improvement though not sufficient to carry on the work. By 1894 the Sisters had to be withdrawn.

Phoenix, Sacred Heart School—1892-1904

Meanwhile the Pastor of Phoenix, Father Francis Jovenceau, also wrote Mother M. Paul requesting Sisters for his parish school. Two Sisters were sent to Phoenix to look over the grounds and determine the prospects. They were very kindly received by the good pastor and his assistant, Reverend Peter Timmermans, who later became the Vicar General of the diocese of Tuscon. After the favorable reports of the Sisters, Mother M. Paul agreed to send Sisters for the fall term of 1892 if the school and furnishings could be made ready by that time. The school building, a two-story brick structure and quite commanding, was put up in record time for the opening of the school. It was then considered to be the finest building in the town.

Phoenix had at this time about two thousand inhabitants, the majority of whom were of Spanish or Mexican descent, though a number of Americans were interested in taking up land, and business was just beginning to stir. We are told that although the site of Phoenix once supported an ancient civilization, it had disappeared long before the days of Coronado, and that as late as 1867, present-day Phoenix did not have a single inhabitant. Its revival started when it became a hay camp, supplying fodder for the cavalry horses of Fort McDowell. Others joined John Smith, who held the military contract, and the small settlement, which they called Phoenix, sprang like the legendary fire-bird from the embers with the vigor of a new life. The name stuck and Phoenix has experienced several revivals. The Sisters who came in 1892 recalled that it had quite a suburban appearance, cottonwood trees lining the streets, and flowers and weeds growing wild.

In his book, *The Southwest, Old and New*, Eugene Hollon gives us this description:

> Early visitors to Phoenix were not impressed by the small agricultural community and its dry climate, dreary location and tremendous number of tarantulas and rattlesnakes. But by 1870 it claimed about three hundred people and by the next year a school, a hotel, a brewery, a bakery, a butcher shop and the inevitable saloon and jail. That year it was dignified by being named the county seat of Maricopa County. The first railroad, the Maricopa—Phoenix, reached Phoenix in 1887 and the second, the Santa Fe, in 1895. The population now approached two thousand, enough for the town to supplant Prescott as the territorial capital.[2]

The Sister annalist of the Phoenix Sisters of Mercy also described the conditions which faced the Sisters on their arrival. The two chief annoyances that tried the Sisters on their arrival at Sacred Heart School, Phoenix, were mosquitoes and the heat. The house had no screens when the Sisters came, and the correction of this condition, so simple a matter, soon brought relief.

School opened the first Monday in September, 1892, and as they were busy with the demands of the moment, the Sisters forgot the heat. The Sisters were housed in the same building as the school and there were also some small apartments for boarders. Because there was no chapel the Sisters went to the church for all their exercises until a convent was built. The schools at Phoenix were so crowded that the Sisters decided to relieve the congestion by building a convent and academy across the street from the brick building.In 1893 the new convent was completed, and the same year a separate school building for Mexican children was put up on the church block. This accommodated two hundred children. By the time the new quarters for boarders were completed, that number had doubled; in fact, there were always as many as could be cared for.

Father Jovenceau became quite ill in 1895. As he got no better, he resigned his charge and went back to France; but missionary life was still in his blood and he returned to Arizona, only to die in Tucson a year later. The scarcity of priests in the diocese caused Bishop Bourgade to give the parish of St. Mary's to the Franciscans of the St. Louis province. With the coming of the Franciscans there came a change in the schools. Up to this time the schools were almost private: children who were able paid tuition to the Sisters, the others were free. The Sisters also conducted music classes. Now the schools became parochial, a better arrangement for the Sisters, who had the academy in the new building, as well as the boarders; otherwise the amount paid by the Franciscans could not support the Sisters. The academy continued in good condition for almost seven years, but it was not satisfactory to the Franciscans, who thought it made the children dissatisfied. The boarding school was well attended and helped much financially, as did the music classes. Father Novatus Benzing, O.F.M., however, did not believe in having any but parochial schools in the parish, although it was almost twenty years before he got a high school for Catholics. Phoenix was growing apace, and likewise the demand for schools. In 1903 Father Novatus, still disturbed about the academy, asked Mother M. Paul for more Sisters for his schools. Because heavy labor in the warm climate had been hard on many of the Sisters, she could not supply the need. He then proposed that she take the Sisters from the academy and let all the boarders and Protestants go. She agreed to accede to his request if he could meet the needs financed by the academy. This he would not think of; in fact, he wanted two Sisters, free, for his schools and the other Sisters to receive a very insufficient sum for their services. She told him that she had no more Sisters to give him at this time and that the academy was the principal means of support for the Sisters. Father was insistent in his demands, and so Mother M. Paul advised him to get other Sisters for his schools, who would be satisfied with his offer. She promised, however, that the Sisters would continue for the year, until he could get some other community to take over the schools.

The new convent had been built in 1899, and the set-up had been successful in every detail: boarding school, music department, and academy. Now all had to be given up. The Sisters were withdrawn in 1904 and were sent to Silver City where there was a great demand.

The Sisters who came to replace them were a community of Franciscan Sisters of the Precious Blood, from Ohio. These Sisters rented the convent building from Mother M. Paul because they did not wish to purchase it until they saw how they were going to get along. They were, however, glad to have a place in Phoenix as some of their Sisters were in very delicate health.

Phoenix, during the Sisters' stay at Sacred Heart Academy, had grown to be a modern city, and the cottonwood trees that lined the streets had to be cut down to make way for progress. Hundreds of business houses and homes were put up, and the town began to show promise of the great and thriving southwestern city it was to become; but to the pioneer Sisters of Mercy the tree-lined and flower-decked suburban town ever remained a cherished memory.

Besides teaching, in all the convents of the Southwest the visitation of the sick was an important apostolate. It was here that the Sisters came to really know these people, their simplicity, their poverty, and their faith. As their knowledge and sympathy grew, so too did their labors become more successful.

Phoenix, St. Joseph's Hospital—1895[3]

The Sisters came to Phoenix in 1892 to teach but remained to minister to a crying need, health services. It came about this way. One day on the way to school, Sister M. Peter McTernan and her companion, Sister M. Alacoque Bambrick, passed a cheap rooming house where they saw a young man sitting on a chair, desperately gasping for breath. They helped him to his bed and promised to return. The next day he was dead. This at first seemed to be an isolated case, but they soon learned that many people who suffered from the "white plague" were coming from everywhere to Arizona, hoping that the dry air and wonderful sunshine might cure them. They were not exactly welcome, and the choice left to them was a tent in the desert or a cot in a boarding house, where for a few cents they might sleep on a germ-infested mattress. Looked upon as intruders, without friends or funds, many found nameless graves.

These two Sisters sought to do something about the health problem. They appealed to Mother M. Paul, who authorized them to undertake the project and sent two more Sisters to

Phoenix to help them. They solicited aid wherever they could find it. Their very compassion loosened the purse strings of the apathetic or sometimes even hostile townsmen. Most of the funds came from medical circles and local businessmen, who came to see the urgency of the need for a hospital in Phoenix. Mr. Gibson offered his horse and buggy, and then others, too, came forward. It was a familiar sight to see two nuns go from home to home and shop to shop, even in outlying towns, to solicit funds for the new hospital in Phoenix. The response was good, and in January, 1895, the Sisters rented a six-room brick cottage on Fourth and Polk Streets. Sister M. Berchmans McCormick and Sister M. Dominic Lyons came from Silver City. The latter, having the experience of a similar work at St. Joseph's Sanatorium, was placed in charge of the tiny institution. With generous help from the school Sisters, the six two-bed rooms were made ready for patients. The twelve-bed hospital was filled immediately, and other patients provided for on a screened-in porch. Everyone seemed caught in a fever of helpfulness. Department stores contributed dry goods as well as cash; the bakery refused to accept payment for breads and cakes. The man in the clothing store was always willing to lend his horse and buggy, and served as an unpaid coachman when anyone needed to go anywhere. True, the little hospital was operated by the Catholic Sisters, but it was obvious from the first that the whole town claimed it; at least, most of them.

The hospital had been in operation two months when the landlord decided it was devaluating his property, and he decided to take the legal procedure to evict them. It became evident to the Sisters that they must secure the hospital property in their name. This took money, and the unofficial chief fund raiser was a devout Presbyterian. In record time the property was purchased, and soon after, two adjoining lots were donated by a fine old Catholic gentleman, General Clark Churchill. Each step of the way seemed to be blessed by God; for not long after, Mother M. Paul was able to buy two more lots from the same gentleman at a very moderate price.

On the Feast of St. Joseph, March 19, 1895, a stake was driven into the ground to mark the site of the new St. Joseph's. By fall, a two-story brick structure for twenty-four beds was completed. After the hospital opened its doors, many tubercular sufferers, especially young men, came to the Sisters to die or in some cases to prevent death by starvation. Some came prepared to meet expenses, others were without a penny, although frequently they "hoped to get money from home." Many a soul was saved by coming to the hospital, but without an appropriation of some sort, the Sisters could not keep this up. The city and county had no provision for sick poor from other places. They thought the towns and cities from which these persons came should defray the expenses. When the people of Albuquerque, however, asked the Sisters to open a hospital there, the physicians of Phoenix made a public statement on the wonderful work and charity of the Sisters, and how they would be obliged to go to some other town where they could at least meet expenses. This opened the eyes of the public; a committee of businessmen pledged to give as much as they could at the time and a stated sum for three years. In the meantime, the city and county would give the Sisters a contract for the care of the indigent sick.

St. Joseph's Hospital, with its twenty-four beds in 1896, did great good and was a blessing for all concerned. This same year the Franciscan Fathers took charge of St. Mary's parish. Their coming was a distinct advantage to St. Joseph's where so many patients were admitted in a dying condition. Father Casimir, O.F.M., spent every available moment of his time at the hospital and was loved by Catholic and non-Catholic alike. Every night before retiring Father Casimir opened his window to bless the Sisters and the hospital.

Measured by the standard of the hospitals of today, St. Joseph's would fail accreditation. But it met a specific need and grew at a pace with medical science. Of course, it was not air-conditioned and electric fans were still a luxury. Doctors came to the hospital in buggies. The Sisters appointed to the work there knew little about caring for the sick according to present-day standards, but they worked faithfully, followed the orders and directions of the doctors, who were wonderfully kind and helpful. It must be remembered, too, that medical science was in its infancy. In all of the United States there were probably no more than a few hundred hospitals. Surgical technique did not include caps, masks, gowns, or gloves. Surgeons merely rolled up their sleeves, washed their hands, donned a rubber apron and began the operation while a nurse swatted the flies. Foundations were being established for diagnosis and exploration of disease processes. Contagion was being studied. Louis Pasteur, Robert Koch, and and Joseph

Lister had made news with the germ theory in the field of bacteriology. Roentgen had learned something about what he called X-rays. The organism that caused tuberculosis had been isolated, and the clinical thermometer had been invented, but the familiar techniques of modern surgery and hospital procedure were just being developed, and the great field of communicable disease was still a "no-man's land." Many who survived accidents and injuries in the western frontier died of pneumonia, typhoid, or some communicable disease. Infection was very commonly fatal. The pioneer Sister in Phoenix often confronted tremendous health problems with little more than their energy and faith.

Phoenix was now a growing town, and many of the medical profession who had come in quest of health for themselves or some member of their family decided to remain and establish a practice. There was a real need for a general hospital, and it was soon evident that the Sisters could not confine themselves to a tubercular sanatorium. In 1897 a group of doctors decided to establish a general hospital. It was when St. Joseph's best men, Doctors Duffield, Scott, Craig, Martin, and Stroud, began sending their medical patients there that the Sisters had cause for alarm. The Sisters sought the solution of their problem in prayer. In less than a year the doctors closed their hospital and one of them said, "Any group can open a hospital but only the Catholic Sisters can manage one." By this time it was evident that the Sisters must make provision for surgical cases.

In 1898 Miss Ida Clouse, a well-trained nurse, was added to the staff to take charge of the surgery department. The Phoenix annalist of this period describes her procedure:

> She prepared the patient's room for the operation by covering the walls with sheets wrung in a carbolic acid solution. She made the dressings, sheets, etc., and sterilized them in a fish kettle. The water and the instruments were boiled on a wood stove. A solid table was moved into the room for the patient. Preparations completed, the surgeons rolled up their sleeves, washed their hands, donned aprons and began the operation.

> Besides attending during the operation, Miss Clouse took charge of the surgical treatment of the patients.

Considering the critical condition of the surgical cases because of late diagnosis etc., the operations were very successful.

Hospital expansion was again an urgent matter in 1900, and again the people of Phoenix responded generously to the Sisters' plea for funds. Construction was soon underway, and an addition to the hospital was completed in 1901. The annex provided for additional private rooms, a ward for surgical cases, an operating room, and a scrub room, all on the second floor. On the first floor were diet kitchens, utility rooms, and storage space. This annex also provided for a small chapel with its carved altar, the work of a Franciscan Brother. The following year, a contract with the Santa Fe Railroad brought more surgical and accident cases.

In 1902 Sister M. Peter McTernan was delegated by the Superior to collect funds for a new wing with twenty-four beds. She and her companion visited a number of Arizona towns—Tempe, Mesa, Superior, Miami, Globe, Stafford, Solomonville, Duncan, Clifton, Florence, and Benson. Then they penetrated into New Mexico, visiting Lordsburg and Deming and returning to the Academy of Our Lady of Lourdes in Silver City.

The hospital, which was crowded for nine months of the year, was usually the reverse during the summer months when the doctors and their clients left Phoenix for cooler climates. This was also an opportunity for the Sisters to go to Silver City or Prescott for retreat and vacation. In the fall of 1902 the Sisters were honored by a visit from Doctor J.B. Murphy of Chicago. Thereafter, each winter while in Phoenix as the guest of Doctor R.W. Craig, the famous surgeon never failed to make a visit to the Sisters' hospital.

Again, in 1903, Sister M. Peter took another collecting trip, visiting Tombstone and Bisbee, where she and her companion were generously treated by the miners. She and her companion then doggedly trekked to Douglas where they went through the smelters, but the Sisters felt well repaid for their climb in the heat. In Old Mexico, they visited Del Rio and Cananea, where they met old friends and were treated most hospitably. Mother M. Paul once cautioned Sister M. Peter about asking people who had already been very generous. Shortly after, Sister met Mr. Charles Korrick, of the New York Store in Phoenix. He had always been most liberal in helping the Sisters. When asked about her work and what she needed, Sister said naively, "Mr. Korrick, Mother M. Paul said I shouldn't ask for any more help, but oh, Mr. Korrick, if you only knew how badly we need sheets and pillowcases!" Needless to say, the sheets and pillowcases, in good supply, were promptly delivered to the hospital.

Although the hospital became more and more a surgical institution, the Sisters did not cease to provide for the tubercular patients, and Phoenix was still a mecca for such victims. They were cared for in the original hospital wing, which had been dubbed "Hogan's Alley" by one of the hands about the hospital. The name stuck, and it was not unusual to have a doctor phone for a room "in Hogan's Alley," for a dying T.B. patient. So many souls took flight for Paradise from here that it might have been called "Gate of Heaven."

Besides much-needed care, a great deal of spiritual good was accomplished in this wing. One day, when the Sisters were returning by cab to the hospital, they were stopped by a stranger who sought aid for a sick man in a nearby rooming house. The concerned man took a seat by the driver and all drove to the place. The very sick man was helped into the cab and brought to the hospital where he was assigned a room in Hogan's Alley. The next day, the patient, a non-Catholic, grew worse and Sister M. Magdalen Noonan said the prayers for the dying. The patient was in such good dispositions that she called the priest and within the space of a few hours this happy soul had received Baptism, the Holy Eucharist and the Last Anointing—a happy prelude to a joyous welcome in his eternal home.

In 1907 Dr. R. W. Craig, a capable and sincere adviser to the Sisters, told Mother M. Paul that the hospital should have another operating room. Accordingly, this surgery and an anasthesia room were included in the new wing of twelve rooms, for the construction of which the doctor loaned the sum of three thousand dollars without interest.

In 1908, still trying to keep abreast with the growth of Phoenix, the hospital added another wing, which increased the capacity of St. Joseph's to sixty beds. Included in this addition was a large chapel, which extended across the entire building on the east end; and sixteen rooms with modern bathrooms, all at a building cost of ten thousand dollars.

Although the Sisters had secured the services of well-trained nurses to supervise and direct the several departments, it became more evident with each passing year that the Sisters themselves should be trained if they were to control and operate the hospital. Dr. J.B. Murphy of Chicago had secured the services of Miss Grace O'Brien, R.N., of Mercy Hospital, Chicago, as surgical supervisor. Mother M. Paul consulted Miss O'Brien about opening a training school for nurses. She also received every encouragement from the doctors. Early in 1910, St. Joseph's School of Nursing was opened, with Miss O'Brien combining the duties of surgical nurse and superintendent of nurses. Miss Ann Sullivan of Mercy Hospital, Chicago, was her assistant. From Mr. Kerr, the Sisters purchased a frame building on the corner of Fifth and Polk Streets to serve as the nurses' quarters. When the school opened in the fall of 1910, Sister M. Gertrude Cruice, Sister M. Ignatius Briody, Sister M. Aloysius Phelan, Sister M. Raphael Gavigan, and Sister M. Patrick Walshe enrolled in the first class.[4]

About this time plans were formed to build an annex on the corner of Fourth and Taylor Streets, to accommodate the patients who were coming to Phoenix every winter in increasing numbers. With the generous help of the doctors and other interested benefactors, a three-story annex containing twenty-four private rooms was completed in 1911. The building cost of the annex was $24,000, of which seven thousand was donated by Mr. D.J. O'Carroll, for a long time the greatest of St. Joseph's benefactors.[5]

On May 4, 1913, Sister M. Cecilia Lujan was called to her heavenly home. After a Solemn Requiem Mass at St. Mary's, she was buried in St. Francis Cemetery, the first Sister of Mercy to be buried in Phoenix. Sister M. Cecilia (Thomasina Lujan) belonged to a prominent Mexican family of Los Alamos, New Mexico. She had entered the community almost two years after the Sisters were established in Mesilla. The talents of this native daughter were a boon to the community when it was starting its work among a foreign people in a missionary country. Sister taught the other Sisters the Spanish language and was instrumental in cementing friendly relations between the Sisters and the people of Mesilla. For many years Sister M. Cecilia taught in Mesilla, later in Silver City, where she also directed the choir, and in Nogales after St. Joseph's Hospital was opened there in 1906.

In 1912 Arizona and New Mexico finally received full

membership in the United States. This promoted a growth in population and a development of industry in both states.

In 1913, Mother M. Paul received word of the proposed division of the diocese of Tucson, which would place the New Mexico convents in the diocese of El Paso. Mother held several conferences during which the future of the community was discussed from every angle. The amalgamation movement of the Sisters of Mercy in the United States was being advanced at that time. Mother M. Paul having obtained the opinions of the Sisters of Mercy of Omaha, Nebraska, Denver, Colorado, Los Angeles and San Diego, went in August to San Francisco to interview Mother M. Euphrasia. At St. Mary's Hospital, Mother M. Paul conferred with Mother M. Pius, and the next day she went to Fruitvale to interview Mother M. Euphrasia, who did not feel ready for such a move. It is to be remembered that the fire of 1906 had swept away the entire Mercy compound on Rincon Hill and that these Sisters were faced with rebuilding a large hospital, as well as providing a new Home for the Aged. Only two years before, in 1911, they had opened the main section of St. Mary's Hospital on Hayes and Stanyan, San Francisco, and in 1912 had completed the Home and novitiate in Fruitvale.

Finally it was decided that as Mother M. Paul's community did not have enough members to stand a division of forces, the Sisters would in due time withdraw from New Mexico and await amalgamation.[6]

Early in 1914, the nurses' home in Phoenix, a two-story fireproof building, was completed and occupied. It provided accommodations for thirty-five nurses, as well as class and recreation rooms. The nurses' home was built entirely by funds from St. Joseph's Sanatorium, Silver City, which sent to Phoenix one thousand dollars a month for a year, and when the building was finished, it was free of debt.[7]

At the elections held in the spring of 1914, Mother M. Stanislaus White became Reverend Mother and Mother M. Paul, Mother Assistant.

Not only did the hospital expand but its reputation for growth in medical services increased from year to year. There was wholehearted cooperation between the medical staff and the Sisters, who kept informed about the ever-changing methods in the field of medicine.

It was in the summer of 1914 that Bishop Granjon asked the

Sisters in the three houses in New Mexico to declare their intention, by vote, to determine whether they wished to be included in the diocese of El Paso or to remain in the diocese of Tucson. When the majority favored remaining under his jurisdiction, he immediately advised the removal of the novitiate from Silver City, New Mexico, to Arizona.[8] Until the convent and chapel at Mercy Hospital, Prescott, were ready, the novices were sent to Phoenix. The hospital adobe cottage that had been vacated when the nurses moved into their new home, now served as a temporary novitiate. In October, 1914, the Mistress of Novices, Sister M. Joseph Anderson, and the novices were welcomed at Phoenix. These were Sister M. Canice Dunne, Sister M. Dominic Fortesque, Sister M. Antonio Heerey, and Sister M. Berchmans McDonnell.

The temporary novitiate in Phoenix lasted only six months. In April, 1915, it was transferred to Prescott up on the completion of the new building. On July 5, 1915, Prescott received its first postulant, Miss Agnes Tamborini, a graduate nurse from Phoenix. She is the only Sister of the Institute received and professed at Prescott, Arizona. This may seem a startling fact unless it is born in mind that the amalgamation of the Arizona Sisters of Mercy with the Sisters of Los Angeles and San Diego, in 1921, necessitated another transfer of the novitiate to San Diego.

On September 15, 1915, Bishop H. Granjon dedicated the new convent and chapel at Mercy Hospital, Prescott.

From time to time Phoenix enjoyed a boom that affected the hospital. In 1915 long staple cotton was introduced by Mr. D.B. Heard, a local businessman, and it was successfully grown in the Salt River Valley. Thousands of acres of desert land were reclaimed and turned into cotton fields. European nations at war bought up the entire crop. Soon more people came to the valley and the hospital facilities were taxed to the limit. Steps were taken to organize a maternity unit in the hospital in 1916, and a new wing was built in 1917.

By the end of the first week in April, 1917, Congress had voted to declare war on Germany.[9] A number of our doctors and nurses, members of the National Guard and the Red Cross, were notified to report for duty.

In the community election of May, 1917, Reverend Mother M. Stanislaus and her council were returned to office for another three years.

Many improvements were made during the summer and St. Joseph's was ready for a record winter season when, on October 5, 1917, the fire demon struck. It was mid-afternoon when the fire was detected; Sisters and nurses were at work in the surgery, and on the floors afternoon snacks were being distributed at 3:00 p.m. Sisters in the operating rooms had had a very strenous morning and were cleaning up for a repetition of the like on the morrow. They did comment on the odor of burnt rubber, but the smell of ether somewhat destroyed the odor and so they went on with their work. The heat was almost unbearable. This, however, was not unsual in Phoenix in pre-air-conditioned days. Suddenly they noticed a commotion in the halls and discovered well organized companies of high school boys carrying the patients from their rooms in orderly fashion. The Sisters, recognizing a patient who had been operated on a few hours previously, asked the meaning of it all. The boys responded, "The building is on fire and we're helping." They had been dismissed from school were playing on a campus close by when they saw the hospital roof in flames. It was they who organized themselves into a fire brigade and began the rescue. Of course, when they arrived at the scene they were directed in transporting the patients. They were splendid, as if trained for hospital work. So carefully and tenderly did they carry out the patients that no one suffered from the effects of removal, although some had been operated on that very day. Everyone was kind; the doctors rushed from their offices to help in every way possible; offers of housing for patients and Sisters came from various quarters. The rector of the Episcopal cathedral offered his church for the use of the patients; but with the annex building, the nurses' home, and the use of the sanatorium close by, offered by the owner, Dr. Gillette, the patients were housed and cared for by the Sisters of Mercy almsot as well as they had been in the hospital building. From many friends came offerings of food and funds to meet immediate demands. While the hospital was still a smoldering ruins the surgical staff was at work in the annex, as though nothing had happened.[10]

The day after the fire a committee of physicians and businessmen of the town was formed to discuss ways and means of building the new St. Joseph's. Mr. D.J. O'Carroll, who had been a great benefactor of the hospital from its beginnings, came forward with an offer to put up a sum equal to that of anyone else, and began by offering $5000. No person accepted his challenge so he added $2000 more to the sum. Probably everyone gave what he could afford.

The building had been insured. The insurance carried was $35,000; of this only $15,000 was allowed, as the company thought the salvaging, etc. was equal to the balance. This sum, with that obtained from the fundraising campaign, made it possible to renew and rebuild the hospital. Ninety days after the fire, the work was well under way. The damaged part was rebuilt and improved so that the patients were soon removed from the Sanatorium.[11]

By the spring of 1918 the new building was completed, just in time to receive hundreds of patients, victims of the "flu" epidemic, which was both general and frightful. Now the people of Phoenix saw how they were rewarded for their generosity to the hospital after the fire. Almost every family in town had one or more victims. The city officials reserved a wing for their patients but very little distinction could be made, as the patients came in by the dozens and had to be placed wherever there was room, regardless of rank or social standing. Whole families came in at the same time, and of these, sometimes two lived out of six or seven. It was heart-rending, but all had to bow to the scourge. In some wards could be found a banker or merchant beside a tramp or a ne'er-do-well, the former glad to be there. Afflictions of this sort make all men equal.

At this juncture, a call came from the Bishop for Sisters to go to Globe, a mining town where the sourge seemed to be almost universal, and where the people were dying without care of any kind as the hospitals were taxed to the limit. The officials of the mines had called for help to some of the nearby towns, but none could be spared. At this crisis the Bishop of Tucson was appealed to, as it was reported that most of the victims were Catholics. The Bishop knew well that everywhere people were fighting for their lives and so he only told Mother M. Stanislaus of the appeal made to him, knowing well that if help were to be had, she would give it. Two Sisters from Nogales and two Sisters from the hospital in Phoenix were sent to Globe. They went to work immediately, and soon conditions improved. The number of deaths was great, and spiritual needs badly neglected, as there was but one priest and he could not see more than a fifth of the victims. Besides ministering to their physical needs, the Sisters had the satisfaction of sending many poor souls, prepared as well as circumstances permitted, to meet their Creator, if not with the blessing of the Last Sacraments, at least with sentiments of contrition and resignation. They remained in Globe for over a month or until the epidemic had abated.

To the reverend chaplain Father Paul Meyers, at St Joseph's in Phoenix, the community owes a deep debt of gratitude for his self-sacrificing attention to the afflicted during the epidemic. He made the rounds of the hospital during the day and often through the night, ministering to all who called upon him. He was always to be found where the most pitiable cases were, and served them when he saw that they needed any service, regardless of race, religion, or rank, except only that he seemed to have special regard for the most afflicted and hopeless cases. As many as twelve victims a day were carried out in the coffin, but the mortality would have been greater were it not for the care bestowed on them. Among the Sisters, not a single death occurred, despite the heavy load of flu cases that taxed the hospital to the limit.

When the scourge abated and only a few cases remained, the work of renewing and refurbishing began, as the wear and tear on the hospital during the epidemic was equal to, if not greater than, the total use of the hospital for years.

In 1920 Mother M. Paul returned to office as Mother Superior. Surgeons were clamoring for space in the surgical department; the hospital, which had just come through the flu siege, sorely needed renovation; and the present chapel, only a room, was inadequate to accommodate the Sisters, nurses and patients who might wish to attend Sunday Mass. Building plans were initiated. After some delays and disappointments, the new building was well underway by the fall of 1921. Mother M. Paul was beginning to see some of her great dreams realized when at the end of 1921 it became evident that God had other plans for her.

Prescott—1893[1][2]

Early in 1893 the Reverend Father Alfred Quetu, brother of Sister M. Xavier and pastor of Prescott, Arizona, asked for two or three Sisters for his little cottage hospital on Marina Street in Prescott, which the Sisters of St. Joseph had been taking care of for him while their schools were very poorly attended. Now that the schools were filling up again, the Sisters were obliged to give up the hospital. Once again the Sisters of Mercy were asked to take up the work left by the Sisters of St. Joseph.

Mother M. Paul felt unable to comply with the request, but under ecclesiastical pressure, an appeal to her missionary spirit and the argument that the summer climate in Prescott would be a boon to the Sisters in Phoenix, she finally agreed "to lend" some Sisters for a period of three years. Immediately after the annual retreat in Silver City, Mother M. Paul, Sister M. Gertrude Keefe, who was to be in charge, and two other Sisters left for Arizona, making the two-day trip from Phoenix to Prescott by stagecoach. On September 8, 1893, the Sisters, popularly known as Mother Paul's Sisters, took over the management of the hospital under Father Quetu.

The cottage hospital consisted of about six rooms, one of them a dining room for the pastor and other visiting priests. The Sisters had a contract with some of the mines in and around Prescott for the care of their injured men. For many months there might not be a single one, or very few, and then some accident at the mine would occur and the Sisters would be crowded out trying to give service to the unfortunate men.

It was a condition such as this, after a cave-in at the Polard mine caused every available space to be requisitioned for the patients' care, that first prompted plans for a proper hospital owned by the Sisters. In fact, Prescott had begun to see the value of the hospital and plans had started toward establishing a permanent institution. Mr. F.M. Murphy, head of the Santa Fe Railroad in Arizona, and a local businessman, donated five lots in the Fluery addition for the hospital. Without consulting the Sisters, a community hospital owned by Mercy Hospital Corporation, with Reverend A. Quetu, as president, and R.E. Morrison, the attorney, as secretary, was organized. However, when the original contract of the Sisters of Mercy was ended, Mother prepared to withdraw her Sisters. Only then did the people of Prescott realize that the Sisters of Mercy were not permanent fixtures. Under no circumstances (not even for a raise of Sisters' salaries to thirty dollars a month) would Mother Paul have anything to do with the proposed Mercy Community Hospital.

It was through the intervention of the future Bishop of Tucson, the Most Reverend P. Bourgade, a personal friend and former pastor in Silver City, that Mother Paul agreed to open a privately owned hospital in Prescott. The Sisters acquired the

260

five donated lots. The property, studded with large pine trees, was ideally located on Grove Avenue on the outskirts of town. The wide view of pine-covered granite mountains in the distance made a background of picturesque beauty. The plans already drawn for a two-story brick building with basement were used. Having no security in the Arizona Territory, the Sisters found it difficult to secure a loan of $10,000. This amount, at eight percent interest, was arranged for in France by Reverend Henry Granjon, later the second Bishop of Tucson.[13] Subsequently this loan was repaid by another, secured in New Mexico at a much lower rate of interest.

Mercy Hospital, Prescott—1897-1940

Building started in the fall of 1896. Local granite was used in the foundation. The severity of the winter of 1896-97 held up construction for almost six months. Nevertheless, the new Mercy Hospital was opened on March 19, 1897, almost four years after the arrival of the Sisters in Prescott. Accommodations for twenty-four patients included both wards and private rooms. For the ambulatory men patients, provision was made in the basement for smoking, recreation and dining rooms.

Insufficient water was a real problem for the new hospital. After unsuccessfully drilling for water on the hospital grounds, they were about to abandon the effort, when Sister M. Gertrude, fortified by earnest prayer, ordered the work resumed. Her faith was rewarded when, only a few feet deeper, they struck water. This supply, in addition to the city water, was sufficient for all hospital purposes.

The old hospital on Marina Street was moved to the new location, where it was used as the Sisters' convent. This gave ample room for the Phoenix Sisters who helped with the hospital work during the summer months. Conveniently, the dull season in Phoenix was the busy season in Prescott. As the Arizona Sisters (the communities in Phoenix and Prescott were so-called) were three days' journey from Silver City, an annual retreat was scheduled for them in Prescott. Here, as in New Mexico, they were privileged to have as directors those masters of the spiritual life, the old Italian Jesuit Fathers from El Paso, Texas.

In the summer of 1898, Sister M. Alphonsus Cox became Superior of the hospital at Prescott, replacing Sister M.

Gertrude Keefe who was transferred to Mesilla, New Mexico. News of the unexpected death of Sister M. Gertrude Keefe, on October 17, 1898, came as a shock not only to the Prescott community but to all of Prescott, where she was beloved by all who had the privilege of knowing her. On her way from Silver City to Mesilla, Sister became ill on the train and stopped off at El Paso, where the Sisters had taught school until 1892. Here Sister died of peritonitis from a ruptured appendix. Her remains were taken to Mesilla for burial, where she rests beside the grave of Mother M. Bernard Connor, victim of smallpox in 1883.[14] The death of this gifted but humble Sister of Mercy left a gap in the ranks which was difficult to fill.

A short time after the hospital was built, Mr. F.M. Murphy, President of the Santa Fe Railroad in Arizona, secured for the Sisters the Santa Fe Railroad contract. Through his influence, Mercy Hospital was made headquarters for all accident cases on the Ashfork-Phoenix line, a contract renewed annually for the next twenty-one years. Success for the hospital now seemed assured, and in 1903 a second building was added on the adjoining lots, which had been wisely acquired for possible expansion and updating.[15]

The railroad opened the resources of Yavapai County. Among those interested in mining and cattle was Thomas Barlow-Massicks, a member of a well-to-do English family. In developing the gold mines at Lynx Creek, he acquired a boom site and called it Massicks. Here his beautiful home became the center of the smart set in and around Prescott. An accidental gun wound brought him to the hospital. Lung complications developed. After lingering a year, and in spite of all that money and medical science could do, he died. His sister, Miss Maude Barlowe-Massicks, a trained nurse, had come from England to care for him. A devout member of the High Church of England, she grieved because of her brother's rebellious state of mind, but was consoled when Dr. McNally assured her that his last words had been a prayer and that Father Quetu had given him conditional absolution.

Miss Massicks became interested in the hospital and offered to give the Sisters a complete course in nursing, which offer was readily accepted. Once, however, her horsemanship almost brought them to grief. Before leaving for Prescott, Father Quetu had given instructions that his pair of spirited horses should be driven by Miss Massicks only. As a compliment to the Phoenix

Sisters, she planned to use these horses for a picnic to Granite Dells. In passing the depot, a gust of wind blew a waste basket containing papers in front of the horses. The frightened animals got out of control. Only prompt help from the railroad employees saved the Sisters from the fate of their crushed picnic baskets.

Later Miss Massicks was admitted into the Roman Catholic Church. She returned to England and in spite of family opposition persevered in her choice. Moved by the inspiration to enter a religious order, she consulted a priest who, knowing something of her father's anti-Catholic bias, advised her to enter "where she saw the light of faith." She returned to Silver City and entered the novitiate. When, however, she discovered that her vocation was to the contemplative life, she was transferred to a convent in St. Louis. Here she completed an earnest novitiate but became seriously ill and was privileged to pronounce her vows shortly before her very edifying death.

Fortunate, indeed, were the Sisters in the appointment of Dr. J.B. McNally as division chief surgeon of the Santa Fe Railroad. Dr. McNally was born in Ireland. On receiving his medical degree, his uncle, Father McNally, of Oakland, California, asked Mother Paul to secure a place for "Johnny" on the Santa Fe medical staff. An instant favorite, Dr. J.B. McNally in time was made chief surgeon. In devotion to the poor he was a modern St. Vincent de Paul. Although the railroad men had their choice of consultation with doctors who had offices in the same building, they preferred to wait, if necessary, for "Mac," as they affectionately called him. Dr. J.B. McNally was intensely Catholic and as intensely Irish; and his inimitable style at the bedsides of his patients often meant more to them than medicine.

In the rush of hospital duties, other works were not neglected. Regular visitation to the County Hospital, to past patients and to homes saddened by death were firmly established. At the "Poor Farm" the Sisters were instrumental in doing much good spiritually. One whose only comfort was the Sisters' weekly visit was Jimmy Geoghan, an Irishman who had been blinded in a mine accident. He keenly felt his affliction and a lack of sympathy at the Poor Farm. Finally, unable to stand it longer, he begged the Sisters to take him back to the hospital with them. Without further to-do, Jimmy was in the hospital surrey and on his way to a new home. Here he spent a holy and retired life for the next quarter of a century.

In the summer of 1912, Sister M. Antonia Kearney, a Sister in Prescott, went to join the community in heaven. Sister had come from Silver City to Phoenix in ill health. When the weather got hot she came to Prescott to rest until retreat. Her condition gave concern to the sisters and they called Father C.A. Buckley, S.J., of San Francisco, who was then giving a retreat at St. Joseph's Academy. Complying with her request, Father administered the Holy Viaticum and Extreme Unction. Two days later she died.

She was the young lady teaching in Moate, Ireland, who had offered herself to go with Mother Josephine Brennan to East St. Louis when recruits were being sought for the American mission. It was she for whom Mother Josephine had waited until she received the habit in Cynthiana, Kentucky, before they answered another call to go to Mesilla, New Mexico, in 1880. Her life in religion paralleled the story of the growth of the Institute in the Southwest. Most of her days were spent in the classroom, for which she had received her credentials before leaving Ireland. An unselfish teacher, she was much loved for her zeal for the welfare of her pupils and for the poor in general.

About this time the hospital, which still enjoyed the benefits of the railroad contract, received a very favorable commendation from the officials for efficiency in handling a major accident at Kirkland, about thirty miles from Prescott, where a passenger train and a "canteloupe special" had collided. Besides rushing doctors and nurses to the scene, the hospital had a staff at the track near the hospital where the injured were taken. The local papers, as well as the railroad company, gave unstinted praise to Mercy Hospital, Prescott.

In the fall of 1914, work was begun on a new chapel and convent building, separate from the hospital but connected to its second floor by an arcade. This structure would provide for the transfer of the novitiate[16] as well as for the need for expanded facilities. In June, Mother Stanislaus came from Silver City to preside over the chapter of the novices who, on August 26, 1915, would make their profession, the first in Prescott.

About this time, Prescott felt the impact of the European War. All the French priests were called to the colors in France, and Reverend Father Pousell had to go. For a while Prescott was without a priest. The Sisters were glad that the new chapel was large enough to accommodate most of the parishioners, and Reverend Father Nicholas, O.F.M., was made chaplain pro tem.

The Prescott house became very important in April, 1917, when the election for Major Superior was held in the new chapel, although there was no change in the administration. Rev. Mother M. Stanislaus White, Superior, Mother M. Paul, Assistant, and Mother M. Vincent, Bursar, were re-elected.

In June, 1917, the Visitation Suite was finished. It was a red brick bungalow providing bedrooms, reception and dining rooms, as well as a kitchenette. This little unit filled a long-felt need for quiet quarters for guests and priests in retreat. Rev. Father Wilx, S.J., who spent four weeks in Prescott as director of two retreats and as chaplain during Father Gerard's vacation, was the first guest in the visitors' suite.

About this time, Dr. Morrison, chief surgeon of the Santa Fe Railroad, notified the hospital that after a given date all railroad patients were to be transferred to Los Angeles, a ruling which would cut off the chief source of Mercy Hospital's revenue. Mr. Drake and Mr. Wm. B. Storey, local railroad officials, and other friends, advised the Sisters to protest the ruling. Sister M. Benedict, Superior of Mercy Hospital, made inquiries and found the railroad men most willing to sign the petition. Mr. Ed Lee and Mr. Ruben Johnson canvassed the line from Ashfork to Phoenix. When Mr. Storey saw that nine-tenths of the employees had signed in protest, he exclaimed, "Delighted! Wonderful!" Sister then remarked, "We notice that one prominent name is missing." "Whose?" he eagerly asked. With a smile she replied, "Mr. Storey's." He signed, as did the others in his office. With the New Year came the answer to their prayers. The contract was given to Mercy Hospital, Prescott, for another three years.

Before the close of summer, 1918, word was received that the chapter votes by the two communities in southern California, Los Angeles and San Diego, were overwhelmingly in favor of amalgamation. The Arizona Sisters took this as a favorable omen and looked forward to union with the California Sisters.

In the fall of 1918, influenza came to Prescott in all its fury. In every available space, in rooms, corridors and on porches, beds and cots were placed. Because of the shortage of nurses, the Sisters, as long as they were physically able, remained on duty day and night. When the epidemic continued with its deadly work, the Sisters found consolation in the number of death-bed conversions and reconciliations, some after a lapse of a half-century and longer. Other recovered and, after finding themselves for the first time acquainted with the Catholic faith, as well as observing the dedication of the Sisters, expressed appreciation for what this had meant to them.

When November came, and with it the news of the armistice, Prescott, like every other town, turned from sorrow to joy. Father Gerard held a special *Te Deum* service for his beloved France. From every heart arose a cry of gratitude to God that peace had come to a war-torn world.

Having completed the second term as Major Superior, Mother M. Stanislaus was made Mother Assistant in April, 1920, while Mother M. Paul once more assumed the guidance of the community. Almost immediately she moved to re-open the question of amalgamation with the Sisters in California.

With the New Year of 1921 came the notification that the Santa Fe contract would not be renewed. As a concession, however, the Santa Fe Railroad employees were given the privilege of choosing between Prescott and Los Angeles. The majority were faithful to the Sisters.

Nogales, St. Joseph's Hospital—1906-1922[17]

After the turn of the century, Reverend Louis Duval, pastor of Nogales, pleaded with Mother M. Paul to open either a school or a hospital in that border town, where many of the Mexican refugees were Catholics. Mother M. Paul was most sympathetic with the cause but unable to undertake either work at the time.

In 1905 the Arizona Sanitorium, an institution built and operated by a group of doctors, had failed, and the property was for sale. Father Duval, seeing an opportunity to forward his project, notified Mother M. Paul. With the encouragement of Bishop Granjon of Tucson, she visited the place and with some reluctance purchased the building for a hospital.

In April, 1906, Mother M. Paul, Sister M. Alphonsus Cox, Sister M. Cecilia Lujan, and Sister M. Gertrude Cruice arrived in Nogales to put the building in order. It was a twenty-room one-story brick structure built to form three sides of a square. Originally it was designed for the treatment of tuberculosis; hence all the rooms opened onto a covered porch and faced one another across an open patio, an arrangement which gave an all-day maximum sun exposure. But much that was most necessary to such an institution had not been provided. Any woman, to say nothing of a nurse, would not have needed to consult an architect to detect what was wrong. There was neither running water nor any kind of sewage outlet. It is no wonder that the doctors had failed in their venture. When the Sisters took over, the very courage and energy with which they began to convert the place into a hospital won the cooperation of the people, who gladly contributed toward the necessary alterations. Besides the new construction for surgery, kitchen, dining and record rooms, provision was made for gas, water and electricity; even plumbing for sewerage was to be installed. The front section of the building was selected for offices, chapel and quarters for the Sisters, which left the other two wings for hospital use.

Now called St. Joseph's Hospital, the infant institution found a real benefactor in its first surgical patient, Mr. Phil Harrold, a local banker who was stricken with acute appendicitis. He got along very well and served as a good advertisement. Through his influence, too, the hospital got a very desirable contract with the Southern Pacific Railroad, which was then extending a line from Nogales to Guymas, Mexico. Except for an occasional official, all the railroad patients were Yaqui Indians employed in the construction work. It was customary for the Southern Pacific to furnish nurses to Mexican hospitals handling their patients, which custom was extended to St. Joseph's, where for several years the S.P. paid the salary of the surgical nurses.

After the first few years in Nogales, the Sisters found that the history of the hospital reflected the history of Mexico, as conditions in that unfortunate country were continually felt north of the border. The hospital itself was only a block from the international line, and the Sisters had to adapt themselves to the customs of a border town. At almost any hour of the day or night there were bugle calls, military commands or even music, which floated across the border from the little town of Nogales, in Sonora, the military headquarters of one of the revolutionary parties then disturbing Mexico.

Business on both sides of the line was conducted in Spanish. All the doctors spoke the language fluently, and so there was no choice for the Sisters but to study Spanish, too. Fortunately, Sister M. Cecilia Lujan spoke the language and she proved an exceptionally good teacher.

The inconvenient arrangement of the building called for much extra walking, but this, too, the Sisters gladly accepted in compensation for a very fruitful apostolate in the healing of souls as well as bodies. Many of the patients were Catholics in name only when they entered the hospital, yet before they left, they had often learned the principal mysteries of religion. The Indians were quite docile and anxious to hear more about their faith.

For years, until diplomatic relations between the United States and Mexico became strained, the Sisters found the church in Mexico more convenient for daily Mass than the Sacred Heart Church on the American side. Although the hours for Holy Mass was often irregular, the fifteen-minute bell gave the Sisters ample time to reach the church in Mexico.

The Sisters did not limit their apostolate to the hospital in Nogales. As soon as it could be arranged, Sister M. Cecilia Lujan took a census by going from house to house. The catechism classes were scheduled at the hospital, and a Sunday school was provided at Sacred Heart Church. This successful missionary effort was challenged by an anti-Catholic group, which had a dilapidated church near the hospital renovated and put in charge a Mexican mission preacher to draw the Mexican pupils. Although this was long before the current guitar strumming popularity, this type of music proved an effective bait. He succeeded in turning many children from the Sisters by the Spanish hymn singing. If the Sisters had so wished, they also could have taken advantage of the lessons and could even have followed the Methodist services from the convent porch.

Early in 1908 the Superior, Sister M. Alphonsus Cox, became so ill with typhoid fever that Father Duval began to make plans for the first funeral of a Sister of Mercy in Nogales. Members of the church choir met at the Brickwood home, across the street from the hospital, to practice the Requiem Mass. When the strains of the *"Dies Irae"* were wafted to her room, the sick Sister suspected they were practicing for her funeral. She recovered, however, and when able to travel was taken to Silver City to recuperate.

From the beginning, the Sisters had to contend with anti-Catholic and Masonic influences. From time to time individuals who were influential with the railroad or in local government diverted patients to the Mexican hospital across the border, or to private homes, in an effort to thwart the work at St. Joseph's.

When Mexican politics became more disturbed, barbed wire was strung along the international border, on both sides of which immigration officers sat to give their nod of approval to tourists or shoppers crossing the line. One day two of the Sisters were stopped by a Mexican officer who questioned them about a package good Sister M. Veronica was carrying very carefully. Sister tried to explain that it was "only a gift from their baker." The officer was skeptical and proceeded to do his duty. She had to hand it over. When he discovered it contained six fluffy cream puffs he was covered with embarrassment and returned them in a hurry. During the revolutionary era that followed, conditions in Mexico became so unsettled that further construction of the railroad from Nogales to Guymas, Mexico, became inpossible, and the work was discontinued. The number of Mexican families seeking refuge in the United States made Nogales a boom town, and the hospital did not miss the railroad revenue.

The little hospital saw something of the tragedy of the revolution. In 1910, when the opposing parties fought for the town of Nogales, Sonora, the town was captured and recaptured between sunrise and sunset. Cannon boomed from the surrounding hills, while machine gun and rifle fire barked from closer range. American soldiers with machine guns were stationed on the roof of the hospital, from which vantage point they had an excellent view of the Mexican lines in Sonora. Others took up positions by the windows of the rooms facing the border. Several bullets struck the hospital or fell in the patio. American soldiers who fired warning shots were answered by a hail of bullets. The patients were moved out of the range of the firing to the Sisters' dormitory, where some protection was afforded by the Methodist church building. When the firing ceased, several Army doctors went over to care for the wounded. At that time there were no hospitals in Nogales, Sonora, and permission was given to cross the line and bring the wounded to St. Joseph's. Soon a procession of American Red Cross and Mexican White Cross stretcher-bearers were crossing the line. Sisters, doctors, Father Duval, Mexican clergy, and lay people were getting the hospital ready to receive the wounded soldiers. When every available bed and cot had been taken, patients were placed, heads to toes, on blankets on the floor. Others, with minor wounds, sat along the porches outside the surgery. "Enemy" officers for the time being forgot party strife, as one aptly remarked, "When we meet here we are all friends."

269

Having lived for weeks in trenches, the uniforms of the Yaqui soldiers were caked with mud and blood. All who were able to walk were taken back after treatment. About 2:00 a.m. the excitement subsided and Father Duval insisted that the Sisters get some rest. But where could they rest? Equal to every emergency, Father contacted one of the U.S. Army officers who ordered an ambulance to bring six Army cots and blankets to the camp. These were arranged in the Sisters' refectory. When Father was assured that the Sisters were provided for, he left for home. The Mexican government, through the U.S. Army, compensated the hospital for all hospitalization services.

In 1911 Father Duval pleaded again with Mother M. Paul for his school, and again she had to refuse him. Undaunted, the good priest engaged an architect, made a successful appeal for funds, and built a convent and school. At the time, Mother Camilla, Superior of the Dominican Sisters of Adrian, Michigan, was a patient at St. Joseph's Sanatorium, Silver City. Mother M. Paul knew the Dominican Sisters were interested in securing a house in the West for their delicate Sisters, and she broached the subject. Mother Camilla visited Nogales, and the Dominican Sisters agreed to take over the Sacred Heart School.

Meanwhile, the hospital was cleaned and renewed after the last soldier had departed. It was a big task, for the hospital looked like a charnel house. Things had just about been restored to normal when another battle took place, in 1912, and again the wounded were brought in, although not in so great numbers as before. Only those very seriously wounded were sent to the hospital. Other leaders were in charge now. The boom of cannon and whine of rifle bullets across the border came to the Sisters all throughout the day and often through the night.

According to a custom the Mexicans sometimes employed in dealing with traitors, the latter were taken at daybreak from the prisons in which they were kept. They were marched to the cemetery, where graves had been dug, and each prisoner was shot into the grave assigned to him by the firing squad. This was a rather frequent practice, and the report of the guns could be distinctly heard at the hospital; at time patients could count the shots and know how many had been sent to their doom that morning. Acts such as this, and the lawlessness that often characterizes a boarder town, kept Nogales from prospering as it might otherwise have done. Of course, there were some periods of comparative quiet—lulls in the storm.

The Mexican revolutionary government that was in control in 1914 had been recognized by Washington.[18] Many prominent families who had been living in Nogales returned to their homes in Mexico. Other families, however, known to be unfriendly to the new regime, came to the United States and established temporary homes in Nogales. Among these latter exiles were the Rodriguez and Tapio families. Miss Maria Tapio, a devout Catholic lady (later the wife of President Obregon of Mexico), was a constant visitor at the hospital, where she spent several hours a day with Sister M. Ignatius Briody helping with the patients or making herself useful in the surgery. Miss Tapio often spoke of the lack of hospital facilities in Mexico. In later years, she built and endowed the Sisters' hospital at Nogales, in Sonora, Mexico.

The situation in Mexico could scarcely have been said to be settled when Carranza was recognized in 1914 as President of Mexico. Opposition forces were still extant, the religious issue being particularly critical. The roots of Mexico were Catholic and millions of Mexicans gave varying degrees of allegiance to the Faith. There was, however, a hard core of political aspirants whose loyalties were Masonic rather than Catholic and who sought to destroy the Church. In November, 1918, Carranza proposed amendments to the Constitution of 1917 which would permit religious liberty. Carranza had promised American President Wilson that he would promote religious liberty, and Wilson was being besieged by Catholic Democratic leaders in the United States to do something about the religious persecution in Mexico. For Carranza's attempt to keep his word, it is thought that he was ambushed while seeking shelter in a wattled hut.[19]

Religious persecution became more severe. Anti-Catholic laws were enforced in the state of Sonora. Priests not of Mexican nationality were expelled and their churches confiscated. A short time later all religious were expelled, and more churches, convents and schools were closed. The Sisters extended hospitality to many of these exiled priests and religious. For months priests made their way to the hospital to offer Mass, and the Eucharistic Lord was constantly invoked by a procession of black-shawled women, lay and religious, who sought the peace of the hospital chapel as they prayed for Mexico's survival.

In 1915, all Nogales grieved when its good pastor, Father Louis Duval, was transferred to the cathedral of Tucson to replace Reverend Peter Timmerman, Vicar General, who had been interned in Belgium by the Germans during World War I. Father Van Goethem took charge of the parish at Nogales. As soon as the new pastor saw the condition of some of the Sisters in the school, he complained to Mother Camilla at Adrian, Michigan. A short time later one of the Sisters at Sacred Heart, Nogales, died of a pulmonary hemorrhage. Parents became alarmed and petitioned the Sisters of Mercy to take over the schools. The pastor was firm in his determination that only healthy Sisters be engaged in the schools, and the Dominican Sisters withdrew to Adrian at the close of the school year.

Sacred Heart School, Nogales—1915-1932

Mother M. Stanislaus was rather unwilling to accept the work, but was finally persuaded to try to meet the needs of Sacred Heart School by sending Sisters from Silver City, where the schools were about to close. In August, 1915, six Sisters[20] arrived to take up the work in the school. Until the convent and school were fumigated and repainted, the Sisters stayed at the hospital. In September the school opened with over two hundred pupils.

In the midst of wars, rumors of wars and exaggerated reports of every kind that helped to create the tense atmosphere along the border, the Sisters learned to carry on their duties from day to day and await events to present themselves. The unexpected usually happened.

One afternoon during lecture the Sisters jumped to their feet when cannon on the surrounding hills began to boom. Recovering her breath, Sister M. Alphonsus Cox looked at her watch and announced: "Five minutes more of lecture," and she continued to read. Outside, patients' bells buzzed and nurses scurried around the veranda. The cannonading kept up. The reading did not last the five minutes, for before this the U.S. soldiers were marching up the front steps of the hospital and out through the patio. From the hospital roof the soldiers took in the full view of Nogales, Sonora. They set up machine guns and awaited developments. When the officer in command saw that the only danger was from stray bullets he ordered everyone to stay under cover. Some sought refuge in the chapel; others, curious to see the fireworks, watched from some point of vantage. In her anxiety to warn these of their danger, Sister M.

Alphonsus apparently did not think the "under cover" order applied to her, for she hurried down the center of the open patio, miraculously escaping the bullets falling around her.

When the noise of the battle, which lasted an hour, had died out, the brick wall of the hospital had a six-inch hole and the roof its share of bullet wounds. Sisters and nurses found a few more bullets for souvenirs. In accord with Mercy hospitality, the soldiers were served refreshments before returning to camp. By tray time the hospital was back to normal, ready for the next surprise. Whatever casualties there were received treatment across the line.

Better hospital accommodations were needed and about this time plans were made for an addition which would be the first unit of a new hospital. By May, 1916, the new unit, which cost $16,000, was completed. The wing, a one-story brick building and basement, contained fourteen private rooms with private baths. In the basement was provision for a laboratory, furnace room, laundry and janitor's quarters. The Sisters and medical staff were very proud of the new addition; the fourteen rooms were furnished by the people of Nogales.

This year saw an increase of border incidents between the American and the Mexican troops. The Sisters, while waiting to board the train, saw one of these incidents at close range. A United States officer, standing on the platform, was shot down by a Mexican soldier across the street. The people on both sides of the line were panic-stricken for a few minutes. The wounded officer was carried to the baggage room for first aid, and thence to the hospital. Some months later another bullet from a Mexican rifle took the life of an American soldier, Stephen Little. Some soldiers of the National Guard arrived to establish a camp in Nogales, which came to be known as Camp Stephen Little. Unaccustomed to army life, many of these young men contracted colds, which developed into pneumonia. The critical cases were brought to St. Joseph's. The new wing was turned into an isolation ward under the supervision of Army doctors and nurses. One epidemic followed another, as gastric infection and acute appendictis swept the camp. These cases were also cared for at the Sisters' hospital. New Army doctors arrived and kept the surgery busy, night and day. These homesick boys, but a short time in the service, were only too happy to be sent to the hospital. For almost six months the hospital was a branch of the Army services. In time the camp was equipped for surgery but the officers and their families continued to come to St. Joseph's. After the last soldier patient had been discharged, the Army orderlies continued to report for duty at the hospital. They explained: "We take orders in the Army, not give them." Until assigned other duties, these men busied themselves around the hospital, painting, repairing, or working in the garden.

The National Guard was composed of splendid young men from the eastern states. Many were Catholics and appreciated contact with the Sisters. Nogales society entertained the officers but left the rank and file to find their own entertainment; hence the hospital became a favorite visiting place where the boys spent their leisure hours folding dressings or cleaning instruments with the nurses. Dear Sister Veronica Crane served lemonade or coffee and fresh bread with plenty of homemade jam, which made their visits even more pleasant. Sister M. Alphonsus was very understanding with the soldier boys, many of whom hailed from her own state, Connecticut; but when their numbers reached the nuisance stage she was forced to discourage the visits. The Sisters had letters from parents letting them know how much their sons appreciated the friendly atmosphere of St. Joseph's Hospital, Nogales.

During the influenza epidemic of 1918, Nogales was one large isolation camp, with every home a hospital. All schools, theaters and churches were closed. The hospital proper was crowded to overflowing. Every morning the school Sisters came to help out and returned to their convent at night. In November, the volunteer services of the city of Globe, Arizona, collapsed in the face of the mounting death toll. The city officials appealed to Bishop Granjon for aid. Three Sisters from the Nogales school, Sister M. Baptist Gavigan, Sister M. Columba Ryan, and Sister M. Evangelist O'Grady, as well as Sister M. Aloysius Phelan, from Phoenix, volunteered for the mission of Mercy. While the epidemic lasted, the four Sisters, two on day and two on night duty, nursed the sick in the public school of Globe. The Sisters occupied convenient quarters at the old Dominion Hotel across the street from Holy Angels Church, where they assisted at daily Mass. A police car brought the Sisters to and from their patients. When the epidemic subsided, a group of citizens requested that the Sisters remain in Globe and conduct either a hospital or a school. Although the Sisters could not accept the proposal, they recognized it as an expression of gratitude. The city officials, likewise, expressed genuine appreciation for their services and generously compensated them for their devoted care of the stricken victims of Globe.

The war over, Father Peter Timmerman was able to return from Europe. He had been interned in Belgium. This made possible the relief of Father Louis Duval, who had been temporary Vicar General, and he gladly returned to his people in Nogales. He was now faced with the perplexing problems of the refugee Mexican clergy. After discussing the question with the immigration officers, the U.S. Government gave Father Duval authority to regulate the visas without the priests having to appear in person. His chief difficulty lay in keeping in touch with the priests who, whenever an opportunity presented itself, slipped back into Mexico without notifying him. Father usually learned of these trips from immigration officials, and then an apology was due, as well as another re-entry form which had to be filled out. The hospital served as a clearing house for the exiles.

Many priests found assignments as hospital chaplains; others came daily to offer the Holy Sacrifice. Although all dressed in secular attire, one easily recognized the priest. Likewise, one could always spot the Mexican nuns, modestly dressed women who singly or in twos came to Mass or to visit the Blessed Sacrament. Lest they faint on the way, the latter were served hot chocolate before leaving. From them the Sisters at St. Joseph's heard later of heroism the equal of any in the long history of the Church.

There is no need to trace the story of the Mexican revolution as one followed another further than to say that true sons of freedom north of the Rio Grande could not condone the almost incessant persecution of the Church by a so-called republican government in a land long dominantly Catholic. Nowhere along the Mexican border were the repercussions of an organized attack on everything Catholic brought to the attention of the American people as in the little border town of Nogales.

Mother Mary Baptist Russell

San Francisco

Mother Mary Camillus McGarr
Rio Vista

Mother Mary Paul O'Grady
New Mexico-Arizona

Mother Mary Bonaventure Fox
Los Angeles

Mother Mary Michael Cummings
San Diego

The Magdalen Asylum
On Poterero Ave., San Francisco
(Opened 1865-Closed 1932)

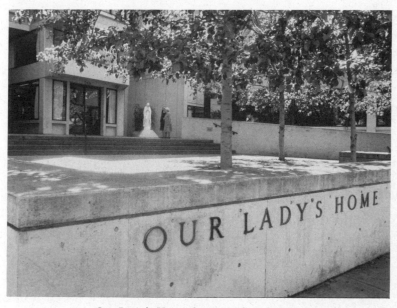

Our Lady's Home for the Aged, Oakland
(Originally opened on Rincon Hill, S.F., 1872)
(Victoria Rouse Photo)

Present Motherhouse
Burlingame, California (Robert Graham Photos)

St. Mary's Hospital, Rincon Hill
San Francisco

Present (Victoria Rouse Photo)

Mercy Hospital and Medical Center today
San Diego

St. Joseph's Sanitorium, circa 1893

St. Joseph's Hospital & Medical Center

Phoenix, Arizona

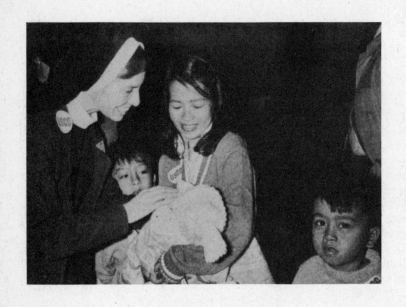

Greeting Southeast Asian Refugees
at San Francisco Airport
(Victoria Rouse Photo).

PART III—GRAFTING FOR GROWTH

Chapter 13

THE AMALGAMATION[1]
1903-1923

The spread of the Institute of Our Lady of Mercy over the English-speaking world has been truly phenomenal. Among the several reasons advanced to explain this is the choice of government[2] made by Mother Catherine McAuley. Instead of the current trend of a centralized organization she preferred to send out foundations which could be independent as soon as they could manage their affairs. Mother Catherine McAuley established a custom of accompanying each founding group and generally remaining with it about a month. Of course, strong ties were continued, but she saw tremendous advantages in leaving decisions to those she had selected to shape the destiny of each new community.

The Sisters of Mercy, in the design of the Holy Spirit, served the nineteenth century Church in meeting the social problems attendant on the Industrial Revolution. The industrial society accelerated urbanization and with it, while the rich grew richer, the poor became poorer. Every growing city spawned its quota of impoverished workers who endured substandard living conditions, conducive to the spread of disease, crime, etc.

From the first, Mother McAuley's daughters were imbued with the spirit of mercy, to meet, as far as it was in their power, every crying need. Constant were the demands of the English and Irish bishops for new foundations of the Institute of Mercy, which was especially designed to meet the growing social problems.

It was in the nineteenth century, too, that waves of immigrants were either lured or driven to find a better life in the new promised land—America. Many were survivors of the potato famine in Ireland or sufferers from religious or political persecution; all looked forward to the opportunities and freedom offered across the sea. The Irish Sisters were prompt to answer the needs of Irish immigrants.

Under the so-called monastic type of government, the independent foundation was also very advantageous during an era of overseas expansion and the western movement across the plains when living conditions were primitive and communications very limited. The type of government of the Sisters of Mercy was conducive to the spread of the Institute from Ireland to England, to Canada, to the United States (from shore to shore), to Latin America, to Australia, to New Zealand, and even to Africa.

And yet as the years passed many of the bishops observed that there were many very small communities of religious who found it difficult to replace their depleted ranks as the strong pioneer Sisters aged or died. Further, the independent communities were duplicating services, such as the training of novices, which work could be more effective if religious of the same Institute amalgamated and established a good novitiate to serve a number of convents.

The following letter of Archbishop Sadoc Alemany, O.P., is indicative of the concern of bishops in 1882:[3]

November 1, 1882

To All the Sisters of Mercy in California

Dearly Beloved:

In our late Provincial Council we took into consideration what we deemed would finally result to your benefit and we now propose it to your minds and hearts for the purpose of obtaining your own views and candid wishes, after mature reflection and earnest prayer.

Our charge extending over large territories in which new settlements are being formed, and in which new towns and churches are continually springing up, new demands for Christian schools likewise arise for the instruction of the many children who, without Christian training, would naturally grow up irreligious and would probably be lost to the Church and to Heaven. Our people being so intermingled with those of other denominations are not always found numerously congregated in one locality; yet oftentimes there are sufficient numbers to support a few, and only a few Sisters, who would generously devote themelves to the great work of saving souls. Earnestly desiring to preserve and perpetuate the Faith among these children of the Church, and anxious to share with the good Sisters the rewards attached to the imitation of Our Blessed Lord, we are always desirous of establishing a house wherever it can be supported, but since, as we have seen, if often happens that in such places only a few Sisters can be maintained, we consider it undesirable to have a novitiate in every small convent and believe it highly useful to the welfare of each to be aided by others. One or more Sisters, for instance, may become incapacitated by sickness, or other causes may render it advantageous to have her placed in a more agreeable situation which in many instances might conduce to the improvement of health and happiness or other benefits of the parties concerned. The above advantages and many others we believe could be secured by having one Superior General or Provincial for all California or for each diocese if you prefer it who, with proper counsel, and not without it, could see to the carrying out of the above objects. After much serious reflection on the foregoing, we thought it would be to your advantage and for the interests of religion to adopt methods like the following provided the Holy Father would deem it proper and approve of it.

After outlining his plan for election and a central administration, Archbishop Alemany concluded:

We would, therefore, request that this be carefully read and considered; and that each Sister. . .ask the Holy Ghost for light and direction. Within three weeks after the receipt of this, she shall freely express her view with her signature in a sealed small note. . . .

Shortly after, in accord with the archbishop's direction, this proposal was submitted to the vote of all the professed Sisters of Mercy. Since a majority opposed the measure voted upon, the matter was dropped for the time being.

Early in 1886, the San Francisco Archdiocese was redivided, and Sacramento was made the episcopal city for the upper diocese under the jurisdiciton of Bishop Patrick Manogue. With the erection of the Diocese of Sacramento, May 28, 1886, Grass Valley was transferred to the newly formed diocese. The San Francisco filiation in Grass Valley was already independent, though from time to time Sisters from San Francisco were loaned. Up to this time, the Sisters of Mercy in Sacramento had been a branch house of the San Francisco Sisters of Mercy. With the erection of the Sacramento Diocese, the Mercy foundation in Sacramento was separated from the San Francisco community. The Sisters in Sacramento were given their choice between remaining permanently or for a specified time in Sacramento, or returning to the Motherhouse at St. Mary's, Rincon Hill.

For many years it had been the great desire of Archbishop Riordan, who succeeded to the see of San Francisco on December 28, 1884, that the Rio Vista community of Sisters of Mercy should be united with that of San Francisco. From the Book of Chapters, we learn that the vocals of the latter community were assembled on May 10, 1894, for the purpose of ascertaining their views regarding the question, and it was recorded that, "the great majority were in favor of a union with the Rio Vista community." To this record the signatures of the Archbishop and the Reverend John J. Nugent, Rector of St. Brendan's, San Francisco, are affixed. Reverend Mother Camillus McGarr, foundress of the Rio Vista community, was a frequent visitor at St. Mary's, Rincon Hill, and on intimate terms with Reverend Mother Baptist Russell. However, the union did not take place at this time. Why was it not accomplished? Rumor had it that Mr. and Mrs. Joseph Bruning, who had furnished the means for the Rio Vista foundation and were still generous benefactors of the institution, were opposed to the amalgamation. This seems possible as these good people had previously tried to get Mother M. Baptist to establish a convent in Rio Vista, and she had been obliged to refuse the request because of a lack of Sisters for the mission. However, neither did the death of Mr. and Mrs. Bruning bring about the desired union.

It was not until May 19, 1917, that the merger of the San Francisco and Rio Vista communities was actually accomplished. Archbishop Riordan, who had urged the first step toward amalgamation in 1894, did not live to see the success of his efforts. His death occurred on December 27, 1914, and he was succeeded by the Most Reverend Edward J. Hanna, June 1, 1915.

Finally, in February, 1917, the Very Reverend John J. Cantwell, Vicar General, called upon Mother M. Euphrasia Sullivan, Superior of the San Francisco community, to press the desire of the archbishop that the Sisters consider anew the question of amalgamation with the Rio Vista Sisters. Soon after, he paid a visit to the Rio Vista community. The Sisters were assembled in the chapel, where he gave an exhortation regarding the desirability of the proposed union. Votes were taken. In the entire community (three houses), only one member voted against the proposition. On May 19, 1917, Mother M. Josephine Campbell resigned the superiorship of the Rio Vista community, and with the transfer of authority to Mother Euphrasia the amalgamation was complete.

At the time of the amalgamation the Rio Vista congregation had under its care: the academy, St. Gertrude's, which was an elementary school for boys and girls and a boarding school for girls through high school; St. Joseph's School for young boys; and Mt. Carmel Academy, Sausalito, a boarding school for girls and an elementary school for boys and girls.[4]

About this same time Mother M. Joachim McBrinn of Los Angeles and Mother M. Michael Cummings of San Diego, superiors of their respective communities of Sisters of Mercy, also sought to effect an amalgamation with the Sisters of Mercy, San Francisco. It has often been stated that Mother M. Euphrasia Sullivan was opposed to the union. The truth is that Mother M. Euphrasia was already overburdened by the crucial responsibilities of her office, and she feared the assumption of additional responsibility at this time.

In 1918, shortly after the Most Reverend John J. Cantwell became Bishop of the Monterey-Los Angeles diocese,[5] he suggested that the two Mercy communities of his diocese, those of Los Angeles and San Diego, unite for greater strength and efficiency. After due deliberation and consultation, the Chapter votes, taken in the summer of 1918, were overwhelmingly in favor of amalgamation, as attested by the Acts of the Chapter of

San Diego August 8, 1918, and that of Los Angeles, August 12, 1918. At both of the Chapters, Bishop Cantwell presided.[6]

Mother M. Joachim McBrinn was appointed Mother Superior, and it was agreed that the Motherhouse be at 4060 West Washington Boulevard, Los Angeles. The novitiate was to be at San Diego for at least three years, with Mother M. Michael Cummings as Novice Mistress.[7]

Early in 1919, Mother M. Paul O'Grady, second foundress of the Sisters of Mercy of the Tucson diocese, visited Mother Euphrasia. Mother M. Paul was also interested in advancing the cause of union. Again Mother Euphrasia gave no immediate promise of effecting an amalgamation with the Sisters of the Tucson diocese.

Her health failing, Mother Euphrasia was succeeded in June by Mother M. Bernard O'Brien, to whom would fall the responsibility of the final amalgamation.

Perhaps it is important to call attention to an angle which may explain the persistence of Mother M. Paul in her desire for amalgamation with the Sisters of Mercy in California. Not until 1912 were New Mexico and Arizona recognized as members of the United States. Besides working in an area not yet developed, the Sisters of Mercy were caught in difficult circumstances due to diocesan changes in the Southwest. Between 1881 and July, 1913, when the Sisters left Mesilla, they opened and closed ten schools. After the creation of the diocese of El Paso,[8] it became evident that not only El Paso and Mesilla would be incorporated in the new diocese, but also Silver City, where the Sisters had their motherhouse and novitiate. This necessitated the transfer of the novitiate to Prescott, Arizona. It also meant the withdrawal from Silver City, the closing of the hospital in 1915 and of the Academy of Our Lady of Lourdes in 1916.

In dealing with the bishops of the Southwest, the Sisters had to contend with the false impression that they were a diocesan congregation. The bishops, too, tended to restrict them to a given diocese; if not, the community in the diocese would become a separate group.

On July 21, 1908, a communique addressed to the Most Reverend Henry Granjon, Bishop of Tucson, from Cardinal Diomedes Falconio, Apostolic Delegate, stated:

> . . .In answer to your favor of the 14th inst. I beg to say that you cannot act any longer on the letter of the S.C. Propaganda addressed to your predecessor in

September, 1894, nor that of the Apostolic Delegate, October 4, 1894. It is evident that they were led to believe that these Sisters of Mercy who are in your diocese had no Constitutions approved by the Holy See. However, since they have Constitutions approved by the S.C. Propaganda, July 5, 1841, for the original Motherhouse, Dublin, you must be governed by its decrees cited in my letter of the 10th inst., and by the *Constitutio Apostolica (Condita a Christo Ecclesia)*.

With sentiments of esteem,
S. Diomedes, Cardinal Falconio[9]

We find no evidence that Mother M. Paul was ever made aware of this letter. It was her concern that the creation of new dioceses would affect her houses that prompted her to leave no stone unturned to secure the amalgamation of her Sisters with a large and stable religious community.

The first step toward such a union was made when the Arizona community joined with the united communities of Los Angeles and San Diego. The Chapter was held in Los Angeles, March 12, 1921, [10] with Bishop John J. Cantwell presiding. Here, too, the votes on the amalgamation of the Sisters of southern California with the Arizona Sisters showed a large majority in favor of the union.

Four months later[11], the houses of Los Angeles, San Diego, and Phoenix were united with the Sisters of Mercy of San Francisco, and the union ratified by a brief received from Rome on March 27, 1922.[12]

The brief which confirmed the union of the Sisters of Mercy of California and Arizona also asked that the constitutions be submitted to the Sacred Congregation for Religious after revision. The changes in Canon Law, regarding government in particular, were included in the new constitution that was submitted to the Holy See.[13]

Meanwhile, in a letter directed to Mother M. Bernard O'Brien, April 19, 1922, the Most Reverend Archbishop of San Francisco stated:

Wednesday of Easter Week
April 19, 1922

Dear Reverend Mother:

283

After taking counsel with the Rt. Rev. Bishop of
Monterey-Los Angeles, I hereby appoint you Mother
General of the United Sisters of Mercy of the
Archdiocese of San Francisco and of the Dioceses of
Monterey-Los Angeles and of Tucson and I confirm
you in all the obligations and privileges of the said
office for a term of six years. Your Council for the
time being will remain as before until the arrange-
ments suggested by the Holy See be put into effect.
You will take the usual means of notifying all the
Sisters in your jurisdiction of this appointment.

I pray upon your dear head new light and new
strength for the great task that lies before you and I
join with Bishop Cantwell in wishing you a most
successful administration.

Always devotedly in Christ,
Edward J. Hanna (signed)[14]

While holding a visitation in Rio Vista in the latter part of
September, 1922, Mother M. Bernard was apprised of the
serious illness of Mother M. Michael Cummings in San Diego. It
was a great shock to her community and to Mother M. Bernard
that her death followed so shortly afterward, on October 6,
1922. Immediately, Mother M. Bernard and Sister M. Vincent
White left for the south and remained until after the obsequies.

It does seem strange that Mother M. Paul O'Grady[15] and
Mother M. Michael Cummings, both of whom had worked so
earnestly to bring about the amalgamation, were called by God
as the union was about to be consummated.

Following the ratification of the amalgamation by the Holy
See, February 16, 1922, and the approval of the new
constitutions, November 21, 1922, the various houses of
California and Arizona chose Chapter delegates in the spring of
1923.[16] The First General Chapter of the Sisters of Mercy,
California and Arizona,[17] was held at St. Mary's Hospital, San
Francisco, July 10, 1923. At this Chapter, Mother M. Bernard's
appointment as Mother General was confirmed for six years,
1923-1929.

Motherhouse and Novitiate

After the amalgamation of the Sisters of Mercy of the Archdiocese of San Francisco and the Dioceses of Los Angeles and that of Tucson, it was deemed wise that the Motherhouse and novitiate be distinct from all branch houses and the works of the Institute.

At the first General Chapter, held July 10, 1923, at St. Mary's Hospital, San Francisco, the subject was discussed and the delegates were unanimous that it was advisable to secure property for this purpose.

Both Archbishop Edward J. Hanna and Bishop John J. Cantwell favored establishing the motherhouse and novitiate in the environs of San Francisco, where the education of the young Sisters would profit by a location so close to centers of learning.

Several pieces of property had been considered when it was learned that The Oaks,[18] the beautiful home of Frederick Kohl in North Burlingame, was on the market. This estate embraced forty acres of land and the Kohl residence, a typical Tudor mansion which rested on the crest of knoll covered with gnarled oaks. The building was red brick and stone with rambling gables and slate roofs. The house itself was surrounded by well kept lawns and broad terraces, and to the rear was a quaint tiled area with a sunken rose garden. It was a perfect building in a perfect setting, and the grounds beyond gave wonderful promise for further developments.

A house with sixty-five rooms put some limitation on the number of prospective buyers. Some real estate men from Los Angeles made a bid, which the executors refused. A country club also considered the purchase of the property. The owner seemed to urge the sale and the executors were impatient to conclude the transaction.

On December first, Mother M. Bernard O'Brien, Mother Gertrude Reid, Sister M. Emmanuel Spelman and Sister M. Paschal Magee visited The Oaks, and Mother Bernard said that to her surprise the description had not been exaggerated. Mr. Alan Maginnis,[12] one of the executors, met the Sisters at the place and was most anxious that they decide at once whether or not to purchase.

For several weeks, the matter was discussed and visits were made to the offices of the archbishop and Mr. John Drum. The deciding factor appears, to have been the recommendation of the archbishop that the Sisters accept the offer, "a chance in a lifetime." They could not think of building elsewhere for the amount demanded for both the land and the house—$235,000.

Negotiations were completed and an inventory made of the articles of furniture that would be considered part of the purchase. These included the fine Aeolian pipe organ, the hall clock, the equipment of the kitchen and storeroom, and the furnishings of the living room.

The Oaks in the Burlingame Hills, was purchased by the Sisters of Mercy for a motherhouse and novitiate on January 24, 1924. Mother Bernard, the General Council and most of the novitiate Sisters from Fruitvale took possession of the place on February 25, 1924.[20]

Although the Kohl mansion was not erected for convent needs, there is evidence of an ecclesiastical note such as is found in much of the architecture of the Tudor period. A large baronial hall, directly ahead of the entrance, formed the predominant feature of the house and was called the music room. Here Mr. Kohl had installed one of the finest Aeolian pipe organs in any private abode on the continent. This spacious and lofty hall, with its wonderful oak paneling and three galleries that overlooked the room, furnished an inspirational design befitting a chapel, the center of religious life.[4]

The library, to the right of the entrance, became a reception room for the Sisters' visitors.

The wing complementary to the library, at the farther end of the music room was the Kohl dining room, a study in green and pale ivory with a perfect mantelpiece of the Adams period. The exquisite dining table, sideboard and brocade drapes were soon disposed of in order to set up a suitable novitiate room.

The terrazzo breakfast room became the Sisters' dining room, while the kitchen and pantry continued to serve their purpose. The billiard room, off the second landing, was used for the community room.

The third and fourth floors offered ample space for the living quarters of the Sisters, at least until 1931 when a new Motherhouse was built on the same property and the Kohl mansion converted into a girls' high school, now known as Mercy High, Burlingame.

The real amalgamation, the creation of a union of dedicated religious, was only beginning, but the Sisters bravely accepted the challenge of the Master, that "all may be one." The history of the next fifty years of the Sisters of Mercy, California and

Arizona, is a testimonial to the success of their combined efforts to promote the greater good of the Institute and the Church by a more effective discharge of the works of mercy.

As the Sisters of Mercy, California and Arizona, look back over more than 120 years of faithful and effective service, they can recognize some goals attained and some worthwhile achievements; but they must note, too, that the vocation of a Sister of Mercy is an ongoing process. Social concerns present an ever widening appeal, and while the Sisters are attentive to the demands of the present they must ever prepare to meet the needs of tomorrow.

NOTES

Chapter 1

1. The three centuries of British rule, roughly speaking, covered the span from the fall of the House of Kildare under the Tudors to the Act of Parliament referred to as the Catholic Emancipation, 1829.

2. The Penal Laws of Ireland were a series of statutes initiated by the Reformation Parliament of 1560, which represented about a third of the people of Ireland. The laws were designed to subject Catholics to increasing penalties for practicing their faith and for not conforming to the Established Church. The Act of Supremacy and the Act of Uniformity were similar to those passed by the English Parliament. By the former, the monarch was recognized as the supreme head of the Church, and an oath accepting the Queen as such was asked of officeholders in the Church, state, all mayors of incorporated towns, and all who sought university degrees. By the Act of Uniformity the new Book of Common Prayer was imposed and attendance at the Established Church was made compulsory each Sunday under penalty of fine. By 1570 Pope Pius V excommunicated Elizabeth and this clearly answered the assertion that the Elizabethan establishment was a reformed but Catholic Church under the direction of the monarchy. It was not.

The story cannot here be given proper coverage, but suffice it to say that, in the years following, laws were enacted under severe penalties to prevent the free exercise of the Catholic religion and to promote the Protestant ascendancy in Ireland by confiscations and plantations, unjust land laws, laws denying inheritance, limitations on Catholics in education, laws forbidding the possession of arms or entry into military service, and finally, in their own country, Catholics could not vote, hold office or serve in the Irish Parliament.

History records that the Penal Laws did succeed in depriving the Irish of their earthly heritage and many were impoverished and degraded to real destitution, but the vast majority of Irish clung to their faith. See Edmund Curtis, *A History of Ireland*, pp. 182-378, and *passim*.

Some writers date the Penal Laws from 1692 to 1829. This is due to the fact that an act passed in the English Parliament in

1691 was extended to Ireland. By it members of both Houses were required to take an oath of allegiance and with it a declaration against the Mass, Transubstantiation, as well as an oath denying the spiritual supremacy of the Pope. No conscientious Catholic could comply with such a disavowal. The law was repealed in 1829, which enabled Roman Catholics to sit in Parliament. See Curtis, p. 275 ff.

3. Edmund Curtis, *A History of Ireland*, Chapter XVII. *Cf.* J.C. Beckett, *The Making of Modern Ireland.*

4. Curtis, p. 317.

5. *Ibid.*, p. 354.

6. *Cf.* Curtis, p. 349, and J.C. Beckett, p. 202 ff.

7. Vesey Fitzgerald vs. Daniel O'Connell for Parliament. See Beckett, p. 302 ff.

8. Catholic Emancipation, see Beckett, pp. 295-305.

9. There has been little agreement on the date of Catherine McAuley's birth, due to lack of records: e.g., the marriage date of her parents, the date of her birth, and even the date of her reception of the Sacraments. Today some consensus has been reached as to the most probable birth date of those suggested, September 29, 1778. This date accords with that given by her earliest biographer, Sister M. Vincent Hartnett, whose *Life of Catherine McAuley* was published by John Fowler, Dublin, 1864.

In Charleville (Rath Luric) there are some interesting papers: annals, the Crimean diary of Mother Joseph Croke, and original letters of Catherine McAuley. Among the papers there is an 1864 advertisement for a publication "Lamp"; the reverse side was used as a practice sheet for printing the title page of the notice of Catherine McAuley's death. It states that she was born in 1778. This information was provided by Sr. M. Celeste Rouleau, S.M.

10. The spelling of James McGauley, father of Catherine, would seem to need some explanation. He spelled his own name McGauley. After his death it was her mother, Elinor Conway McGauley, who decided to drop the "G" and in imitation of their mother the children followed suit. The youngest child, James, later became a physician and he chose to spell his name Macauley. To further complicate matters, Mary, the sister of Catherine McAuley, married a Doctor William Macauley. From time to time reference has been made to their children. They spelled their name Macauley (See Neumann, p. 2).

11. Extant deeds of ownership attest the fact that James McGauley was a man of property.

12. James McGauley's will, according to the Public Records of Ireland, went through probate August 2, 1783, and carried the date of his death as July 18, 1783.

13. According to all reports this incident seems to have left a deep impression on Catherine. It is probably her most vivid recollection of her father.

14. Savage, pp. 22-23 and pp. 92 *seq.*

15. *Ibid.*, p. 24 ff. Life at the Conways.

16. *Ibid.*, p. 27. Father Lube's influence.

17. *Ibid.*, p. 26 ff. Life with the Armstrongs.

18. *Ibid.*, p. 29 ff. Life with the Callaghans.

19. According to all biographers Catherine was well received and even highly esteemed by both Mr. and Mrs. Callaghan. What the biographers do not seem to agree on is the conversion of Mrs. Callaghan. Father Savage tells us that the latter feared to displease her husband but consented to see a priest during his absence at Apothecaries' Hall. Father Michael Keogh readily agreed to come. Because of her advanced years and her long illness he decided that, with her dispositions as good as they were, he would baptize her without delay. He promised, however, to return in a few days to bring her the Holy Viaticum and anoint her. See Savage, p. 38.

Mother Hartnett says (p. 32) that because the patient was in no immediate danger of death he deferred the administration of "the Last Sacraments." She adds, however, that a few hours after "her reconciliation" and "before the return of the priest" she expired, "assisted by her affectionate daughter." Even if she had not been baptized, what could have prevented Catherine from supplying the need? And yet we read in more than one subsequent biography that Mrs. Callaghan died "before she could receive Baptism."

20. Mary Ann Powell was a relative of Mrs. William Callaghan and she, too, had lived at Coolock House before she married Robert Moore Powell. The original will named Catherine McAuley and Mary Ann Powell as sole residuary legatees. A codicil of the same date, however, changed this and named Catherine the sole residuary legatee. Mr. Powell had spoken too soon and was overheard by Mr. Callaghan. See Degnan, p. 40. See also Neumann for a copy of the will and note the codicil, pp. 50-53.

21. Savage states in his book, *Catherine McAuley*, p. 40, that the estate she received was more than £ 25,000, and he added "equivalent to more than £ 200,000 in present day values." According to the copyright of his book, that was more than thirty years ago, 1949.

22. See Savage, pp. 49-50 for details of the acquisition of the Baggot Street property and the building plans. The work was completed in September, 1827.

23. One date is established concerning the death of Mary Mcauley, Catherine's sister. She was buried in St. Mark's Churchyard August 11, 1827. Apparently she died a Protestant. Catherine herself, however, was able to supply the real facts. She visited her at Stillorgan during her illness, and she tells us that her sister had not forgotten the faith of her childhood. It was Father John McCormick of Booterstown parish who visited her. She was reconciled to the Church about three weeks before her death. Catherine bided her time to tell the grief-stricken husband, but she finally did so. *Cf.* Savage, p. 68; Hartnett, p. 32; or Mother M. Bertrand Degnan, pp. 52-53; and more recently, *Catherine McAuley* by Sister M. Angela Bolster, p. 23.

24. Catherine McAuley was surely "led by the Spirit." Without even adverting to the choice of the day, she began her work at Baggot Street on the Feast of Our Lady of Mercy, September 24, 1827. Savage, p. 62.

25. She did not leave the Macauley home until provision was made for the five children.—Savage, Chapter IV, Family Ties. Catherine's concern extended to each of her sister's children and to Doctor Macauley, too. Savage, pp. 69-72. See also Degnan, *Mercy Unto Thousands*, pp. 80-82. Here a statement made by Doctor Macauley when at the point of death indicates a strong Christian faith. It is a pity that Mother Bertrand did not clearly state where she got the quotation ascribed to the doctor.

26. After taking care of the needs of those near and dear to her, Catherine turned to her life work. As early as September 10, 1828, in a letter to Rev. Francis L'Estrange she states the object of her charity: the education of poor girls, the instruction of and safe haven for young women, and the care of the sick. Neumann, p. 69.

27. In the same month she sought and received the approval of the Archbishop to dedicate the House to Our Lady of Mercy, September 24, 1828. Savage, p. 75.

28. Even her difficulties with Canon Matthias Kelly seemed to initiate the steps that led to the choice of religious life. Savage, pp. 104-105.

29. "Learning the Ways of Christ," Savage, Chapter VII.

30. See Neumann, *Letters of Catherine McAuley*, p. 32.

31. This is the first instance when the Sisters of Mercy were called upon by public officials to meet a health crisis. It would occur again and again. See Sister M. Rose McArdle's *California's Pioneer Sister of Mercy, Mother Baptist Russell*, Academy Library Guild, Fresno, California, 1954. Sister describes the cholera epidemic in San Francisco in 1855 and the smallpox epidemic in 1868. For a general picture of the contribution of the Sisters of Mercy to nursing, see *The Way of Mercy* by Sister M. Beata Bauman, Vantage Press, New York, 1958. See also the *Crimean Diary of Mother M. Francis Bridgeman, War Companion of Florence Nightingale, 1854-1865*, an unpublished Master dissertation by Sister Marie Jeanne d'Arc Hughes, R.S.M., Catholic University of America, 1948.

32. Savage, p. 414: Cardinal Fransoni's letter. See also Savage, pp. 133-134 and pp. 262-266; and finally p. 415 for the Decree of the Sacred Congregation, July 5, 1841.

33. *Letters of Catherine McAuley, 1827-1841*, edited by Sister M. Ignatius Neumann, R.S.M., Helicon Press, Baltimore, Md., 1969.

34. Since the House of Mercy, Baggot Street, is considered the first foundation, St. Patrick's Convent is regarded as the second foundation.

35. The second branch house was St. Anne's Convent, Booterstown, on Dublin Bay.

36. Savage, pp. 201-202.

37. Secondary education for the middle class began at Carlow. Savage pp. 202-203; see also the manuscript annals of the San Francisco Community, Vol. I, pp. 176-177; Letter from Mother M. Vincent Hartnett to Mother M. Baptist Russell.

38. Mother Catherine's reply to Mother De Pazzi Delaney, Savage, p. 221.

39. Savage, p. 238.

40. Hartnett, p. 133.

41. Savage, p. 240: Miss Helen Heffernan, benefactor of Limerick.

42. Mother M. Bertrand Degnan, p. 227.

43. Savage, p. 400.

44. Neumann, p. 169.

45. Neumann, p. 186-187.

46. Neumann, p. 195-196.

47. Letter of Rt. Rev. Thomas Walsh, Vicar Apostolic of Birmingham, England, Savage, pp. 295-297.

48. A problem of dowry, Neumann, pp 214-215.

49. Savage p. 316.

50. Neumann, p. 139, Letter of Mother Catherine to Sister Teresa White, October 12, 1838.

51. Neumann, p. 267, new foundations in Florida.

52. Savage, p. 339, Mother Catherine writing from Birr to Mother Cecilia Marmion in January, 1841.

53. Savage, pp. 411-421, Translation of the documents.

54. The Bermondsey Manuscript was written by Mother Catherine McAuley at the time of the Bermondsey difficulties. The original treatise is still in the possession of the Bermondsey Community. Sister M. Bertrand Degnan, when in Bermondsey, copied it by hand. When Mother M. Dominic Foster, the Superior of Carysfort Park, learned of it, she succeeded in getting it microfilmed. Mother M. Maurice, Superior General of the Sisters of the Union, had the prints photostated.

The difficulties in Bermondsey arose following the installation of Mother M. Clare Agnew as the Superior. A brief explanation of the case has been offered, as well as a brief account of how Mother McAuley handled it.

The quotation used is but an excerpt of a much longer article. The lines were chosen because they are Mother McAuley's own explanation of the Spirit of the Institute and its twofold aim. See also Newmann, pp. 385-391.

55. Neumann, p. 238. A supplement letter dated October 14, 1840, was addressed to James Philip, Cardinal Fransoni, concerning the confirmation of the Rule. It stated that two houses had since been added to the twelve then in operation, and one hundred and forty-two Sisters were now devoted to the works of mercy.

56. The three Sisters professed with Sister Juliana Hardman were Sister M. Xavier Wood, Sister M. Vincent Bond, and Sister M. Cecilia Edwards. See Neumann, p. 344. The group signed the letter addressed to their Bishop, Rt. Rev. Thomas Walsh of Birmingham, June 14, 1841.

57. Neumann, pp. 357-358, Mother Catherine's letter on August 3, 1841 to Sister M. Teresa White concerning the

Liverpool foundation.

58. Bishop George Hilary Brown of the Liverpool Diocese, of which Doctor Thomas Youens was the Vicar General, should not be confused with Doctor George Joseph Plunket Browne, Bishop of Galway (1790-1858).

59. Savage, pp. 370-371. Two phrases are especially note-worthy in her lines to Mother M. Frances Warde:

> "You will not forget
>
> Yours ever affectionately,
> M.C. McAuley"

and "I wish Rev. Mr. Maher would bring you to me." Apparently Mother Frances Warde did not appreciate the seriousness of Mother Catherine's illness or she would have made every effort to reach her before her death.

60. Neumann, pp. 383-384.

61. Degnan, p. 340.

62. Hartnett, p. 169.

Chapter 2

1. The story of the San Francisco foundation is based on the details furnished by the first volume of the manuscript annals of the Sisters of Mercy, cited as *ASMB*. We are fortunate to have the details of arrangements, the journey and the early history of the foundation written by Mother Baptist Russell herself.

2. For a more complete picture of the Spanish period of California history, see Caughey. *California*, Chapters 8, 9, and 10.

3. Hanna, Phil Townsend, *California Through Four Centuries*. The brief account offered on pp. 48-76 marks the beginning of the Mexican period, 1822-1846.

4. "Secularization of the Missions"—see Hanna, pp. 52 and 59, as well as p. 60 for the *Reglamento Provisional para la Secularizacion de las Misiones de la Alta California*, August 9, 1834, by Governor Jose Figueroa.

5. Hanna, p. 96.

6. *Ibid.*, p. 121. August 21, 1856.

7. *ASMB*, 1854.

8. The day was significant to American Catholics because on that day Pope Pius IX promulgated the dogma of the

Immaculate Conception and it is under this title that she is invoked as the patroness of our country.

9. Some twenty years later the little convent of the Sisters of Charity on Market Street, San Francisco, was chosen as the site of the quite celebrated Palace Hotel.

10. *ASMB*, 1854.

11. See Walsh, pp. 16-36 and also McGloin, *passim*, but especially Chapter 8, "The First Decade in the See of San Francisco, 1853-1863," pp. 147-191.

12. Russell, *The three Sisters of Lord Russell of Killowen*, p. 31.

13. The story of Mother Baptist Russell's early life follows the account given by her brother in *The Life of Mother Mary Baptist Russell* published in 1901 and supplemented by Father Russell's *Three Sisters of Lord Russell of Killowen* published in 1912. See p. 16 of the latter for the quote on p. 79.

14. The "Discreets," p. 82—a term sometimes used to designate members of the General Council of the Sisters of Mercy.

15. The exchange of letters between Mother M. Francis Bridgeman and Rev. Hugh Gallagher have been carefully preserved in the San Francisco *Annals* of the period, Burlingame Archives.

16. *The Arctic* was lost at sea with all on board. The Sisters were fortunate to have had to transfer to *The Canada* because of the size of their party. *ASMB*.

17. Mother Austin Carroll, *Leaves from the Annals of the Sisters of Mercy*, Vol. 3, pp. 471-472.

18. Not the Isthmus of Panama, but the Isthmus of Nicaragua. They traveled on one of the ships of the Nicaragua Steamship Company. There is a narrow strip of land between the Lake and the Pacific.

19. *ASMB*, 1854; the details of their journey.

20. *ASMB*, 1854; their arrival in San Francisco.

21. *The Christian Advocate*, December 9, 1854.

22. *The San Francisco Herald*, January 18, 1855.

23. Hanna, pp. 119-120.

24. *ASMB*, 1855. The first convent of the Sisters of Mercy in San Francisco.

Chapter 3

1. It is important to note that the Sisters were in San

Francisco from Dec. 8., 1854, until July 27, 1857, before establishing St. Mary's Hospital on Stockton Street. *ASMB.*

2. An instrument for measuring blood pressure.

3. Harris, Henry, M.D., *California's Medical Story*, pp. 104-106.

4. The account of the purchase of the State Marine Hospital by the Sisters of Mercy on Aug. 17, 1855, is given in the Annals of the Sisters of Mercy, Burlingame, 1855.

5. *Ibid.,* 1855.

6. The County Hospital was the old State Marine Hospital the Sisters purchased for $14,000 in Aug., 1855. The terms of the contract between the Board of Supervisors and the Sisters are given in *ASMB*, 1855.

7. *ASMB*, 1857.

8. The opening of St. Mary's Hospital of Stockton Street, July 27, 1857. *ASMB*, 1857.

9. Archives, Sisters of Mercy, Burlingame.

10. Harris, p. 368.

11. *Ibid.,* pp. 369-370.

12. *ASMB*, 1857.

13. Copy of letter in Archives, Sisters of Mercy, Burlingame.

14. Archives, Sisters of Mercy, Burlingame.

15. *Ibid.,* 1859 and 1860.

16. *Ibid.,* 1860.

17. *ASMB*, 1864-65. Provision for the Magdalens.

18. Rev. Matthew Russell, *The Life of Mother Baptist Russell*, p. 64.

Chapter 4

1. Rev. James Bouchard is the "Eloquent Indian" of Father McGloin's book. As early as 1862 he was chosen as the speaker of the day, for the dedication of St. Mary's. *ASMB*, 1862.

2. Letter of Mother Baptist Russell to her aunt in Dunback, Ireland. A copy is in the Archives, Sisters of Mercy, Burlingame.

3. Hittell, p. 433.

4. Hanna, Phil Townsend, *California Through Four Centuries*, p. 130.

5. *Ibid.,* p. 126.

6. *Ibid.,* p. 141.

7. *Ibid.,* p. 145. "The Octopus" is a reference to the expanding of the railroads by the "the Big Four." The word "octopus" was used by Frank Norris in his book to describe the

railroads.

8. Benjamin E. Lloyd, *Lights and Shadown in San Francisco*, p. 323.

9. Dr. Isaac Rowell, Health Offices, *Municipal Report 1869-70*, p. 199. See also Dr. Henry Harris, *California's Medical Story*, p. 326.

10. *San Francisco Call*, July 27, 1868.

11. *Daily Evening Bulletin*, Aug. 5, 1868, from the minutes of the Board of Supervisors, Aug. 4, 1868.

12. Copy of the Archbishop's letter is in the Archives of the Sisters of Mercy, Burlingame.

13. Also in the burlingame Archives is a copy of the letter of Mother Gabriel Brown.

14. A copy is in the Archives of the Sisters of Mercy, Burlingame.

15. The account of the work of the Sisters: *Annals of the Sisters of Mercy, Burlingame*, 1868-1869.

16. Copy of the report in the Archives of the Sisters of Mercy, Burlingame; also published in the *Alta California*, Jan. 28, 1869.

17. *San Francisco Morning Call*, Feb. 9, 1869.

18. California Statutes 1869-70, p. 234. A city-wide tradition however, persists to this day that the city offered to give free transportation to the Sisters of Mercy for their heroic services during the smallpox epidemic and that Mother Russell asked that all Sisters be granted the use of City transit without charge. The privilege has existed even to this day. No other reason has been found concerning the legislation cited.

19. Copy of Governor Haight's reply, Archives of the Sisters of Mercy, Burlingame. This permission was subsequently withdrawn sometime after the death of Mother Baptist (Aug. 6, 1898).

20. *ASMB*

21. The San Francisco *Monitor*, Dec. 7, 1894.

22. *ASMB*.

23. Copy in Archives of the Sisters of Mercy, Burlingame.

24. *San Francisco Post*, March 23, 1879.

25. San Francisco *Call*, October 22, 1881.

26. *ASMB*.

27. The eight acres on Bray Avenue, now 34th Avenue, Oakland, is the site of the present home for the aged, Our Lady's Home, Oakland.

28. Fruitvale was the earlier name of this section of the city of Oakland.

29. San Francisco *Post*, March 23, 1879.

30. *AMSB*.

31. Report to Archbishop Alemany on November 23, 1877. Archives of Sisters of Mercy, Burlingame.

32. *ASMB*.

33. *ASMB*.

34. Copy of letter in Archives, Sisters of Mercy, Burlingame.

35. *ASMB*.

36. "The first object of the institute is education." See the *San Francisco Herald*, June 21, 1856.

37. Father Matthew Russell, S.J., *The Life of Mother Baptist Russell*, p. 32.

38. St. Rose School, Sacramento, *ASMB*.

39. The Grass Valley foundation under Sister M. Teresa King was made August 20, 1863, and was called Convent of the Sacred Heart. The schools opened in September. St. Joseph's was for the girls; St. Aloysius for the boys. It was Mother de Sales Igo who in 1878 changed the name of Academy of the Sacred Heart to St. Mary's Academy, now a State landmark.

40. The Rincon Hill School, 1871, *ASMB*.

41. Old St. Brendan's School.

42. *ASMB*, 1855-1898.

43. Copy of the letter in the Burlingame Archives.

44. Copy in Archives of Sisters of Mercy, Burlingame.

45. *Ibid*. Six years; i.e., two terms. Mother Baptist Russell was elected for three years in 1879 and reelected in 1882.

46. There is a copy of the letter in the Archives of Sisters of Mercy, Burlingame.

47. Sir Charles Russell, 1832-1903—*Dictionary of National Biography*, Vol. XXII Supplement, pp. 1199-1204, Oxford University Publishers.

48. See *Catholic Directory*.

49. Copy of the letter in Burlingame Archives.

50. See Sister M. Clement Manion's unpublished theses, *Principles of Catechetical Instruction According to Rev. Peter C. Yorke, 1953*. Copy in Russell College Library. See also the more recent biography of Father Yorke by Rev. Joseph S. Brusher, S.J., *Consecrated Thunderbolt*, 1973.

51. *Ibid*.

52. Copy of letter in Archives of Sisters of Mercy, Burlin-

game.

53. *Ibid.*

54. Father Matthew Russell, S.J., *Life of Mother Baptist Russell*, pp. 172-179.

55. *Loc. cit.*, p. 172.

56. *Loc. cit.*, p. 173.

57. *Loc. cit.*, pp. 174-175.

58. Father Russell's statement of the cause of Mother Baptist's death, p. 175.

59. San Francisco *Call*, August 6, 1898.

60. The letter of the Archbishop to Father Matthew Russell, S.J., may be found as the introduction to "Part One: Mother Baptist Russell" in Father Russell's *The Three Sisters of Lord Russell of Killowen* published in 1912.

61. San Francisco *Chronicle*, August 10, 1898.

62. Copy in Archives of Sisters of Mercy, Burlingame.

63. *Ibid.*

64. *ASMB* 1900-1903.

Chapter 5

1. *ASMB*, 1902.

2. *Ibid.*, *1905*

3. *Loc. Cit.*

4. See Dr. Elwood Topham's own account in his book *St. Mary's Hospital and the Sisters of Mercy, 1903-1949.*

5. *ASMB*, 1906.

6. Topham, *loc. cit.*

7. *Leader*, April 28, 1906.

8. A journalistic commemorative: *Call, Chronicle* and *Examiner*, April 19, 1906. The three morning papers sent a request to the *Oakland Tribune* for use of their facilities, and according to Byington and Lewis, p. 417, the request was granted and the plant put at their disposal.

9. Byington and Lewis, *The History of San Francisco*, Vol. 1, p. 414.

10. Details of the fire as it affected the Sisters of Mercy have been culled from the *ASMB*, 1906-1907.

11. For assistance from overseas see Gordon Thomas and Max Morgan Witts, The *San Francisco Earthquake*, p. 167.

12. Copy in Archives, Sisters of Mercy, Burlingame.

13. *ASMB*, 1906-1912.

14. Copy of letter in Burlingame Archives.
15. *ASMB*, 1917-1923.
16. Copy of letter in Burlingame Archives.
17. *ASMB*, 1920.

Chapter 6

1. For the story of the early Church in Yreka, see Walsh, *Hallowed Were the Gold Dust Trails*, Chapter XVI.

2. Bishop Eugene O'Connell was in charge of the Vicariate of Marysville cut from the San Francisco Archdiocese in 1860. See Walsh, pp. 35-45.

3. See Sister M. Benignus Doherty, R.S.M., *The First Hundred Years of the Manchester Sisters of Mercy*, pp. 40-44, "The Yreka Foundation."

4. Data from the Life Records of the Rio Vista Community, Burlingame Archives.

5. See Doherty for details of the journey West, pp. 40-43, supplemented by Rio Vista Annals. Arrival in Yreka February 2, 1871. Both letters of Bishop Eugene O'Connell to Mother Frances Warde are quoted by Mother Eulalia Herron, pp. 173-175, *The Sisters of Mercy in the United States, (1843-1928)* and by Sister M. Benignus Doherty, pp. 41-43, *The First Hundred Years of the Manchester Sisters of Mercy, 1858-1958. Rio Vista Annals* and Life Records are now in the Burlingame Archives.

6. The story of the July 4 fire is recounted in the *Yreka Journal*, Bancroft Library, Berkeley, California.

7. *ASMRV* Burlingame Archives.

8. *Ibid.*

9. The Sisters who did not accompany Mother Camillus discontinued, after a few years, the school at Yreka and transferred to Red Bluff on the advice of Bishop Patrick Manogue. Sister M. Helena Dickson was the Superior of this group. In 1930 the Red Bluff Sisters of Mercy affiliated with the Sisters of Mercy of the Union and now belong to the Omaha Province. Doherty, *loc. cit.*, pp. 43-44.

10. *ASMRV*, in Burlingame Archives.

11. *Ibid.*

12. Archives of Sisters of Mercy, Burlingame; Life Records and *Annals of Sacred Heart Convent*, Ukiah.

13. Life Records, Ukiah, now in Burlingame.

14. A.P.A., the American Protective Association, very hostile to Catholics.

15. The Ukiah Foundation, 1883-1903. See *Annals* and Ukiah Life Records, now in the Archives of the Sisters of Mercy, Burlingame.

16. St. Joseph's Boys' School, Rio Vista, 1903, was the Rio Vista school for boys that became St. Joseph's Military Academy in 1923. In 1932 St. Joseph's Military Academy was moved to Belmont. Captain Edward Dougherty served as Commandant during the twenty years (1932-1952) on its Belmont Campus.

17. *Annals of Mount Carmel Academy*, 1910-1940.

Chapter 7

1. For some of these land grants see Phil Townsend Hanna's *California Through Four Centuries;* e.g., Sutter's Grant, *New Helvetia*, p. 69; and *Rancho San Antonio* granted to Luis Peralta, p. 114. The latter grant comprised a good part of the present city of Oakland. Also see Caughey's *California* (pp. 160-170) who on p. 167 states that between 1830-1846 eight million acres were in the hands of eight hundred grantees.

2. McGloin, *California's First Archbishop* (July 29, 1853), pp. 92-95.

3. Walsh, *Hallowed Were the Gold Dust Trails*, p. 17.

4. McGloin, *op cit.* pp. 144-145.

5. Caughey, *op. cit.*, p. 261 seq.

6. *Ibid.*, pp. 402-404.

7. *ASMLA*, now in Burlingame Archives.

8. Life Records of the Sisters of Mercy in Los Angeles, Burlingame Archives, supplemented by an exchange of letters with several New York communities, as well as with the Sisters of Mercy, Grand Rapids, Michigan. On February 12, 1972, Sister M. Lucille Middleton, R.S.M., Grand Rapids, wrote concerning Sister M. Bonaventure:

"Professed member of the Sisters of Mercy, Greenbush, New York, was admitted as a member of this community, June 16, 1881."

Greenbush was a lead since it was the old name of Rensselaer, New York. Two years later, July 26, 1974, Sister Marjorie Elizabeth Allen, R.S.M., wrote from Farmington Hills, Michigan. She had found my letter of February 12, 1972, and she promptly offered the following:

"Elizabeth Fox, daughter of John and Bedelia Fox of County Galway, Ireland, entered the Convent of Mercy, New York, February 2, 1868. Received the Holy Habit August 4, 1868, taking in religion the name Sister M. Bonaventure. Made her Holy Profession September 11, 1870, Convent of Mercy, Greenbush, New York. Excerpt from the Convent of Mercy Chapter Book, East Greenbush (Rensselaer) New York.

9. Bishop N. Chrysostom Matz, Coadjutor to the Most Reverend Joseph Machebeuf, the first Bishop of Denver; *Catholic Directory.*

10. Bishop Francis Mora, the Coadjutor to Bishop Thaddeus Amat, Cm., Bishop Alemany's successor to the See of Montery; *Catholic Directory.*

Chapter 8

1. Details for the Los Angeles foundation were supplied by the records of the Sisters of Mercy, Los Angeles: Life Records, Chapter Books, Reports, Letters and Annals, referred to as *ASMLA;* all now in the Burlingame Archives.

2. Sister M. Philomena Coe offered as a postulant to assist Sister M. Bonaventure Fox in the Salinas project. Early in 1888 the two left Grand Rapids, Michigan, and made their way to Durango, Colorado, where Julia Coe served her postulancy beginning February 4, 1888. On September 2, 1888, she received the habit and the name Sister M. Philomena. (From the records of the Sisters of Mercy, Durango, Colorado)

From June, 1889, until April 7, 1890, she worked with Sister M. Bonaventure in the school in Salinas, California. Sister M. Philomena made her vows on September 24, 1890, in the Cathedral of St. Vibiana, Los Angeles. Sister M. Philomena was appointed Superior and she also served as administrator of Mercy Hospital, Bakersfield, on February 9, 1910. In 1913 she was named Superior and administrator of old St. Thomas Aquinas Sanatorium at Mentone, California. Sister was chosen Mother Superior of the Los Angeles Community in May, 1914, and served until 1917, when she became Mother Assistant. She died at Mercy Hospital, Bakersfield, March 30, 1932. (*ASMLA* and Life Records)

3. St. Martha's Home for Working Girls, established in 1890, was the first work of the Sisters of Mercy in Los Angeles. (*ASMLA*)

4. The Care of Aged Women, 1891. (*ASMLA*)

5. Mercy Hospital, San Bernardino, 1891-1897. According to the Sister Annalist, the closing was prompted by a change of conditions and needs. *(ASMLA)*

6. The Home of the Guardian Angels, 1895-1918. *(ASMLA)*

7. The new Mercy Motherhouse at 326 Boyd Street, Los Angeles, was provided in 1896. *(ASMLA)*

8. A larger home for God's little ones had to be opened in 1895, South Figueroa Street, which served its purpose until the quarters on West Washington were built in 1906. *(ASMLA)*

9. Evidence of the growth of the Los Angeles Community in nine years was recorded at the time of the death of Mother M. Bonaventure Fox, April 6, 1899.

10. It appears from the records that Father Joachim Adam left Spain entertaining the hope of returning to California, when death overtook him in England.

11. See John Walton Caughey, *California*, 1953 edition, pp. 419-421, for evidence of the leadership of E.L. Doheny in the oil industry of Southern California.

12. Consult Caughey also for other industrial developments in Los Angeles, especially pp. 486-487 for the automobile industry; pp. 497-500, the film industry; and pp. 545-546 and 562 for the airplane industry. Because of the numbers employed, these industries are often called "blotting paper industries."

13. *Ibid.*, pp. 450-455 for the story of the San Pedro Harbor improvement.

14. *Ibid.*, pp. 423-424, The Los Angeles Aqueduct.

15. *Ibid.*, pp. 496-497 and pp. 522-523, the Boulder Dam Project.

16. *ASMLA*, 1906—Our Lady of Mercy Convent, 4060 West Washington, Los Angeles, which opened June 30, 1906.

17. St. Martha's Home for Working Girls, 1626 South Figueroa Street, Los Angeles, opened in 1908, and continued as such until its closing in 1918 at the suggestion of Bishop John J. Cantwell. The twenty-eight years of service referred to include the years before they moved to South Figueroa Street. *(ASMLA, 1918)*

18. Sacred Heart Elementary School, Redlands, 1908, and Our Lady of Mercy, 1918, are evidence of an effort by the Sisters of Mercy to meet the most urgent needs of the diocese at the time. The latter school was established to provide for the

many Mexican children even then coming in good numbers. *(ASMLA,* 1908 and 1918)

19. Mercy Hospital, Bakersfield, was established by the Sisters of Mercy Los Angeles in 1910 at the request of Bishop Thomas James Conaty. (See *(ASMLA,* 1910, and also the subsequent Annals, Records, Reports, Letters, etc. of the Sisters of Mercy, Bakersfield).

20. United Airlines no longer provides this service and transportation is, at present, not too promising.

21. In 1922 Bishop John J. Cantwell was transferred from Monterey to Los Angeles. By 1936 Bishop Cantwell became an Archbishop of the Archdiocese of Los Angeles. About this time there was a reorganization of dioceses, and Bakersfield was in the Diocese of Monterey-Fresno until the split of this Diocese in 1967. Bakersfield has since been in the Fresno Diocese. *Catholic Directory.*

22. A copy of the letter of Mother M. Joachim McBrinn is the Burlingame Archives; the original is in the Convent of Mercy Hospital, Bakersfield.

23. These two Sisters also came from the Los Angeles Community of the Sisters of Mercy. *(ASMLA)*

24. *ASMLA,* as well as the *Annals* of St. Francis Convent, Bakersfield.

25. Ireland was a fruitful source of vocations during these pioneer days. *(ASM Bak)*

26. See *ASM Bak* for details of the $45,000 gift which made possible an up-to-date hospital by november 1, 1912.

27. *Ibid.,* completed November 9, 1913.

28. *Loc. cit.,* the three-year nursing program.

29. *Ibid.*

30. The St. Thomas Sanatorium, Mentone.*(ASMLA,* 1911-1917)

31. *ASMLA* and also records of the Academy, e.g., Yearbooks, press reports, etc., for the story of St. John's Military Academy.

32. The Watsonville Orphanage, an interim assignment, 1919-1921. *(ASMLA)*

33. The story of the Florence mission St. Aloysius, *ASMLA* and its House Annals.

34. *ASMLA, passim* for the evidence of Mother M. Joachim McBrinn's contribution to the Los Angeles Community and her leadership during the period of the amalgamation.

Chapter 9

1. *ASMSD—Annals of the Sisters of Mercy, San Diego*—are the chief source of material for Chapter 9. The Annals are supplemented by Life Records, Chapter Reports, the Annals of the branch houses, e.g., St. John's Hospital Convent, Oxnard, and by a number of letters in the possession of the San Diego Community, now in the Archives in Burlingame.

2. Copy of the letter of Bishop Mora may be found in the Burlingame Archives.

3. Sister M. Eulalia Herron, *Sisters of Mercy in the United States*, 1843-1928: p. 178, Mother M. Michael's early religious life; p. 338, Mother Michael was one of the five Sisters who left St. John's Hospital, St. Louis, February 8, 1882, to bring the works of Mercy to the Diocese of Denver; p. 341; Durango, its school in 1882; Mercy Hospital, Durango, 1883, p. 344, St. Joseph's Hospital at Ouray, Colorado, in 1887.

4. Copy of Sister M. de Pazzi Bentley's letter; Burlingame Archives.

5. The original St. Joseph's Hospital, 1891; *ASMSD*, 1891.

6. *Ibid.*, the Home for the Aged, 1892.

7. *ASMSD*, 1898.

8. *Ibid.*, 1900.

9. Copy in Burlingame Archives.

10. See Caughey, p. 412-416, George Chaffey's irrigation project to bring water from the Colorado River.

11. *ASMSD*, 1910-1917.

12. See both *ASMSD*, 1912, and the *Annals* of the Sisters of Mercy, Oxnard.

13. *Ibid.*, and the local daily papers.

14. The letter of Cardinal Falconio, December 22, 1916, Burlingame Archives.

15. Much of the story of Mother Michael's early life has been gleaned from the *Short Life of Mother Michael* by Rev. Henry Brinkmeyer. For her life in religion there is the testimony of history preserved in the Annals of the Sisters of Mercy and the memory of her daughters.

Chapter 10

1. The excerpt is from Howard R. Lamar, *The Far Southwest*, 1846-1912, a book jacket epitome which concisely

explains the late admission of New Mexico and Arizona as states. The same author also gives a good account of the work of Bishop Jean Baptist Lamy, especially pp. 102 and 103.

2. Rev. Henry Walsh, S.J., in his book, *Hallowed Were the Gold Dust Trails*, pp. 16-17, made note of the fact that these names had been submitted to Pope Pius IX by the Seventh Provincial Council of Baltimore in May, 1849, as a part of the arrangements for the creation of a permanent episcopate in California.

3. In Salpointe, *Soldiers of the Cross*, edited by Odie B. Faulk, pp. 4-6, we are told that it was at this same Council that the American Bishops petitioned the Holy See to establish a Vicariate Apostolic in the New Mexico Territory separate from the See of Durango, Mexico, and that they nominated Father Jean Baptist Lamy, pp. 6-7. Salpointe, Chapter II, pp. 6-18, states that Pope Pius IX on July 19, 1850, created the New Mexico Vicariate and on July 25 of the same year appointed Lamy Vicar Apostolic.

4. Rev. Joseph Machebeuf, companion of Bishop Lamy to Santa Fe, later became Vicar Apostolic of Colorado and Utah, and subsequently (in 1887) the first Bishop of Denver. Salpointe, pp. 10-15.

5. Chapter IV, p. 25 seq. The Vicariate of New Mexico was raised to the rank of an Episcopal See July 29, 1853, with the city of Santa Fe, the See of Bishop Lamy.

6. See Salpointe, p. 65, for the account that Colorado and Utah became a Vicariate Apostolic and Rev. Joseph Machebeuf was appointed the Vicar Apostolic February 5, 1868. Note, too, that on February 12, 1871, Utah was placed under the jurisdiction of the Archbishop of San Francisco.

7. Salpointe, Chapter XI, pp. 111 seq. Arizona was made a Vicariate Apostolic September 25, 1868, and Rev. J.B. Salpointe was named Vicar Apostolic. The Bishop-elect went to France for his episcopal consecration and at the same time to secure much-needed recruits for the Arizona missions. In France Salpointe was joined in a journey to Rome by the Vicar Apostolic of Colorado and Utah, the Right Rev. J.P. Machebeuf, who had also gone to France to secure volunteers for his missions. Salpointe, p. 113.

8. The first Sisters to open schools and hospitals in the Southwest were Sisters of Loretto, among them a relative of Bishop Lamy. Chapter XIV of Salpointe's book, *Soldiers of the*

Cross, gives a skeletal survey of the work of the Sisters of Mercy in New Mexico and Arizona. It was at the invitation of Bishop Salpointe that the Sisters of Mercy came to New Mexico (Mesilla) in 1880. See p. 158 seq., Salpointe, *Soldiers of the Cross*, edited by Odie Faulk.

Chapter 11

1. The story of Mother Josephine Brennan and the New Mexico foundation has been based on the original manuscript annals of the Sisters of Mercy, New Mexico and Arizona, Archives of the Sisters of St. Joseph's Hospital Convent, Phoenix, Arizona.

2. Rev. Augustin Morin, pastor, Mesilla, was one of the six French missionaries whom Bishop Salpointe brought from Clermont, Ferrand, France, in 1869. In the same group was Rev. Peter Bourgade, later Bishop of Tucson. Much credit for the evangelization of the United States in the Southwest should be conceded to the French missionaries. See Salpointe, *passim*, especially Chapters VI, VII, XIII, and the lists of its missionaries. Salpointe, pp. 152-157.

3. At the time of the creation of the Vicariate of Arizona, Mesilla belonged to this ecclesiastical division. It is a bit confusing, since Mesilla is in New Mexico. See Salpointe, Chapter XI, p. 116:

The Vicariate of Arizona at the time of its creation comprised the Territory of that name and its parish of Las Cruces in New Mexico. Soon after the parish of Mesilla, also in New Mexico and that of Isleta and San Elizario in El Paso County, Texas, were added to the Vicariate of Arizona by decision of the Holy See. These parishes, with the exception of Las Cruces, had been under the jurisdiction of the Bishop of Durango, Mexico. The decree ordering the change had come from Rome to the Vicar Apostolic of Arizona, but nothing was heard from Durango to make it effective. . . .

Finally on p. 118 Salpointe says: "The Mexican prelate wrote that the Pontifical Decree had been received at last, and transferred its jurisdiction of the parishes already mentioned to the Vicar Apostolic of Arizona toward the end of the year 1871."

Salpointe also tells us that because of the revolution which was going on in Mexico, all mail communication had been stopped.

4. Evidence that Mesilla was a re-location from Cynthiana, Kentucky, is supported by two very reliable accounts:

1) The obituary of Mother M. Josephine Brennan which appeared in *The Southwest*, a Durango Weekly, January 19, 1884. It states:

"She came to America and located in a convent in Cynthiana, Kentucky, where she remained for two years and then came west to New Mexico."

2) There is also a letter of Mother M. Paul O'Grady, June 23, 1894 to the Most Rev. Peter Bourgade, Vicar Apostolic of Arizona, and written from Phoenix, which supports this contention.

"Your letter was received, and I hasten to reply. . .Our Community was established in 1880 (December 24) by Mother M. Josephine Brennan from Cynthiana, Kentucky."

5. Eugene Hollon, in his work, *The Southwest, Old and New*, p. 281, tell us that President Rutherford B. Hayes appointed Major General Lew Wallace Territorial Governor in 1878. Federal troops were ordered to the scene to stop some local lawlessness. Before the troops took any action, Pat Garrett, the Sheriff shot "Billy the Kid." Probably Wallace stayed on to maintain peace. At any rate, his special achievement during his stay in New Mexico was the completion of his well-known novel, *Ben Hur, a Tale of the Christ*, 1888.

6. Paul Horgan in *The Centuries at Santa Fe*, p. 271, provided the interesting detail of Susan Wallace's prose sketches of "Indian Life in the Southwest" for the *Atlantic Monthly*. He also states that Lew Wallace not only wrote well, but that he had a flair for drawing, which he used to make more graphic his wife's magazine articles. Horgan, p. 272.

7. It was the coming of the railroad, more than anything else that brought fundamental changes in the Southwest. The first such change was effected when the Santa Fe Trail was

replaced by the Atchison, Topeka and Santa Fe Railroad. About the same time the Southern Pacific advanced slowly from the West. By 1881 the Santa Fe joined the Southern Pacific at Deming and gave New Mexico her first transcontinental line. See Riegel, *America Moves West*, pp. 557-560.

8. Details of the story of the Sisters of Mercy in New Mexico and Arizona *ASMA*.

9. Sister M. Paul O'Grady was one of the aspirants who came from Ireland in the summer of 1881. Hers was the first religious reception in Mesilla, March 1, 1882. On May 17, 1884, Sister M. Paul O'Grady was professed in Mesilla. This was also the last Profession ceremony at Mesilla. By August 22, 1884, the Sisters were held the first religious ceremony in Silver City, New Mexico, the new Motherhouse of the Sisters of Mercy.

10. Annals and Records in the Phoenix Archives, also reports of Sister M. Cecilia Barry of the Omaha Province. In gathering material she had come on some interesting details in Durango, which she shared.

11. *Ibid.*

12. Shortly after Mother M. Paul became Mother Superior of the New Mexico Community, she had the Motherhouse changed from Mesilla to Silver City. The change was quite wise because it was more convenient for all the houses. After January 1, 1890, the Annals stem from Silver City until the Sisters withdrew from Silver City in 1915 and the convent in Phoenix, Arizona, became the new Motherhouse. *ASM NM & Ariz.*

13. Salpointe, pp. 158-167.

14. *Silver City Enterprise*, August 10, 1883. Bancroft Library, U.C., Berkeley.

15. *Annals of the Sisters of Mercy, Silver City, New Mexico. ASMSC*

16. Salpointe, p. 136-137.

17. *Ibid.*, p. 137.

18. *Loc. cit.*, p. 165. In 1898 the Arizona Vicariate became a regular diocese, with its See at Tucson, and the Most Rev. Peter Bourgade its first bishop.

19. *Annals of the Sisters of Mercy, New Mexico.*

20. *Ibid.*

21. *Ibid.*

22. See Los Alamos foundation, 1882-1893.

23. It was at Los Alamos that Emilio Gene Segre, a nuclear physicist of the University of California, spent much of his time working on the Manhattan Project which exploded the first

310

atom bomb in 1945. As an atomic research center, Los Alamos has drawn some 20,000 interested in nuclear physics. See also Caughey, pp. 549-550.

24. See Salpointe, Chapter XIV: "The Sisters of Mercy in New Mexico and Arizona" but for the dates see the *Annals of the Sisters of Mercy.*

25. *Annals of the Sisters of Mercy, Arizona;* Archives, Convent of St. Joseph's Hospital and Medical Center, Phoenix.

26. When Pope Pius IX created the Metropolitan See of Santa Fe, with the Rev. J.B. Lamy its first Archbishop, February 12, 1875, the Vicar Apostolic of Colorado and the Vicar Apostolic of Arizona became suffragans. It was some time, however, before the Diocese of Denver and that of Tucson were established, the former August 16, 1887, and the latter May 8, 1897. Even before the creation of the See of Tucson the Vicar Apostolic of Arizona, the Most Rev. J.B. Salpointe, was called to Santa Fe, April 22, 1884, to serve as Coadjutor with the right of succession to Archbishop Lamy. Upon the resignation of the latter on July 18, 1885, Archbishop Salpointe succeeded to the See of Santa Fe.

On January 7, 1899, the Most Rev. Peter Bourgade was transferred by Pope Leo XIII from the See of Tucson to the Metropolitan See of Santa Fe, New Mexico, as its new Archbishop. At his departure Very Rev. Edouard Gerard was named Administrator of the Diocese of Tucson until the appointment of Right Rev. Henry Granjon who was consecrated bishop by James Cardinal Gibbons on June 17, 1900.

The Diocese of El Paso was erected March 3, 1914. It embraced Mesilla in Dona Ana County as well as Silver City in Grant County, New Mexico. The creation of the Diocese of El Paso led the Sisters of Mercy to withdraw from Mesilla and Silver City and to concentrate their forces within the Diocese of Tucson; Sources: Salpointe, *passim* and the *Catholic Directory.*

Chapter 12

1. The Chief sources of information for Chapter 12, the story of the Sisters of Mercy in Arizona, has been supplied by their own annals, now in the Archives of St. Joseph's Medical Center, Phoenix, and alluded to: *ASMA.*

2. W. Eugene Hollon, *The Southwest Old and New*, pp. 444-445.

3. *ASMA.*

4. In 1913 St. Joseph's School of Nursing held its first graduation. Among the graduates were Sister M. Ignatius Briody, Sister M. Aloysius Phelan, Sister M. Benedict O'Grady, Sister M. Raphael Gavigan. The other Sisters who had started with the class and had been called to duty in other houses graduated at a later date.

5. *ASMA*

6. *Ibid.*

7. *Loc. cit.*

8. See *Prescott Annals*, bound volumes now in Burlingame Archives, p. 10.

9. President Wilson's War Message was given April 2 and Congress responded with a decisive vote April 6, 1917. See Schlesinger, pp. 414-418.

10. Details from the *ASMA*, Phoenix.

11. *Ibid.*

12. Details in the *Prescott Annals*, Burlingame.

13. Bishop Henry Granjon succeeded the Most Rev. Peter Bourgade when the latter was transferred to the Metropolitan See of Santa Fe, January 7, 1899; *Catholic Directory*.

14. These two Sisters are the only Sisters of Mercy interred at Mesilla, New Mexico.

15. In 1901 additional lots #3, #10, #11, #12, #13 were purchased from Mr. Murphy at $250.00 a lot. In this way provision was made for inevitable expansion. The second addition to the building was begun in 1902 and completed in 1903. *Annals of the Sisters of Mercy, Prescott*, now in Burlingame.

16. On April 10, 1915, Mass was celebrated in the new chapel in Prescott, and in less than two weeks Mother Joseph Anderson and her novices were transferred from Phoenix to Prescott; *ASM Prescott*.

17. The story of the Sisters of Mercy in Nogales has been supplied by the Nogales Annals, which are found in the bound volume of the *Prescott Annals*, Burlingame Archives.

18. It seems to have been a choice between Huerta and Carranza following the murder of President Francisco Madera. Wilson would not recognize Huerta, who was alleged to have been implicated in Madera's death. For this reason, the American President decided to lift the embargo so that munitions could flow to Huerta's rivals. Huerta resigned in the summer of 1914 and withdrew to Spain. He was succeeded by

Carranza. See Schesinger, pp. 388-390.

19. Carranza was subsequently murdered for his efforts to abolish "restrictive clauses" from their Constitution—or so it has been explained. See Parsons, *Mexican Martyrdom*, pp. 15-16 and *Blood Drenched Altars*, pp. 291-292, by Francis Clement Kelley. Both state that Carranza was shot for trying to change 130 of the Mexican Constitution, a step in the direction of freedom of religion.

20. The six Sisters were Sister M. Paul O'Grady, Sister M. Aloysius Bambrick, Sister M. Peter McTernan, Sister M. Raphael Gavigan, and the newly professed Sister M. Berchmans McDonnell. *ASM Nogales*, Burlingame, Archives.

Chapter 13

1. Material for this chapter, "The Amalgamation," has been taken from the Annals of the Communities of the Sisters of Mercy involved in this study, and the facts as supplied by those of the Chapter Books, Reports, Records, and pertinent letters. They are now in the Burlingame Archives of the Sisters of Mercy.

2. See Savage, *Catherine McAuley, The First Sister of Mercy*, Chapter XV, "Catherine's Views on Government," p. 260 seq.

3. A copy of Archbishop Alemany's letter of November 1, 1882, is in the Burlingame Archives.

4. It will be recalled that the Academy in Rio Vista was established in 1876, and St. Joseph's School for Small Boys was opened in 1903, after the amalgamation of the Ukiah Sisters of Mercy with the Sisters of Mercy, Rio Vista, in 1903.

5. The Most Rev. John J. Cantwell was appointed Bishop of Monterey—Los Angeles on September 21, 1917, and was consecrated December 5, 1917.

7. On September 2, 1918, the Most Rev. Bishop appointed Sister M. Joachim McBrinn Superior of the United Los Angeles and San Diego Community. Letters confirming the appointment of Mother M. Joachim McBrinn and Mother M. Michael Cummings are in the Archives of the Sisters of Mercy, Burlingame.

8. The El Paso Diocese was erected March 3, 1914. Catholic Directory.

9. A copy of the letter of Cardinal Falconio, July 21, 1918,

can be found in the Burlingame Archives.

10. For the vote of the Los Angeles Chapter, see the Los Angeles Chapter Book, March 12, 1921. Burlingame Archives.

11. The Los Angeles Sisters had taken the vote July 1, 1921. See Los Angeles Chapter Book now in Burlingame. The vote of the San Francisco Sisters of Mercy was held July 29, 1921; all these Chapter Books are now in Burlingame Archives.

12. Given at Rome on February 16, 1922. (N. 8304 - 21)

13. The Constitutions were examined by the Sacred Congregation for Religious and approved by Pope Pius XI, November 21, 1922. (N. 8304-21 M 98)

14. Letter of Archbishop Hanna, April 19, 1922, Burlingame Archives.

15. Mother M. Paul O'Grady died January 1, 1922, after a very brief illness.

16. At the time of the Amalgamation of the Sisters of Mercy, California and Arizona, the following membership is attested by their own records:

The Rio Vista Community, including the seven Ukiah Sisters who had joined the Rio Vista Sisters in 1903, and two Sisters in temporary vows:	30
The Los Angeles Community	60
The San Diego Community	54
The Arizona Community	36
The San Francisco Community	121
Total at the time of the Amalgamation of 1922	301

17. The name, Sisters of Mercy, California and Arizona, was the corporate title at that time.

18. A description of "The Oaks" at the time of purchase by the Sisters of Mercy may be found in a forty-three page booklet printed by Bruce Brough, San Francisco, for the Mercantile Trust Company and entitled, *The Oaks*, Burlingame Hills, San Mateo County, Howard and White, Architects.

19. Alan Maginnis, representative of the Mercantile Trust Company.

20. *ASMB Annals of the Sisters of Mercy*, Burlingame, 1924.

21. This history, which has been developed in detail by the author, is too long to be included in this volume; but interested researchers may contact the archivist at the motherhouse of the Sisters of Mercy, Burlingame, California, for use of the collated materials covering the history of the community from the time of the amalgamation until the present.

BIBLIOGRAPHY

Basic Sources:
Documents and Original Manuscripts

A.

Documents of Vatican II 1963-1965. Guild Press, New York, General Editor Walter Abbott, S.J., American Press, 1966.
Documents on Renewal of Religious. Daughters of St. Paul, Boston, Mass. 1979.

B.

1. *Annals of the Sisters of Mercy*
   Original Communities:

San Francisco	1854-1979
Rio Vista	1876-1917
Ukiah	1883-1903
New Mexico-Arizona	1880-1923
Los Angeles	1890-1923
	1890-1923

2. *Annals of the Sisters of Mercy*
   California-Arizona, 1924-1979
3. Reports, Official Records, Life Records, Chapter Books, Letters, etc.

C. Rescripts from Rome

Additional References:

Atherton, Gertrude, *My San Francisco.* Bobbs-Merrill, New York, 1941.

Bailey, Thomas, *The American Pageant.* Fourth Ed., Heath, Lexington, Mass., 1971.

Bancroft, Hubert H., *History of California,* A.L. Bancroft, San Francisco, 1884-1890.

Bauman, Sister M. Beata, S.M., *The Way of Mercy: Catherine McAuley's Contribution to Nursing.* Vantage Press, New York, 1958.

Bean, Walton E., *California: an Interpretive History* McGraw, Hill, New York, 1973, Second Edition.

Becket, J.C., *The Making of Modern Ireland: 1603-1923.* Alfred Knopf, New York, 1966.

Behlmeyer, Karl and Herman Fuckle, *Church History*, vol. III: *Modern and Present Times.* Newman Press, Westminster, Md., 1966.

Bolster, Sister M. Angela, *Catherine McAuley in Her Own Words.* Published by the Dublin Diocesan Office, John English & Co., Ltd., Wexford, 1978.

Bolton, Herbert Eugene, *Outpost of Empire: The Story of the Founding of San Francisco.* Alfred Knopf, New York, 1931.

Brinkmeyer, Rev. Henry, *Life of Mother M. Michael Cummings* (privately printed, n.d.).

Brusher, Rev. Joseph S., S.J., *Consecrated Thunderbolt: Father Peter C. Yorke.* San Francisco. Joseph F. Wagner, Inc., Hawthorne, N.Y., 1973.

Byington, L.F. and Oscar Lewis, *The History of San Francisco*, 3 vol. A.J. Clark Co., San Francisco, 1931.

Carroll, Mother Austin, S.M., *Life of Catherine McAuley*, second edition, 1874. Vicentian Press, St. Louis, Mo., 1860.

————, *Leaves from the Annals of the Sisters of Mercy*, 4 vol. The Catholic Publication Society, New York, 1881-1895.

Caughey, John Walton, *California*, second edition. Prentice-Hall, Inc., New York, 1953.

Chapman, Charles E., *A History of California: The Spanish Period.* Macmillan, New York, 1955.

Cleland, Robert Glass, *From Wilderness to Empire: A History of California*, edited by Glenn Dumke. Alfred Knopf, New York, 1962, new edition.

————, *California in Our Times, 1900-1940.* Alfred Knopf, New York, 1947.

Cronin, Rev. Bernard, *California Caravan of Charity: An Historical Sketch of Nursing Sisterhoods and Their Hospitals.*

Curtis, Edmund, *A History of Ireland.* Barnes & Noble, New York, 1961.

Degnan, Sister M. Bertrand, R.S.M., *Mercy Unto Thousands: The Life of Mother Catherine McAuley.* Newman Press, Westminster, Md., 1957.

Diamond Jubilee of St. Anthony's Parish, 1871-1946. Harrington McGinnis, Oakland, 1946.

Dictionary of National Biography. Oxford University, England. (For account of the work of Lord Charles Russell of

Killowen).

Doherty, Sister M. Benignus, R.S.M., *The First Hundred Years of the Manchester Sisters of Mercy, 1858-1958.* Published by Manchester Sisters of Mercy, Manchester, N.H., 1968.

Edwards, Robert Dudley, editor, *The Great Famine, 1845-1852.* (Studies edited by Robert D. Edwards & T.D. Williams) New York University Press, N.Y., 1957.

Evans, Sister M. Daniel, S.M., *From the Letter to the Spirit: A Study of the Charism of Mother M. Catherine McAuley.* Based on the Letters. Sisters of Mercy, Burlingame, 1968.

Gilliam, Harold, *San Francisco Bay.* Doubleday, New York, 1957.

Gilsdorf, Sister Helen Marie, S.M., *The Contribution of the Sisters of Mercy to Music Education in California.* Unpublished Thesis for M.A., Holy Names College, Oakland, 1969.

Hanna, Phil Townsend, *California Through Four Centuries: A Handbook of Memorable Historical Data.* Farrar & Rinehart, Inc., New York, 1935.

Harris, Henry, M.D., *California's Medical Story.* Grabborn, San Francisco, 1932.

Hartnett, Mother M. Vincent. S.M., *Popular Life of Catherine McAuley.* Edited by the Sisters of Mercy, St. Louis, Mo. Original Dublin Ed., 1863. Baltimore Publishing Co., 1887.

Healy, Kathleen, *Frances Warde, American Foundress of the Sisters of Mercy.* The Seabury Press, New York, 1973.

Herron, Sister M. Eulalia, *The Sisters of Mercy in the United States, 1843-1928.* Macmillan Co., New York, 1929.

Hittell, John S., *A History of the City of San Francisco and Incidentally of California.* A.L. Bancroft, 1878.

Hittell, Theodore H., *History of California* N.J. Stone & Co., San Francisco, 1898.

Hollon, W. Eugene, *The Southwest, Old and New.* Alfred Knopf, New York, 1961.

Horgan, Paul, *The Centuries of Santa Fe.* E.P. Dutton, New York, 1956.

Huggims, Dorothy, *Continuation of the Annals of San Francisco, 1854-1855.* A.L. Bancroft, 1878. Supplement to the City Annals of San Francisco by Soule, Gihon and Nesbit.

Hunt, Rockwell, *California the Golden.* Silver-Burdett, San Francisco, 1911.

Jacobsen, Pauline, *City of the Golden Fifties.* University of

California Press, Berkeley, 1941.

Jones, J. Roy, M.D., *Memories, Men and Medicine.* Society of Medical Improvement, Sacramento, California, 1950.

Kelley, Francis Clement, *Blood Drenched Altars.* Bruce, Milwaukee, 1936.

Lamar, Howard Robert, *The Far Southwest, 1846-1912.* Yale University Press, 1966.

Lewis, Oscar, *San Francisco, Mission to Metropolis.* Howell-North Book Co., Berkeley, California, 1966.

Lloyd, B.E., *Lights and Shadows in San Francisco.* A.L. Bancroft, 1876.

Madden, Rev. James, Bernadette S. Desmond, and Sister Barbara Cavanaugh, *Where Your People Are.* Report submitted to Albert J. Koenigsnecht, M.M., Apostolic Administrator of July Prelature, Peru, 1976.

Manion, Sister M. Clement, S.M., *Principles of Catechetical Instruction According to Rev. Peter C. Yorke.* Unpublished Thesis for Master's Degree, Dominican College, San Rafael, 1953.

McArdle, Sister M. Aurelia (Rose), S.M., *California's Pioneer Sister of Mercy, Mother M. Baptist Russell, 1829-1898.* Academy Library Guild, Fresno, California, 1954.

MacDonagh, Oliver, *Ireland.* Prentice-Hall, Inc., Englewood Cliffs, N.J. 1965.

McGloin, J.B. S.J., *California's First Archbishop.* Herder & Herder, New York, 1966.

——————, *Eloquent Indian: The Life of Rev. J. Bouchard.* Stanford Press, 1949.

Morgan, Sister M. Evangelist, S.M., *Mercy, Generation to Generation.* Fearon Publishers, San Francisco, 1957.

Nadeau, Remi, *Ghost Towns and Mining Camps of California.* Ward Ritchie Press, Los Angeles, 1965.

Neumann, Sister M. Ignatius, R.S.M. (edited by) *Letters of Catherine McAuley, 1827-1841.* Helicon Press, Baltimore, Md., 1969.

O'Brien, Robert, *This Is San Francisco.* McGraw-Hill, New York, 1948.

Parsons, Wilfred, S.J., *Mexican Martyrdom.* Macmillan, New York, 1936.

Riegel, Robert E., *America Moves West,* third edition. Henry Holt, New York, 1956.

Royce, Josiah, *California.* Peregrine Press, Santa Barbara, 1870.

Russell, Matthew, S.J., *The Life of Mother Baptist Russell.* (First Ed. 1901) Academy of California Church History, Fresno, California, 5th Ed.

——————, *The Three Sisters of Lord Russell of Killowen.* Longmans, Green, London, New York, Bombay, 1912.

Savage, Rev. Roland Burke, S.J., *Catherine McAuley, The First Sister of Mercy.* M.H. Gill & Son, Dublin, 1949.

Salpointe, Jean Baptiste, *Soldiers of the Cross: Notes on the Early History of the Church in New Mexico, Arizona and Colorado.* Original publication by St. Boniface Industrial School, Banning, California, 1898.

——————, *Soldiers of the Cross*, edited by Odie B. Faulk. Published by the Diocese of Tucson, Arizona, 1966.

Sisters of Mercy, San Francisco, *Golden Jubilee Souvenir of the Sisters of Mercy, San Francisco, 1854-1904.* Moore-Hinds, San Francisco, 1904.

Sisters of Mercy, Oklahoma Diocese, *The Spirit of Mary Catherine McAuley.* Sisters of Mercy, Mt. St. Mary's Academy, Oklahoma City, Oklahoma, 1921.

Soule, Frank, John H. Gihon and James Nisbit, *The Annals of San Francisco.* Appleton, New York, 1855.

Schlesinger, Arthur M., *Political and Social Growth of the American People, 1865-1940*, third edition. Macmillan, New York, 1941.

Thomas, Gordon and Max Morgan Witts, *The San Francisco Earthquake.* Stein & Day, New York, 1971.

Topham, Edward, M.D., *St. Mary's Hospital and the Sisters of Mercy, 1903-1949.* San Francisco, 1950.

Walsh, Rev. Henry J., S.J., *Hallowed Were the Gold Dust Trails.* University of Santa Clara Press, 1946.

Warner, Louis H., *Archbishop Lamy: An Epoch Maker.* New Mexico Publishing Co., Santa Fe, 1936.

Wright, Kathleen, *Fifty Years of the Sisters of Mercy in San Francisco, 1904-1954:* An unpublished thesis offered in partial fulfillment for the Master's Degree at the Catholic University of America, 1955.

INDEX